Katherine Mansfield
and the Bloomsbury Group

Also Available from Bloomsbury

Katherine Mansfield and Literary Modernism,
edited by Janet Wilson, Gerri Kimber and Susan Reid
Virginia Woolf's Late Cultural Criticism,
Alice Wood

Photo of Katherine Mansfield at Garsington, by Lady Ottoline Morrell, 1916–1917. Photographs Collection, NPG Ax140568. National Portrait Gallery, London, with kind permission. © National Portrait Gallery, London.

Katherine Mansfield
and the Bloomsbury Group

Edited by
Todd Martin

BLOOMSBURY ACADEMIC
LONDON • NEW YORK • OXFORD • NEW DELHI • SYDNEY

BLOOMSBURY ACADEMIC
Bloomsbury Publishing Plc
50 Bedford Square, London, WC1B 3DP, UK
1385 Broadway, New York, NY 10018, USA

BLOOMSBURY, BLOOMSBURY ACADEMIC and the Diana logo
are trademarks of Bloomsbury Publishing Plc

First published 2017
Paperback edition first published 2019

© Todd Martin, 2017

Todd Martin has asserted his right under the Copyright,
Designs and Patents Act, 1988, to be identified as Editor of this work.

For legal purposes the Acknowledgements on p. ix constitute
an extension of this copyright page.

Cover design: Eleanor Rose
Cover image © Erin Bannister Townsend

All rights reserved. No part of this publication may be reproduced or
transmitted in any form or by any means, electronic or mechanical, including
photocopying, recording, or any information storage or retrieval system,
without prior permission in writing from the publishers.

Bloomsbury Publishing Plc does not have any control over, or responsibility for,
any third-party websites referred to or in this book. All internet addresses given in
this book were correct at the time of going to press. The author and publisher
regret any inconvenience caused if addresses have changed or sites have
ceased to exist, but can accept no responsibility for any such changes.

A catalogue record for this book is available from the British Library.

Library of Congress Cataloging-in-Publication Data
Names: Martin, W. Todd, editor.
Title: Katherine Mansfield and the Bloomsbury group / edited by Professor Todd Martin.
Description: London ; New York : Bloomsbury Academic, 2017. | Includes
bibliographical references and index.
Identifiers: LCCN 2016048846 | ISBN 9781474298971 (hb) | ISBN 9781474298995 (epdf)
Subjects: LCSH: Mansfield, Katherine, 1888-1923–Friends and associates. |
Bloomsbury group.
Classification: LCC PR9639.3.M258 Z73246 2017 | DDC 823/.912–dc23
LC record available at https://lccn.loc.gov/2016048846

ISBN: HB: 978-1-4742-9897-1
PB: 978-1-3500-9461-1
ePDF: 978-1-4742-9899-5
ePub: 978-1-4742-9898-8

Typeset by Integra Software Services Pvt. Ltd.

To find out more about our authors and books visit
www.bloomsbury.com and sign up for our newsletters.

To Brigitte, Meghan, and Elise

Contents

Acknowledgments ix

1 Introduction: Networking Modernism—Katherine Mansfield and the Garsington Connection
  Todd Martin 1

Part 1 Katherine Mansfield and Bloomsbury Friendships

2 "I wonder if you know what your visits were to me": Mansfield, Woolf, and Modernist Hospitality
  Christine Darrohn 17
3 A Critical Duet: Katherine Mansfield and Virginia Woolf Reviewing their Contemporaries
  Sydney Janet Kaplan 39
4 Katherine Mansfield and Aldous Huxley: A Blighted Friendship
  Gerri Kimber 53
5 "Feuille d'Album": Katherine Mansfield's Prufrockian Encounter with T. S. Eliot
  Janet Wilson 73
6 "Memorials of the Dead": Walter de la Mare, Katherine Mansfield, and the Literary Afterlife
  Jenny McDonnell 91
7 Mansfield and Dunning: An "important and shadowy" Friendship
  Erika Baldt 107
8 Turning the Tables: Katherine Mansfield and W. L. George
  Ann Herndon Marshall 125

Part 2 Katherine Mansfield and Literary Bloomsbury

9 Katherine Mansfield: A Fauvist, Colonial Outsider Encounters Bloomsbury
  Mary Ann Gillies 145

10 Modernist Emotions: The Critical Writings of Katherine Mansfield
    and Virginia Woolf
    Chris Mourant   161
11 Space of Debate, Debating Space: A Look at Irreverent Bloomsbury
    through the Lens of Mansfield's Stories
    Ruchi Mundeja   181
12 Performances of Knowledge in Mansfield's Bloomsbury Satires
    Alex Moffett   201
13 An Invitation to the Table: Katherine Mansfield's "A Cup of Tea"
    and Literary London
    Richard Cappuccio   219

Selected Bibliography   235
Contributors   238
Index   242

Acknowledgments

Special thanks go to Gerri Kimber, whose passion for Katherine Mansfield extends beyond her own scholarship to the numerous others whom she encourages and promotes in various ways, and especially for her role as mentor and friend. I would also like to thank Huntington University for awarding me the Emeriti Fellows Research and Artistic Creation Fund stipend for the summer of 2015, the award that enabled me to pursue this project and helped fund the purchase of the permissions and rights for the images used for this book.

I would also like to thank Erin Bannister Townsend for granting permission to use her beautiful painting of Garsington for the front cover, and to the National Portrait Gallery for permission to reproduce the photo of Katherine Mansfield for the frontispiece.

Further acknowledgment goes to the following for granting permission to quote from published and unpublished works by Katherine Mansfield and Walter de la Mare: the Literary Trustees of Walter de la Mare and the Society of Authors as their representative; the Society of Authors as the Literary Representative of the Estate of Katherine Mansfield; Oxford University Press; and the Newberry Library, Chicago (Special Collections).

1

Introduction: Networking Modernism—Katherine Mansfield and the Garsington Connection

Todd Martin

To begin a book on the Bloomsbury Group by discussing the difficulties of defining the group—whether its membership or its aims—seems almost clichéd. And Clive Bell's comment that there was never such a group followed by attempts to either qualify or refute the statement is a mainstay. But while one must contend with the notion of Bloomsbury, the goal of this volume is not so much to focus on the group itself, and certainly not to lay out its parameters. Instead, the approach of this book is to hover around the periphery, exploring the Bloomsbury Group from the outside-in, with the hope that by sketching the borders we might reveal—through relief—a new perspective. More particularly, this study focuses on Katherine Mansfield and her place on the fringe of the group both in her associations and interactions with key Bloomsbury figures such as Virginia Woolf and Roger Fry as well as other fringe figures like T. S. Eliot, Aldous Huxley, and, further afield, Walter de la Mare, W. L. George, and Millar Dunning.

Both Leon Edel and R. S. Rosenbaum work to establish a more definitive Bloomsbury by emphasizing the relational aspects of the group, restricting it through both proximity and close personal ties. Limiting the group to nine key members (Maynard Keynes, Leonard Woolf, Virginia Woolf, Lytton Strachey, Clive Bell, Desmond McCarthy, Roger Fry, Vanessa Bell, and Duncan Grant),[1] Edel emphasizes geographical proximity, especially their interrelationships with one another in the salon fashion of their early meetings, as the group's primary tie; he places the ending of Bloomsbury in 1916 when the group was dispersed—in part due to the war—to the respective personal residences of its members, never fully to regroup.[2] Likewise, Rosenbaum emphasizes that the group's "affinities came with the friendships, not the other way round,"[3] most likely drawing on Leonard Woolf's comment in "Old Bloomsbury" that "we were and always remained primarily and fundamentally a group of friends" to bolster his contention.[4] Rosenbaum, though, is more willing to concede the role of nonmembers in the development and evolution of Bloomsbury, especially looking beyond the limited purview of Edel's chronology. Looking beyond 1916, Rosenbaum's exploration of the group during the Georgian years draws attention to Lady Ottoline Morrell:

> Of greatest importance to the development of Bloomsbury, however, were the people gathered into the circles created by Lady Ottoline Morrell. Much has been sometimes made of Bloomsbury's ridicule of this extraordinary aristocrat. But underneath the mockery and amusement there was considerable fondness for her extravagant personality, if not for her sentimental affinities [....] More than any other individual or group that Bloomsbury encountered during their Georgian years, Ottoline Morrell both expanded Bloomsbury's middle-class perspectives and at the same time reaffirmed them in their different ways of life.[5]

Rosenbaum stops short of including Morrell within the group, but his acknowledgment of her role in introducing various members of Bloomsbury to some of the other key thinkers, artists, and writers of the time recognizes that Bloomsbury, despite the insularity of its interpersonal makeup, did not exist in isolation and must therefore be considered within this larger context.

One could contend, then, that while the Bloomsbury Group was a key proponent of the ideological foment of the day, its views were not all necessarily original to the group. In her essay "Local Modernity, Global Modernity: Bloomsbury and the Places of the Literary," for example, Sara Blair reverses the tendency to expand the notion of modernism beyond national boundaries and turns instead to the local, claiming that "modernism is among other things a determined response to the specific spaces in which it takes shape, advertises its cultural value, and contests for social power."[6] Blair explores the geographical and social spaces of the environs of Bloomsbury itself, arguing that "by 1905, long before 'Bloomsbury' as a class fragment, oppositional culture, bohemian enterprise, or whatever we choose to name it as crystallized, Bloomsbury as an urban living space already embodies certain key contradictions of class, mobility, transnationalism, and cultural emplacement."[7]

Blair questions the possibility of defining the group based on relationships, which she argues are too fluid. She notes the difficulty of "drawing a confident circumference around a cultural phenomenon constituted through networks of conversation, contact, and exchange."[8] However, by showing the Bloomsbury Group within its spatial context, she reinforces the idea that the group did not exist in isolation—that it was not only a part of the social and cultural milieu of the neighborhood where it was formed, but also the product of its interactions with other individuals who may or may not have been a part of the inner circle. And like Morrell, whose Bedford Square residence would have likewise made her a product of the influence of the Bloomsbury district, many of the various frequenters of her Garsington Manor shared a common view of the shifting tides of society, eliciting a cross-fertilization of ideas and expanding their social relationships.

Thus, a study of the fringes of the Bloomsbury Group can work on two levels. It can outline the borders of what is and is not Bloomsbury, but more significantly, it reveals the permeability of the group and the various interpersonal relationships the members had outside the group, relationships that helped to reaffirm and even define their broader beliefs. In his book *Networks of Modernism*, Wesley Beal addresses the general tension between fragmentation and totality inherent in the "cultural logic of modernism" by suggesting that this dialectic can be mediated through understanding social discourse, specifically the concept of the network.[9] Of course, notions of networking are not new to modernist studies; one need only consider Bonnie Kime Scott's diagram of the "Tangled Mesh of Modernists" in which she links key modernist writers to one another and argues that "the value of literary connections, for anything from creative stimulation to contact with publishers, seems indisputable."[10] Beal, though, proposes a more spatial perspective; no longer simply a web of personal and professional relationships (though these are a part of it), he emphasizes the expansion of public spaces in the early twentieth century where more heterogeneous interactions transpire. Beal emphasizes a distributive model in which each locale becomes connected to other locales through the individuals who circulate between them.

Beal focuses primarily on American modernism, particularly how the concept of network theory helps to reconcile the paradox of a growing nationalism among Americans even as enclaves of immigrants were growing.[11] Network theory enables one to understand distinct, often homogeneous communities in relation to the larger, more diverse whole because these communities are conjoined by a system of various links, including communications, trade, and artistic influence. This shift in social space, Beal argues, manifests itself in modernist aesthetics. But rather than leave the tension of fragmentation and totality unresolved, in either the aesthetic or the social context, he proposes that one must draw on "distributive aesthetics" which provides a new model of community, one of interconnecting nodes which are expanded through a network of connecting links, allowing for a "cultural logic of centralization and dispersal."[12]

Beal suggests that a similar "cultural logic holds in global modernisms."[13] Simply put, one can map out the interrelationships between individuals and groups in which groups become "nodes" and the individuals "edges" connecting the various groups. Thus, if one considers Bloomsbury and Garsington as two distinct nodes, then they are connected socially and intellectually through individuals such as Lytton Strachey and Virginia Woolf. This distributive model of network theory, then, with its nodes and edges, allows one to acknowledge the insularity of the Bloomsbury circle while simultaneously expanding it beyond its basic relational and geographical limits. Using a slightly different metaphor, Peter Brooker notes that Bloomsbury was "less the still-point of a vortex in the image of its rival modernism than a wandering rhizome":

> The philosophy, as it were, undermined the physical walls of Bloomsbury and led on to passageways and tunnels which surfaced in another place in the country, or someone else's garden party or drawing room. Once there, from Ottoline Morrell's house in Bedford Square, for example, or from Garsington manor […] it might have looked as if the Stephen sisters' Bloomsbury was more the annex than the main building—particularly since one of them lived in Richmond and one in Sussex.[14]

As Brooker's image of the "wandering rhizome" implies, though, social networks are not quite as stable as the distributive model suggests. Theories of technological networks (such as the distributive model) and social networks are distinct in that the former tends to limit the network to a series of interconnected nodes in which the "agency is attributed to the active nodes [and the] carrying out of actions is attributed to the passive edges."[15] Sociologists and anthropologists, though, desire to attribute agency to the individual actors. Bruno Latour, for example, a proponent of Actor-Network-Theory (ANT), contests social scientists who use network theory merely to describe and map out the interrelationships between groups and individuals.[16] While Latour acknowledges the necessity of using identifiers for social groups as well as the complexity of tracing the individual actors, he argues:

> In situations where innovations proliferate, where group boundaries are uncertain, when the range of entities to be taken into account fluctuates, the sociology of the social is no longer able to trace actors' new associations. At this point, the last thing to do would be to limit in advance the shape, size,

heterogeneity, and combination of associations. To the convenient shorthand of the social, one has to substitute the painful and costly longhand of its associations.[17]

Such a view of social groups—not as they are defined collectively but as individual actors—captures the complexity of the Bloomsbury Group and even questions attempts to define it. Certainly, it was an enclave of ideas and a watershed of cultural change, broadly unified by values such as "the primacy of personal relations, an aesthetic focus on what Fry dubbed 'significant form,' pacifism and anticolonialism, and a commitment to social reform in matters of sexuality and gender."[18] However, studying networks as the broader interaction of individual actors, limiting them not to a narrowly defined group but showing the social activity of the various individuals to understand the larger social matrixes, allows one to discuss Bloomsbury not so much as a closed group, but to explore the social connections members of the group had outside of the group. Assuming that the group existed in isolation ignores the complexity of influence and professional relationships of its members. Whereas one can conceive of the Bloomsbury Group as an individual node, its members' interactions with the more permeable node of Garsington makes defining the group more complicated, but it also reveals a more nuanced understanding of its members' influence beyond the group.

Latour acknowledges the relativistic character of moving beyond the more structured understanding of network theory and giving agency to individuals, for "social links have to be traced *by the circulation* of different vehicles which cannot be substantiated by one another."[19] According to Alexander Galloway and Eugene Hacker, while groups (nodes) are capable of individuation, making them distinct and knowable—like the Bloomsbury Group—networks can "auto-individuate" as well, which in social network theory equates to the systems of "small worlds" or "friends of friends" theory,[20] or what Beal calls the "six degrees of separation theory" which shows how seemingly disparate lives "intersect, entangle, and diverge."[21] Thus, exploring the individual actors reveals another, more complicated network beneath the often artificially imposed groupings. But as Beal explains, something as relativistic as the six degrees model provides a way of "rethinking the physical boundaries of a knowable community, as well as the degrees of intimacy needed to maintain it."[22] Although less directly verifiable, such theories expand social relationships to include individuals only distantly connected, revealing potential personal and professional connections which, while they might not be direct, may be significant.

The point is not to ultimately discount the significance of the Bloomsbury Group as an entity or its impact on the social, economic, and cultural milieu of its time. Social theories of this nature do, however, reveal that the individuation of the group does not preclude its interaction with others; they even validate links of influence with others who may or may not have had direct contact with the members of the group—such as Walter de la Mare, W. L. George, and Millar Dunning—but who were linked to the group indirectly through Garsington and more specifically through their relationship with Katherine Mansfield.

Lady Ottoline Morrell began her "Thursdays" salon in her Bedford Square residence in 1907, hoping to link writers, painters, and musicians with potential patrons, and when she moved to Garsington in 1915, she continued to host a variety of artists, providing them with a refuge—quite literally for the numerous conscientious objectors she housed—and an opportunity to exchange ideas. As Miranda Seymour notes, this gave her "the chance to live a life of active benevolence outside the conventions."[23] The Bloomsbury Group factored significantly in these gatherings, but Morrell would always be an outsider. Her relationships with the members of Bloomsbury were contentious, and she often played the role of reluctant hostess out of a sense of obligation, both to her larger view of the world and to her understanding of her class role. There are many instances of her guests' lack of appreciation for her hospitality, for which many, especially members of Bloomsbury, repaid her with derision. It was in this context that Katherine Mansfield was introduced to Morrell and Garsington. Her husband, John Middleton Murry, was invited to Garsington in December of 1915 at the request of D. H. Lawrence, and Mansfield began frequenting Garsington in the summer of 1916. There, she would have run into the likes of Lytton Strachey, Maynard Keynes, Vanessa and Clive Bell, Virginia and Leonard Woolf, and Desmond and Mollie McCarthy, among the other frequent visitors.

Despite a brief falling out, attributed by Morrell to Murry's misreading her desire for friendship as a profession of love,[24] there appears to have been an affinity between the two women. Both certainly knew the sting of being excluded from Bloomsbury. Seymour points out that Morrell was made painfully aware of their disloyalty in January 1918.[25] Morrell wrote in her journal: "I am told by several people that many in London think me a dangerous and designing woman, immoral and unclean, and that no one likes me for myself, only for what fun they can get out of Garsington, and that they enjoy making fun of me."[26] Even before this discovery, though, she empathized with Mansfield's place as an outsider. Writing in her journal after a soiree at Garsington in 1916, she notes:

I think Katherine feels unsure of her position, partly because she is a New Zealander and is not as yet very easy or natural in England and she is constantly playing different parts. We were playing a game after dinner when she was here, describing people by symbols, such as pictures and flowers and scents; unfortunately Katherine was described by some rather exotic scent such as stephanotis or patchouli, and although her name was not mentioned, we all knew and she knew who was meant. It was dreadful. The spite that was in the company maliciously flared out against her and hurt her.[27]

Perhaps where the two shared the greatest affinity, though, was in their favoring the simple pleasures of life over the intellectualization seemingly embodied in the "Blooms Berries." Seymour notes that Morrell's relationships with Strachey and Lawrence appealed to two different interests. She suggests that Strachey provided her with the opportunity to discuss books and ideas while she appreciated Lawrence's enjoyment of the countryside.[28] Although interested in developing a life of the mind, Morrell seems to have preferred being out in nature:

> I have grown to love these natural things of life. They mean much more to me since I have been here [Garsington], and I find purely intellectual people who are not aware of the earth and country and nature very dull. They seem almost as if they are just bodies or boxes encasing a very alert machine that is wound up each morning and tick-ticks mechanically until it runs down in sleep. The very intense intellectuals seem only to know the pleasure of their own mental velocity—almost apart from life—and seldom do they escape from their own mechanisms or begin to be aware of beauty, of nature, or earth moods, or indeed of the richness and humour of life.[29]

These "bodies or boxes encasing a very alert machine" sound very much like Bertha Young's resentment at feeling encased like a rare fiddle in Mansfield's celebrated short story "Bliss." More to the point, it is very similar to Mansfield's reflections in her letters, such as the following to Sarah Gertrude Millin, where she wrote:

> My husband and I are determined never to live in cities, always to live "remote"—to have our own life—where making jam and discovering a new bird and sitting on the stairs and growing the flowers we like best is—are—just as important as a new book. If one lives in literary society (I dont know why it *is* so but it is) it means giving up one's peace of mind, one's leisure—the best of life.[30]

Further, when Morrell reflected on Mansfield in her memoir she notes their common interest in her garden, suggesting that Mansfield "was the one person there who felt their poetry and beauty as I did."[31] But this common spirit is more clearly captured in a shared moment between Morrell and Mansfield. In her memoirs, Morrell recalls a time when she and Mansfield went out to cut lavender to make potpourri:

> The lavender was ripe for cutting and Katherine and I with knives and scissors cut and cut and made great piles of it, laying it out on a sheet to dry. How we both loved that strong aromatic smell which would permeate the house when it was brought in. Then she would linger round me when I was collecting the herbs, sweet geranium and verbena, the rose leaves and rosemary for *pot-pourri*. She would wander about and come back with a handful of green herbs to throw into my basket. She really loved the garden [...].[32]

While Morrell believes that Mansfield associated such experiences with the garden in Tolstoy's story "Family Happiness," it is equally likely that it was a reminder of the gardens she left behind at the various Beauchamp family homes in Wellington, where she lived as a young girl.

Morrell must have been quite astute in her observations, for while one must concede that her perspective is certainly her own, she appears to understand Mansfield as much as anyone. It seems, then, that Ottoline Morrell and Katherine Mansfield had much in common, and had circumstances been different—perhaps without the social intrigue and competing egos, not to mention the geographical distances imposed by Mansfield's illness—the two could have developed a more intimate relationship than they had. Mansfield certainly seems to appreciate the friendship that they shared in her letters. And it is at this nexus of their common sympathies for the simple things in life and a common distaste for supercilious intellectualism that this volume begins. For Mansfield's relationship with Bloomsbury was ambiguous at best. She shared a passion for writing with Virginia Woolf, but one couldn't really call them intimates. There appears to be too much jealousy and competitiveness. And, to the others, she was the "little colonial," not quite of their set. Yet, Mansfield's interactions with Bloomsbury and among those on its fringes were formative for both.

Part One of this volume emphasizes specific relationships between Mansfield and intimates of the Bloomsbury Group as well as other fringe members. While the essays vary in their approach, exploring thematic, biographical, and aesthetic connections, they all provide direct or indirect insight into the significance of Bloomsbury in the development of modernism as well as locate Mansfield within that context. Because we are dealing with relationships—both personal and professional—it seems apropos to begin with Christine Darrohn's discussion of hospitality in Katherine Mansfield and Virginia Woolf. Darrohn, drawing on the ethics of Emmanuel Levinas and Jacques Derrida, explores what it means to welcome the other, especially as it occurs across social barriers. In so doing, she exposes the contexts for Bloomsbury's distinctive practices of hospitality, manifest in Mansfield's and Woolf's friendship, and, more broadly, the self's relation to others. Like Darrohn, Sydney Janet Kaplan considers the relationship between Mansfield and Woolf, but she explores how each woman's personal ties with Frank Swinnerton affected their reviews of his novel *September*. She contends that their contrasting attitudes toward his novel reveal their view on the project of reviewing itself. Kaplan raises questions about literary politics, including the different levels of involvement each woman had with the publication process of the *Athenaeum*.

Gerri Kimber shifts the focus from Woolf to figures who weren't official members of Bloomsbury, but who factored significantly in the group, in her essay on Mansfield's contentious relationship with Aldous Huxley. Noting that the connection between Mansfield and Huxley has not received adequate attention, she sets to redress the oversight. Kimber traces the relationship from Huxley's initial acquaintance with Mansfield to the fictionalizing of each other in their works, revealing a difficult relationship blighted by the friendships—and enmities—of those around them. The pattern that we see here seems to be common to many of her relationships with other writers, as Janet Wilson reveals further in discussing Mansfield's fraught relationship with T. S. Eliot in which Mansfield's initial admiration turned to wariness, and his attitude toward her became openly hostile. Wilson examines their literary rivalry as revealed in their coded comments on each other in their prose writings, though Eliot's experimental modernism also influenced Mansfield's artistic practice at the time. Jenny McDonnell turns our attention to Mansfield's less contentious friendship with Walter de la Mare. Exploring the friendship between these two writers, McDonnell uses it to reveal their anxieties about posthumous publications and their literary afterlives, displaying both writers' conflicted relationship with the literary marketplace.

Erika Baldt and Ann Marshall turn our attention to less famous relationships with individuals further away from Bloomsbury than Huxley, Eliot, or de la Mare. But in doing so, they both continue to reveal the ambiguity Mansfield had in her view of Bloomsbury. Baldt, in her exploration of Millar Dunning, reveals Mansfield's spiritual side, something that Bloomsbury would have derided. As Baldt demonstrates, Mansfield counted on Dunning to help Murry come to a greater understanding about her interest in the Eastern spiritualism which eventually led her to George Gurdjieff. But Baldt also attempts to illuminate the parallel strategies in the form and content of both writers' work. Marshall, on the other hand, in her discussion of Mansfield's growing disdain for W. L. George's posture as a feminist and more particularly his pandering to the market, reveals a perspective most likely shared by Bloomsbury. According to Marshall, by looking at the social theories and family narratives of W. L George, one sees a triumphal feminism that annoyed Mansfield and which she challenged in her own fiction.

Part Two shifts the focus from specific relationships toward Mansfield's views of Bloomsbury. Two of the chapters emphasize her aesthetics, with particular attention to how hers compares to that of the Bloomsbury Group, while the others explore her portrayal of the group in her fiction. Mary Ann Gillies borrows from contemporary neuroscience theories that claim early childhood experiences—perception, cognition, affect—play a profound role in structuring how we perceive people, places, and things later in life. Thus, she posits, the New Zealand landscape of Mansfield's childhood would have drawn her to Post-Impressionist art and aesthetics. For Roger Fry, however, she suggests that Post-Impressionism was more of an intellectual pursuit rather than a lived experience. Chris Mourant, on the other hand, like Kaplan in an earlier chapter, explores Mansfield's reviews in the *Athenaeum* to reveal a more detailed and extensive material record of her sustained engagement with Woolf's ideas. Their critical writings highlight the degree to which their professional relationship was revealed by a shared vocabulary of empathetic emotion and deep feeling.

The final three essays in the section turn to Mansfield's fiction and her engagement with Bloomsbury through satire in such stories as "Bliss," "Marriage à la Mode," "A Dill Pickle," and "A Cup of Tea." Ruchi Mundeja argues that Mansfield was able to see through some of Bloomsbury's apparent nonconformist stances, revealing their view of the other as a consumable commodity. She foregrounds Mansfield as both a woman and a colonial, demonstrating how she qualifies the irreverence of the "Blooms Berries" toward the other by acknowledging the liberatory potential for women of their views. Alexander Moffet, in a corollary to Darrohn's discussion of knowing the other, posits that knowing is constant with the narrative arc of Mansfield's short stories, many of which culminate in some sort of epiphanic moment. However, he suggests that Mansfield contrasts these modes of knowing characterized by interior revelation with other moments in which characters display knowledge through showing performances; the latter comprise a large part of Mansfield's satire of Bloomsbury mores. The volume concludes appropriately with Richard Cappuccio's discussion of Mansfield as an outsider, particularly in her relationship with Virginia Woolf, serving as a bookend to Darrohn's discussion of hospitality and reinforcing the implications of many of the other essays of Mansfield's not belonging, particularly among the Bloomsbury set. Focusing on Mansfield's "A Cup of Tea," Cappuccio suggests that the focus on the privileged Rosemary Fells and the lower-class Miss Smith reflects the relationship between Woolf and Mansfield, making the case that the story is Mansfield's published response to the privilege of Woolf, Bloomsbury, and the Garsington circles of which she never felt a part.

* * *

In his discussion of ANT, Bruno Latour shifts his discussion away from networks proper and to the text, the reports which attempt to capture the nature of the social. He suggests that a good account of social interaction is "one that *traces a network*": "A good text elicits networks of actors when it allows the writer to trace a set of relations defined as so many translations."[33] By allowing individual actors agency, good texts "render the movement of the social visible to the reader. Thus, through many textual inventions, the social may become again a circulating entity that is no longer composed of the stale assemblage of what passed earlier as being part of society."[34]

Such is the hope of this book: not to attempt to identify any pervasive ideology of the Bloomsbury Group nor even to try to argue for a particular roster of members or nonmembers, but rather to examine the personal interactions between Katherine Mansfield and key members of the group itself as well as others who, like Mansfield, hovered on the fringe of Bloomsbury, suggesting their individual agency. If Morrell's Garsington serves as a node linking the various artists of her coterie to those of Bloomsbury, then for this volume, Katherine Mansfield serves as a nexus, uniting the individual actors. The influences, then, are not always direct, and in some ways they show a reaction against Bloomsbury, against whom they could unite.

There are certainly key members of the Bloomsbury Group who interacted with Mansfield who are not discussed here (e.g., Lytton Strachey and E. M. Forster), and others on the periphery who could likewise have been included; further, there are those who are at best only tentatively tied to the group, mostly through chance meetings at Garsington, or even indirectly through Katherine Mansfield, individuals who had little to do with the members of Bloomsbury. But the goal here is not to be exhaustive nor is it to be exclusive, for Mansfield had many literary friendships and acquaintances, and part of the influence of Bloomsbury on her was her exclusion from it and the solace she took in finding others ostracized from the inner circle of the group. Her ambiguous feelings for the group, which ranged from warm friendship, such as that she briefly had with Woolf, to disdain of the intellectual snobbery of the group, are all evident here, both in discussions of her friendships and her aesthetics as well as manifest in her stories.

Notes

1. Leon Edel, *Bloomsbury: A House of Lions* (Philadelphia and New York: J. B. Lippincott Company, 1979), 12.
2. Edel, *House of Lions*, 205.
3. S. P. Rosenbaum, "Preface to Literary History of the Bloomsbury Group," *New Literary History* 12, no. 2 (December 1981): 332.
4. Leonard Woolf, "Old Bloomsbury," in *Bloomsbury: A Collection of Memoirs, Commentary and Criticism*, ed. S. P. Rosenbaum (Toronto and Buffalo: University of Toronto Press, 1975), 112.
5. S. P. Rosenbaum, *Georgian Bloomsbury: The Early Literary History of the Bloomsbury Group, 1910–1914* (Houndmills, Basingstoke, Hampshire: Palgrave MacMillan, 2003), 6.
6. Sara Blair, "Local Modernity, Global Modernism: Bloomsbury and the Places of the Literary," *ELH* 71, no. 3 (Fall 2004): 814.
7. Blair, "Local Modernity," 825.
8. Blair, "Local Modernity," 815.
9. Wesley Beal, *Networks of Modernism: Reorganizing American Narrative* (Iowa City, IA: University of Iowa Press, 2015), 3.
10. Bonnie Kime Scott, "Introduction to *The Gender of Modernism*," in *Gender and Modernism*, ed. Bonnie Kime Scott (London and New York: Routledge, 2008), 55, 54.
11. Beal, *Networks of Modernism*, 7.
12. Beal, *Networks of Modernism*, 18, 20.
13. Beal, *Networks of Modernism*, 7.
14. Peter Brooker, *Bohemia in London: The Social Scene of Early Modernism* (Houndmills, Basingstoke, Hampshire: Palgrave MacMillan, 2004), 164.
15. Alexander R. Galloway and Eugene Thacker, *Exploit: A Theory of Networks*, Electronic Mediations, vol. 21 (Minneapolis: University of Minnesota Press, 2007), 33.

16　While Latour's version of social network theory may be ideal, others point out the impracticality of such a method. See Mark Newman, Albert-László Barabási, and Duncan J. Watts, introduction to *The Structure and Dynamics of Networks*, Princeton Studies in Complexity, ed. Mark Newman, Albert-László Barabási, and Duncan J. Watts (Princeton and Oxford: Princeton University Press, 2006), 4–6.

17　Bruno Latour, *Reassembling the Social: An Introduction to Actor-Network-Theory*, Clarendon Lectures in Management Studies (Oxford: Oxford University Press, 2005), 11.

18　Victoria Rosner, introduction to *The Cambridge Companion to the Bloomsbury Group*, ed. Victoria Rosner (New York: Cambridge University Press, 2014), 10.

19　Latour, *Reassembling the Social*, 12, 36.

20　Galloway and Thacker, *Exploit*, 38–39. However, "these processes of individuation are always accompanied by processes of deindividuation, for each individuation is always encompassed by the 'mass' and aggregate quality of networks as a whole, everything broken down into stable, generic nodes and discrete, quantifiable edges" (39).

21　Beal, *Networks of Modernism*, 25.

22　Beal, *Networks of Modernism*, 25.

23　Miranda Seymour, *Ottoline Morrell: Life on the Grand Scale* (New York: Farrar, Straus, Giroux, 1992), 75.

24　Robert Gathorne-Hardy, ed., *Ottoline at Garsington: Memoirs of Lady Ottoline Morrell, 1915–1918* (New York: Alfred A. Knopf, 1975), 192. The book consists of both later reflections on as well as specific journal entries from the Garsington period, thus the journal entries are distinguished from the reflections by quotation marks.

25　Seymour, *Ottoline Morrell*, 292–93.

26　Gathorne-Hardy, *Ottoline at Garsington*, 234.

27　Gathorne-Hardy, *Ottoline at Garsington*, 150.

28　Seymour, *Ottoline Morrell*, 241.

29　Gathorne-Hardy, *Ottoline at Garsington*, 82.

30　Katherine Mansfield to Sarah Gertrude Millin, early March 1922, in *The Collected Letters of Katherine Mansfield*, 5 vols., ed. Vincent O'Sullivan and Margaret Scott (Oxford: Clarendon Press, 1984–2008), 5:80.

31　Gathorne-Hardy, *Ottoline at Garsington*, 187.

32　Gathorne-Hardy, *Ottoline at Garsington*, 186.

33　Latour, *Reassembling the Social*, 128, 129.

34　Latour, *Reassembling the Social*, 128.

Part One

Katherine Mansfield and Bloomsbury Friendships

2

"I wonder if you know what your visits were to me": Mansfield, Woolf, and Modernist Hospitality

Christine Darrohn

"I wonder if you know what your visits were to me—or how much I miss them," Katherine Mansfield wrote in what would prove to be her last letter to Virginia Woolf.[1] Mansfield's sentence, though apparently simple, points subtly and powerfully to the issues at the heart of this chapter. Mansfield is asserting the profound value of Woolf's visits while simultaneously capturing the limits of her knowledge of her friend, for Mansfield wonders—she does not know—if Woolf knows how she feels (and, thereby, Mansfield also is raising the possibility of her friend's limited knowledge of her). Just prior to this sentence, Mansfield expresses her desire for a visit from Woolf by imagining it: "If Virginia were to come through the gate & were to say 'Well—Katherine'— oh, there are a thousand things Id like to discuss."[2] Unlike the sentence that directly addresses Woolf ("I wonder if *you* know what *your* visits"), this one refers to Woolf in the third person, demanding that Woolf as the reader of the letter slip into Mansfield's point of view, experiencing her imagined arrival from Mansfield's perspective. In these two sentences, with their delicate flickering of point of view, Mansfield not only leads Woolf to share her perspective but also registers her own inability to comprehend her friend's perspective fully, all the while conveying her welcome of this unknowable friend. In short, the sentences grapple with the vexed issue of the relation between self and other in a way that calls to mind hospitality as defined by late twentieth-century theorists: the welcome of an other who remains other.

This chapter explores hospitality in Mansfield's and Woolf's fiction and in their turbulent friendship. In analyzing key representations of hospitality in the fiction, I will take a twofold approach. I will explore texts' representations of hospitality, probing what they suggest about the welcome of others who can and cannot be known. I will also explore texts' strategies by which readers' own encounter with the other is guided. Through this multipronged analysis, I aim to show Mansfield's and Woolf's ceaseless questioning of the dilemma of the self's relation to the other.

A customary way of conceiving of hospitality is that it is the welcome of a stranger who becomes known and familiar.[3] A very different conception of hospitality, which is offered by Emmanuel Levinas and Jacques Derrida, asserts it is the welcome of the other who remains utterly other, in excess of what the self can know. This encounter between self and other (which occurs not merely in overt acts of hospitality but in humans' essential existence in the world) is what enables the self to take shape and assume responsibility for the other. It is at the heart of ethics. In fact, as Derrida asserts, "hospitality is not some region of ethics [...]: it is ethicity itself, the whole and the principle of ethics."[4] This late twentieth-century understanding of hospitality is key in Rachel Hollander's *Narrative Hospitality in Late Victorian Fiction: Novel Ethics*. Hollander argues that a shift occurs between the Victorian and late Victorian novel. Victorian novels promote an ethics defined by the ability of the self to sympathize with and understand others because they are similar to oneself. In contrast, late Victorian fiction conveys an ethics that acknowledges the limits of knowledge; it exemplifies hospitality as Levinas and Derrida will theorize it in the next century. Though Hollander studies primarily late Victorian fiction, she briefly—through a reading of Woolf's *Jacob's Room* (1922)—suggests that the modernist novel insists even more thoroughly than the late Victorian novel on the gap between self and other. I take inspiration from Hollander's study, but I believe keeping in play both definitions of hospitality—welcome of an other who becomes known, and welcome of an other who remains other—provides the supplest framework for uncovering the manifold hospitality in the work of Mansfield and Woolf, two modernist writers who are unsurpassed in their ability to ponder the many ways selves stand in relation to others.

The challenges and pleasures of hospitality are evident in Mansfield's and Woolf's textual record of their friendship. Woolf's diaries afford us glimpses into the women's fluctuating closeness. "As usual we came to an oddly complete understanding. My theory is that I get down to what is true rock in her, through the numerous vapours & pores which sicken or bewilder most of our friends," Woolf writes.[5] Less than a year later, Woolf uses contrasting geologic imagery as she puzzles over a two-month silence from Mansfield: the friendship "was almost entirely founded on quicksands. It has been marked by curious slides & arrests;

for months I've heard nothing of her; then we have met again upon what has the appearance of solid ground."[6] In her very next entry, she amends her assessment because she has received Mansfield's invitation to tea.[7] Five months later, Woolf reports on the solidity and permanence—"some kind of durable foundation"—of their friendship.[8] In fact, though, as later diary entries attest, the friendship remained unstable.

Many factors troubled Mansfield and Woolf's friendship—professional jealousy, personal jealousy, differences in lifestyle.[9] My purpose is not to rehash those causes, but rather to explore this friendship as an enactment of hospitality. To be more precise, I will explore how Mansfield and Woolf in textual products about their friendship enact a welcome of an other who becomes familiar but also to a substantial degree remains ineluctably other. The products that are my focus are Mansfield's letters to Woolf and Woolf's diary writings about Mansfield. The two genres are, of course, very different, but only a couple of Woolf's letters to Mansfield have survived, and Mansfield did not write about Woolf in her notebooks, creating an imbalance in what is available for study.

Mansfield and Woolf relished their commonalities, the most important of which was their shared dedication to and vision of writing, yet even as they vividly represent that commonality, they indicate the limitation of their knowledge of each other. As early as her first letter to Woolf, just several months after the women met, Mansfield underscores commonality as she imagines and seeks to overcome Woolf's possible resistance to the label of friend:

> My God I love to think of you, Virginia, as my friend. Dont cry me an ardent creature or say, with your head a little on one side, smiling as though you knew some enchanting secret: "Well, Katherine, we shall see" … But pray consider how rare is it to find some one with the same passion for writing that you have.[10]

Mansfield emphasizes their identical commitment to writing even as she pictures Woolf in possession of a secret unknown to Mansfield. Moreover, she casts herself essentially in the role of host when she refers to her desire "to give you the freedom of the city without any reserves at all."[11] Clearly, Mansfield is aware of differences in her and Woolf's lifestyles, a point that matches Woolf's statement to her sister after her next conversation with Mansfield ("She seems to have gone every sort of hog since she was 17, which is interesting"[12]). For Mansfield, differences, mixed with a fundamental identicality, constitute the basis for operating as host.

A month later, after spending the weekend with Woolf at her Sussex home, Asheham, Mansfield again draws attention to their common aims as writers.

She adds, "We are [seeking the same thing] you know; there's no denying it."[13] Mansfield not only underscores her and Woolf's identical view of writing, but in saying, "you know," she claims to know what Woolf knows, a bit of rhetorical maneuvering in the face of Woolf's possible denial and the threat of others' gossip: "But dont let THEM ever persuade you that I spend any of my precious time swapping hats or committing adultery," Mansfield urges Woolf.[14] Along with these intermixed expressions of commonality, limited knowledge, and feigned knowledge, there are statements, similar to this chapter's titular quotation, that compactly convey Woolf's importance to Mansfield and Woolf's inability to grasp this point: "You do not know, Virginia, how I treasure the thought of you" and "You would not believe me if you knew how often you are in my *heart & mind*."[15] Mansfield's pattern of conveying simultaneously the intensity of her feelings for Woolf and the inability of Woolf to know these feelings suggests the two points are inextricably entangled: the unknowability marks the depth of those feelings.

Woolf, too, eventually was recording her and Mansfield's remarkable sameness, especially (but not only) in their approaches to writing, yet her reflections on their sameness are intermixed with confessions of incomprehension that parallel acknowledgments of limited knowledge in Mansfield's letters. Woolf refers to "the queerest sense of echo coming back to me from her [Mansfield's] mind the second after I've spoken" and ascribes this to the "rare[ness]" of "[a] woman caring as I care for writing."[16] Despite this identicality, Woolf notes in the same entry that only "God knows" if Mansfield "really want[s]" Woolf to review her book, which she has pressed Woolf to review. The paragraph concludes, "Strange how little we know our friends."[17] In another entry Woolf refers to "a common certain understanding between us—a queer sense of being 'like.'"[18] The visit described in this entry began awkwardly, Woolf seeing Mansfield as "of the cat kind: alien, composed, always solitary & observant," but then, paradoxically as the two "talked about solitude," their disconnection dissolved: "I found her expressing my feelings, as I never heard them expressed."[19] A recurrent word used by Woolf to describe Mansfield is "inscrutable." It appears in Woolf's notorious description of Mansfield:

> We [Woolf and her husband, Leonard] could both wish that ones first impression of K.M. was not that she stinks like a—well civet cat that had taken to street walking. In truth, I'm a little shocked by her commonness at first sight; lines so hard & cheap. However, when this diminishes, she is so intelligent & inscrutable that she repays friendship.[20]

The street walking civet cat calls to mind utter otherness—animality, sexual deviance, and foreignness (civet cats are native to Africa and Asia)—but ultimately Woolf embraces Mansfield's unknowability. A year and a half later, Woolf appreciatively uses "inscrutable" again: Mansfield is "[t]he inscrutable woman" who "remains inscrutable I'm glad to say; no apologies, or sense of apologies due."[21] The word appears yet again when Woolf reflects on Mansfield a few days after she learns of her death.[22] To sum up, Mansfield and Woolf each welcome the other, who is and is not known. Even as Mansfield and Woolf insist they are alike, they value the limits of their knowledge of the other: Woolf is pleased Mansfield is inscrutable, and Mansfield expresses the depth of her feelings for Woolf by asserting Woolf cannot know them.

Mansfield and Woolf's friendship was forged across apparently great social divides. Mansfield was a New Zealand expatriate. Woolf was a native-born and well-connected Londoner, the granddaughter of James Stephen, who, as permanent undersecretary in the Colonial Office, shaped England's imperial policy. Mansfield was not merely an expatriate, someone who chose to leave her native land, but also an exile, compelled by illness to search nomadically for healthful residences:[23] "I seem to spend half my life arriving at strange hotels," where "[t]he strange door" is her room door "shut[ting] upon the stranger," which is her.[24] In contrast, Woolf was blissfully rooted, at least as Mansfield saw it: "How I envy Virginia [...] [H]er roof over her—her own possessions round her—and her man somewhere within call."[25] However, the divide between Mansfield and Woolf was not so simple. Janet Wilson explains Mansfield's "interstitial" location. As a subject from a white settler colony, Mansfield was defined by dual ties: to the "imperium" ("Home," as Andrew Gurr notes, "still automatically meant Britain" for New Zealanders) and to the "indigene," the Maori culture. She was "between both but not fully belonging to either."[26] In an oft-quoted passage in her notebook, Mansfield captures the unwelcome that can be felt in the interstices: she is "the little colonial walking in the London garden patch—allowed to look, perhaps, but not to linger," "a stranger,—an alien," who merely pretends that her garden and her house are her own.[27] The passage evinces an unstable boundary between self and other, for Mansfield does not simply describe herself but nimbly views herself the way English flowers view her. Woolf's tie to the imperium was not troubled by a conflicting tie to the indigene, yet her keen sense of patriarchy illumined her interstitial location in English culture due to gender. Akin to Mansfield's unwelcome in a garden, the narrator of Woolf's *A Room of One's Own* is pleasurably walking "across a grass plot" when "[i]nstantly" an official of the university explains that "[o]nly the

Fellows and Scholars are allowed" on the grass.[28] As for Woolf's experience of home, it was not always idyllic, as Mansfield yearningly imagined. Before Woolf and her siblings moved to Bloomsbury, Woolf's home was the site of incestuous molestations by her half-brothers: "There would be a tap at the door; the light would be turned out and George [Duckworth] would fling himself on my bed, cuddling and kissing and otherwise embracing me."[29] In their varied ways, Mansfield and Woolf were unwelcome in the interstices and at home.

Arguably one divide between the women was the Bloomsbury Group. From its earliest days, the group was for Woolf a release from conventions and power structures that restricted one's speech and made one vulnerable to violation. In her memoir "Old Bloomsbury", she contrasts the pleasurable freedom of Bloomsbury's intellectual conversation and frank discussion of sex to George's scolding her for talking too much at parties and his molesting her (and then rationalizing his behavior when he talked to Woolf's doctor).[30] The Bloomsbury Group was in the most profound way hospitable to Woolf. For Mansfield, Bloomsbury talk was virulent gossip. Just a few days before Mansfield stayed with the Woolfs at Asheham, she wrote to a friend, "To Hell with the Blooms Berries."[31] Mansfield was primarily distressed by the number of social engagements that were distracting her from her writing, yet her vehemence is notable. Later when Mansfield thanks Woolf for the visit, her reference to the untruths told by "THEM" is specifically to Bloomsbury gossip.[32] After this reference, Mansfield pivots to the beautiful scenery at her home, enticing Woolf to join her domain and put aside Bloomsbury tittle-tattle.[33] Mansfield also expresses disdain for the Bloomsbury Group in a letter to her husband, in which a metaphor relocates the Bloomsbury Group to New Zealand: "I feel I would get into the very middle of a Bloomsbury tangi and remain untouched."[34] A *tangi* is a Maori ceremony to mourn the dead, so Mansfield is transmogrifying the elite English group into New Zealand's indigenous culture while envisioning her ability to be in its midst yet impervious to it (as well as exhibiting mastery over the group by riffing on the "bury" of Bloomsbury).

Though Mansfield's and Woolf's social locations were far from identical, especially in regards to the Bloomsbury Group, both women knew the unwelcome of being not wholly at home; both knew a fluid boundary between self and other. In their hospitality toward each other—not just literal visits but also the essential act of attending to the other as an unknowable but familiar being—they exemplify the manifold hospitality that I am suggesting is modernist hospitality. In their friendship, this hospitality may not have reached ethical heights—each woman seems mindful of what she will gain from the friendship (e.g., Mansfield "repays friendship"[35]) rather than suspending her needs to attend to those of the other—but the dynamics of knowing and not knowing the other that play out in the friendship emerge in more complex ways in the writers' fictions.

Small but striking verbal connections between Mansfield's and Woolf's letters and diaries and their fiction suggest that friendship and fiction were arenas in which they grappled with similar issues regarding the relation between self and other. Mansfield imagines Woolf's resistance to the term "friend" in an image of Woolf "with [her] head a little on one side, smiling as though [she] knew some enchanting secret."[36] In "Bliss" (1918), which Mansfield wrote eight months later, Bertha describes her new friend similarly: "[T]he way she has of sitting with her head a little on one side, and smiling, has something behind it."[37] "Inscrutable" is a key term in Woolf's descriptions of Mansfield and also in *Mrs. Dalloway* (1925), which Woolf wrote during a period that straddled the final months of Mansfield's life and nearly two more years when Woolf continued the friendship posthumously, writing about Mansfield repeatedly in her diary, including on the day that she describes finishing the novel. "Inscrutable" is one of a pair of terms that captures the ambiguity of Clarissa Dalloway to a longtime friend: "so transparent in some ways, so inscrutable in others."[38] Clarissa's daughter, Elizabeth, has "inscrutable mystery."[39] Turning to Mansfield's and Woolf's fiction, we should not be surprised that the dynamics of hospitality that have been traced thus far reappear, embedded in texts that even more capaciously register the dangers, pleasures, and ethics of hospitality.

Mansfield's fiction exposes hospitality gone awry, spotlighting fundamental failings of both guests and hosts. For example, parasitical guests in "Marriage à la Mode" (1921) take advantage of their hosts, greedily enjoying William's and Isabel's food, money, and home while disdaining William and converting William's wife to their values (William worries that the guests will usurp his presents for his children, but actually his wife does, and in the story's crisis, she fails to reciprocate her husband's heartfelt concern for her and their marriage). In "Bliss," Pearl Fulton stokes the bliss and sexual desire of Bertha, but Pearl duplicitously has been having a clandestine affair with Bertha's husband.

In addition to unscrupulous guests, Mansfield's fiction features hosts who are unscrupulously self-serving. Jacques Derrida notes the possible "violence of the host":

> To dare to say welcome is perhaps to insinuate that one is at home here, that one knows what it means to be at home, and that at home one receives, invites, or offers hospitality, thus appropriating for oneself a place to *welcome* [*accueillir*]

the other, or, worse, *welcoming* the other in order to appropriate for oneself a place and then speak the language of hospitality.[40]

Bertha of "Bliss" has a precarious relation to her home, as well as to her child and body: although she feels bliss as she "turn[s] the corner of [her] own street,"[41] she often accidentally locks herself out of her house,[42] her child's nurse dominates her,[43] and her body is similar to a rare fiddle kept in its case.[44] However, as Pearl Fulton, her new "find," arrives at her party, Bertha displays a "little air of proprietorship," that last word suggesting Bertha's claim of exclusive rights to Pearl whether or not she possesses her.[45] In "The Doll's House" (1921), the young Burnells' invitations to classmates to view their new dollhouse function as an exercise in social prestige and power (with one notable exception, to be discussed below). In "A Cup of Tea" (1922), when upper-class Rosemary invites to her home the young stranger who approaches her on the street for the cost of a cup of tea, Rosemary's hospitality is driven not by an overt desire to reinforce her social power, but certainly by a self-centered desire to have a "thrilling" experience, "such an adventure," which undercuts any genuine concern for the other.[46] Even those of low socioeconomic status can gain dominance through seemingly hospitable acts, as evident when Kezia and Lottie Burnell of "Prelude" (1917) join the Samuel Josephs for tea. Mrs. Samuel Josephs kindly offers to look after the girls until they can travel to their family's new home. At the start of tea, one of the Samuel Josephs' boys "lean[s] across the table very politely, and smile[s]" as he says to Kezia, "Which will you have to begin with—strawberries and cream or bread and dripping?" Mimicking the wealthy by pretending to have their luxurious items to offer guests, he is setting up Kezia to be the butt of the family's humor. When Kezia chooses the strawberries and cream, everyone laughs, for she has been "foxed" and "take[n] in."[47] The latter phrase, in its multiple meanings, succinctly reminds us that to be received as a guest is to run the risk of being cheated.

Clearly, Mansfield's fiction fits the long literary tradition of exposing the falsity—and even treachery—that is possible in the interactions between hosts and guests.[48] An additional feature of some of her hosts—their desire to know the other—requires careful note. This desire is not treacherous in relation to a traditional definition of hospitality, for the point of hospitality as traditionally conceived is to transform the stranger into the known, but this desire does run counter to Levinas's and Derrida's understanding of hospitality. For Levinas and Derrida, ethics is rooted in one's encountering an other who cannot be known. In this encounter, the self is formed as it becomes responsible for the other. Rosemary and Bertha attempt to subvert such a process. Rosemary, in explaining how she will help her guest, says, "[Y]ou'll tell me everything."⁴⁹ Bertha, too, seeks intrusive knowledge. She finds it "provoking" that she cannot figure Miss Fulton out and is determined to do so.⁵⁰

Detailed examination of "The Doll's House," one of Mansfield's most expansive and nuanced examinations of hospitality, enables us to consider hospitality in which the host does not presume to know the other. This story traces hospitality as a pervasive exercise in social power that reinforces hierarchies while the story's ending showcases a very different kind of hospitality. In the climactic, Levinasian act of hospitality, a character discovers her agency as host while nurturing the agency of her guests, and Mansfield evokes the persistent otherness of a guest even as a bond between guest and host is manifest.

The story begins with the arrival of a magnificently well-appointed dollhouse, a gift to the Burnell children from a recent house guest of the family. Accounting for the dollhouse as someone's reciprocation for hospitality that she has received, the story from its beginning points to complex protocols of hospitality. In a story that will explore acts of welcome and unwelcome, it is significant that this dollhouse, a house guest's gift, is unwelcome in the house. Due to its strong scent of paint, which is noxious to adults although negligible to the delighted children, it is kept outside. The story's network of hospitable acts grows as the children desire to share their house with others. Soon (indeed, over the course of just one sentence) we see the way such a desire can veil—rather thinly—a desire to exhibit social supremacy: the children "burned to tell everybody, to describe, too—well—to boast about their doll's house."⁵¹ Hospitality to reinforce social prestige is evident in the Burnells' relation to their classmates. It is also evident among the Burnell sisters. The eldest, Isabel, confidently claims her prerogative within the hierarchy of sisters: she informs her younger sisters Lottie and Kezia, "I'm to tell [...] because I'm the eldest. And you two can join in after. But I'm to tell first."⁵² Isabel's claim of social privilege leaves her younger sisters silent: "There was nothing to answer. Isabel was bossy, but she was always right, and Lottie and Kezia knew too well the powers that went with being eldest. They brushed through the thick buttercups at the road edge and said nothing."⁵³ When Kezia wants to add her perspective on the part of the dollhouse that she thinks is best—the little lamp—apparently "nobody paid any attention" because all the focus is on Isabel as she selects the first girls to view the dollhouse.⁵⁴

Beyond the sororal hierarchy, Mansfield shows the vicious hierarchy of social class that operates in the school and in the larger society, of which the school is a reflection—and she shows, in particular, how hospitality, offered and denied, reinforces that hierarchy. Because there is only one school in the area, the elite do not have the option of separating their children from other children; however, "the line had to be drawn somewhere. It was drawn at the Kelveys," and everyone—students, parents, and teacher—cooperates in excluding the Kelveys.[55] Given the absolute shunning of the Kelveys, invitations to view the Burnells' dollhouse are extended to all the girls *except* the two Kelveys until the end of the story when Kezia, disobeying her mother, extends hospitality to them. The dollhouse's liminal location—in the courtyard but not in the Burnells' house—makes it suitable for nearly all the classmates—but not the Kelveys—to be invited to see it, "[n]ot to stay to tea, of course, or to come traipsing through the house. But just to stand quietly in the courtyard while Isabel pointed out the beauties, and Lottie and Kezia looked pleased."[56]

There is irony in the physical connections of Mrs. Kelvey and her daughters to the houses of the Burnells and the others who shun them. As a washerwoman, Mrs. Kelvey goes "about from house to house."[57] Moreover, she makes her daughters' clothing from "bits" given to her from her employers, including cast-off home furnishings: Lil Kelvey's dress is "made from a green art-serge table-cloth of the Burnells', with red plush sleeves from the Logans' curtains."[58] These clothes, which make the girls "conspicuous" and laughable,[59] convey the girls' simultaneous connection to and disconnection from their society. Lil's hat, "turned up at the back and trimmed with a large scarlet quill," a cast-off item from the postmistress, is the finishing touch to the impression that Lil creates: "What a little guy she looked!"[60] "Guy" here means "[a] person of grotesque appearance, especially with reference to dress."[61] Because this meaning derives from Guy Fawkes, infamous participant in a seventeenth-century Catholic plot to blow up Parliament, it recalls a thwarted revolution by those on the social fringe.

In the society that is represented in "The Doll's House," can hospitality function as more than an exercise in social power? Yes. Kezia's act of hospitality, the climax of the story, shows us how.

Near the conclusion of the story, visitors come to the Burnell home, and Isabel and Lottie, "who liked visitors," are upstairs changing their pinafores, but Kezia, who (by implication) does not like visitors—at least not socially sanctioned ones—sneaks out the back of the house.[62] In fact, the verb that denotes her action is "thieve[s]," as though to avoid one's role in socially sanctioned hospitality is to steal something.[63] In this illicit moment without anyone overseeing her behavior, what does Kezia do? She positions herself on a threshold, "the big white gates of the courtyard."[64] Moreover, she "swing[s]" on the gates, an image of one's ability to welcome or not welcome others.[65] As though merely to make oneself receptive at a border is to call forth the other, Kezia looks down the road and sees two dots that crystalize into the Kelveys. Levinas says that the encounter with the other "calls" the freedom of the self "to responsibility and founds it."[66] In essence, this is what happens for Kezia. She wavers and "hesitates"—she even gets off the gate for a while—but ultimately Kezia assumes responsibility when she climbs atop the gate again, swings it open, and addresses the Kelveys.[67] Significantly, just before she does so, the Kelveys' shadows stretch into the buttercups—a detail that we first saw when Kezia and her sister silently acknowledged their eldest sister's supremacy as they walked in the buttercups. Whereas earlier Kezia felt a lack of freedom, now she recognizes her freedom, and she uses it.

Unlike the use of power by Isabel and those of her ilk, Kezia grants the Kelveys agency. Kezia's invitation is nonchalant. "Hullo," she says. "You can come and see our doll's house if you want to."[68] This is not the boastful hype of Isabel. This invitation—"*You can* come and see our doll's house *if you want to*"—underscores the freedom of her guests. When Lil repeatedly refuses, Kezia continues to emphasize her guests' desires, asking, "Don't you want to?"[69] Ultimately, "our Else" communicates with her sister in her typically silent fashion, "twitch[ing]" her sister's skirt and "looking at her with big imploring eyes."[70] When Kezia shows the Kelveys the dollhouse, she barely begins to highlight the features of the house—is on the verge of referring to the item that means the most to her, the lamp—when the hospitality is abruptly ended by Aunt Beryl, who scolds and shoos the girls.

Aunt Beryl's rebuke not merely terminates Kezia's hospitality but also unsettles the narrative. Suddenly the narrator diverts the reader's attention from the three girls to Aunt Beryl in a paragraph-long account of Aunt Beryl's motivation for and experience of her outburst. The shift in perspective is startling, for Aunt Beryl has not figured in the story since the opening paragraph, where she briefly conveyed an adult's distaste for the odorous dollhouse. Now we learn she has received "a terrifying, threatening letter" from a male acquaintance who demands that she meet him.[71] If she does not, he will "come to the front door and ask the reason why!"[72] This account points again to the power dynamics of hospitality. Willie demands—does not invite—Aunt Beryl to meet him, and his unwelcome visit to the front door of the house is his threat for lack of compliance. When Beryl reprimands her niece, "frighten[s] those little rats of Kelveys," and "slam[s]" the dollhouse, she relieves her anxiety about Willie by exercising her power over what she can control—the children and the children's house—even if in the adult world of inequalities (in this instance, gender inequalities), social encounters are not so easily managed.[73]

Is Kezia's hospitality a failure? Far from it. The hospitality has been surreptitious and fleeting, yet potent. After the Kelveys hurry far away from the Burnells', Lil's "cheeks [are] still burning" in shame[74] (recalling the gleeful "burning" of the Burnell children as they anticipate boasting about their splendid dollhouse), and they sit on a drainpipe, that device for channeling away sewage or excess water, which signifies their society's view of them. However, our Else, forgetting the scolding, does what she so rarely does: she smiles and speaks. In what she says—"I seen the little lamp"—we realize that despite all the social obstacles, she and Kezia have communicated and reached a common understanding.[75] Most important of all, in regards to Levinas's definition of hospitality, the infinity of our Else—her exceeding the familiar and knowable—is also evident. Mansfield prods readers to recognize this as the narrator asks about our Else and her sister, "What were their thoughts?"[76] The question comes at the end of a paragraph that is almost entirely limited to an exterior view of the Kelveys—and this exterior vantage point is especially noticeable, for this paragraph immediately follows the unexpected delving into Aunt Beryl's interior state. The question is followed by a brief dipping into our Else's mind: "By now she had forgotten the cross lady."[77] Though brief, the sentence requires the reader to pivot radically from the extended description of Aunt Beryl's mental state. Thus, like our Else, who has "nudged up close to her sister," readers now have been nudged close to our Else.[78] But then we are yanked back to the exterior of our Else, an exterior that enables us to feel the infinite depth of her interiority: "She put out a finger and stroked her sister's quill."[79] Throughout the story, the little lamp has been the special detail—and it remains as such—but here another object assumes importance. What it means to our Else is not explained. We can imagine the feather is pleasurably soft to her finger. The stroking of it appears a contented gesture, unlike the anxious gripping of her sister's skirt when she and her sister are in society. Perhaps we see in the quill the symbolism of flight and of writing. But most of all, we can recognize our Else's freedom to privilege one object over others, just as Kezia prized the lamp, and we have the choice to pay attention to our Else as our Else did to Kezia. Importantly, Kezia is no longer in the story. If there is a host at this point—someone taking responsibility for the other—it must be the reader. By now, the significance of our Else's name should be clear. Although "Else" is presumably a shortened version of Elsie and "our" simply an affectionate embellishment within her family, our Else is to us both else and ours.[80]

Mansfield's deft handling of point of view, especially the limited representation of our Else's interiority, is noteworthy in relation to Mansfield's much-remarked-upon ability to impersonate and merge. In explaining her experience of writing, Mansfield repeatedly described her capacity for merging with diverse characters, animals, and even inanimate objects ("When I pass the apple stalls I cannot help stopping and staring until I feel that I, myself, am changing into an apple, too."[81]). Certainly, Mansfield could imagine and present our Else's thoughts if she chose, but, instead, she chooses to position the reader to welcome the unknowable other.

Mansfield's *oeuvre* exposes the potential treachery of hospitality while also offering notable exceptions, such as that of Kezia. The same is true of Woolf's fiction. William Bankes, a summer guest of the Ramsays in *To the Lighthouse* (1927), feels "treacherous" because during dinner he "feel[s] nothing" for his hostess and instead wishes he could be alone. The host, Mr. Ramsay, behaves rudely, "scowling and frowning, and flushing with anger" because a guest requests a second bowl of soup.[82] While these treacheries may appear innocuous, seemingly trivial acts of hospitality are often manifestly linked to significant social matters. For example, Mrs. Ramsay, concerned about one guest, persuades (via a glance) another guest to play the traditional role of women and "say something nice to that young man."[83] Lily complies, but she is displeased by the insincerity of what she says and dissatisfied that she has been prevented yet again from breaking away from society's gender conventions, and readers can see how the protocols of hospitality rigidify the status quo.[84] Woolf often links the dynamics of hospitality on two levels: the interpersonal and the intercultural, especially within England's empire. Lady Bruton admits to her guests that "[s]he had got them there on false pretences" to help her to promote her cause.[85] It is therefore not unreasonable for readers to suspect there are "false pretences" in her social agenda. In fostering emigration of the "superfluous youth of our [Britain's] ever-increasing population" to Canada, specifically those "born of respectable parents," she consolidates her power by presuming to determine who is worthy of support but also of expulsion.[86]

Woolf, like Mansfield, not only exposes the possible treacheries of hospitality as traditionally defined, but also registers humans' desire for knowing the other, a bypassing of Levinasian hospitality. Like Bertha of Mansfield's "Bliss," who is dissatisfied with her partial knowledge of Pearl Fulton, Peter Walsh in *Mrs. Dalloway* recalls his and Clarissa's youthful "dissatisfaction" in "not knowing people; not being known."[87] Like Bertha, who is exhilarated when she believes (erroneously) she and Pearl are feeling exactly the same as they look at her pear tree, Lily Briscoe in *To the Lighthouse* desires a profoundly intimate union. In a physical position that recalls ancient Greek social protocols (think of Priam kneeling down and clasping the knees of Achilles as he begs for the return of his son's dead body in *The Iliad*), Lily "[sits] on the floor with her arms round Mrs. Ramsay's knees, close as she could get," pondering, "What device for becoming, like waters poured into one jar, inextricably the same, one with the object one adored?"[88] Peter, Clarissa, and Lily desire hospitality in which the stranger becomes known and familiar.

Surely one of the most intriguing acts of knowing an other in Woolf's *oeuvre* is the meditation of Clarissa Dalloway, the well-to-do hostess of a Westminster party, on Septimus Smith, the clerk and shell-shocked Great War veteran whom she never meets but instead hears of as two party guests discuss his suicide. Although this climax to *Mrs. Dalloway* has been examined and debated superabundantly in Woolfian scholarship, I believe another examination, specifically in relation to the work of Mansfield, will be fruitful. Rachel Hollander has convincingly shown that *Jacob's Room*, the novel that Woolf wrote before *Mrs. Dalloway*, revises the traditional form of the novel in order to represent more fully than late Victorian novels an ethics founded on others' unknowability. When Hollander contrasts the representations of begging women in *Jacob's Room* and *Mrs. Dalloway*, we glimpse these two novels' different stances toward hospitality. My extended discussion of Clarissa's meditation on Septimus below helps us to grasp more fully the manifold hospitality in Woolf's *oeuvre*.[89]

Clarissa's meditation begins with a key feature of Levinasian hospitality. Not initiated by the self, the act begins with an other's interruption and confrontation. When Sir Bradshaw, the doctor whom Septimus consulted, and his wife talk of the suicide, Clarissa's first reaction is dismay and indignation: "Oh! thought Clarissa, in the middle of my party, here's death, she thought" and "What business had the Bradshaws to talk of death at her party?"[90] She attempts to avert the topic by going into another room. However, there is no one in that room to distract her, and soon Clarissa is vividly encountering Septimus by imagining his suicide. Thus, like Kezia's act of welcome, which occurs beyond the home in which her sisters are preparing for visitors, Clarissa's act of welcome occurs when she absents herself from the form of hospitality that is driven by social protocols. This point is underscored when Sally and Peter erroneously assume Clarissa's absence is due to her attendance on "people of importance, politicians [...] whom Clarissa had to be nice to, had to talk to."[91]

Clarissa's welcome of Septimus begins in a Levinasian way, but as it unfolds, it appears the very opposite of a Levinasian encounter with the other. Rather than the unknown and utterly other, Septimus is for Clarissa accessible and assimilable. In her meditation she readily and accurately explains the motivation of his suicide, expressing points, such as "Death was defiance,"[92] that are in accord with the earlier scene of the suicide that was focalized through Septimus. Moreover, her meditation intermingles thoughts about Septimus and about herself, eroding the distinction between self and other. Even before she thinks about Septimus's motivation, Clarissa's uncanny experience of his suicide dissolves differences. "Up had flashed the ground" is Clarissa's experience of the plummet from Septimus's perspective.[93] The compacted focalization here—Clarissa's view of Septimus's view—enacts what Lily Briscoe craves: the poring of waters "into one jar so that they become inextricably the same, one with the object." "There he lay" seems to suggest distance, but as this sentence continues, Clarissa, in fact, intimately registers Septimus's inner bodily workings, the final pulsing of his blood in his head: "with a thud, thud, thud in his brain, and then a suffocation of blackness."[94] The value of Clarissa's empathic fusion is manifest in the gain to the narrative: the representation of Septimus's final moments is extended (the earlier scene ended with his throwing himself out the window before the downward plummet) and acquires more precise details ("through him, blundering, bruising, went the rusty spikes" was not part of the earlier brief mention of his landing on a railing[95]). Near the end of the meditation, Clarissa "felt somehow very like him"—yet one more indication that the climax to *Mrs. Dalloway* celebrates sameness, not otherness.[96]

However, more careful examination of Clarissa's response to Septimus uncovers some affinity between it and hospitality as expressed by Levinas and Derrida. While readers recognize the keenness of Clarissa's insights into Septimus's suicide, these insights, from her own perspective, are tentative, some of them expressed as questions. Moreover, the flow of her thoughts suggests a generative process that is virtually infinite, one possibility followed by another that does not consolidate it. At one point, for example, the conjunction "or" at the start of a paragraph suggests an alternative to the previous thought.[97] At this point, Clarissa reaches beyond her own experiences. She has been thinking about one of her youthful days at Bourton ("'If it were now to die, 'twere now to be most happy,' she had said to herself once"), but here she considers people whom she presumably thinks of as different from her, "the poets and thinkers."[98] Clarissa's expansive encounter with Septimus leads her to conclude "she did not pity" Septimus,[99] a stance that, as it were, respects

Septimus's otherness to society, for it avoids seeing suicide as the kind of "tragedy" that Septimus (in the scene that is focalized through him) ruefully realizes the doctors, who represent coercive society, like.[100] With all this in mind, we might reconsider Clarissa's "[feeling] somehow very like him."[101] The vague word "somehow" creates a measure of unknowability: she feels very like him, but how exactly? Clarissa may or may not be assuming responsibility for the otherness of Septimus, but she surely takes responsibility for herself in her relations to others. She rebukes herself for her failings: "She had schemed; she had pilfered. She was never wholly admirable."[102] Then she returns to her responsibilities to others, in particular Peter and Sally; these are not merely her longtime friends but also two guests whose status on the party's guest list is equivocal, for Peter was invited at the last minute after Clarissa teases him that she will not invite him, and Sally came uninvited.[103] Clarissa's responsibility to her guests, which brings her meditation to an end, is articulated with an important word that recurs prominently in the novel: "[S]he must go back. She must assemble. She must find Sally and Peter."[104] Throughout the party, "must" has conveyed the social duties of a hostess that drive Clarissa: "[S]he must speak to that couple,"[105] "Clarissa must speak to Lady Bruton,"[106] "But she must leave them,"[107] "She must go up to Lady Bradshaw."[108] For Septimus, the word has conveyed society's coercive power: "'Must,' 'must,' why 'must'? What power had Bradshaw over him? 'What right has Bradshaw to say "must" to me?' he demanded. [...] So he was in their power! Holmes and Bradshaw were on him! The brute with the red nostrils was snuffling into every secret place! 'Must' it could say!"[109] When Clarissa feels compelled to return to Peter and Sally, has "must" metamorphosed from an indication of society's coercion to the self's ethical responsibility to others? Yes—or at least, given the difficulty of reaching categorical conclusions about this remarkable scene, it is a possibility we need to consider.[110]

Overall, in Clarissa's climactic response to Septimus, Woolf validates the process of attempting to know the other and specifically doing so by exploring affinities between self and other. Woolf represents a welcome that encompasses some features of Levinasian ethics but also contrarily and emphatically values sameness. Paralleling the hospitable encounter that forms the novel's climax are the demands that are placed on readers by the novel's overall dynamics. Throughout *Mrs. Dalloway*, readers are propelled along an expansive range of shifting streams of consciousness. This access to an overabundance of interiority flouts a Levinasian treasuring of unknowability. In addition, attentive readers recognize (perhaps only gradually) the links between characters, which are cued by deliberately repeated images and echoed language. For example, the suffering of Peter Walsh, a British official in India, and of Rezia, an Italian immigrant to England, are articulated nearly identically: "Never, never had he [Peter] suffered so infernally!" and "Never, never had Rezia felt such agony in her life!"[111] Discovery of sameness among such varied characters is surely one of the most profound readerly satisfactions offered by this novel. At the same time, the streams of consciousness position readers to be ever open in their encounters with the characters. Shifts in the streams are frequent, sudden, and so erratic that readers cannot predict the next one—thereby positioning readers in a perpetual state of openness to the next other. Only in the novel's final sentence do the flows cease. "There she was" directs our attention to Clarissa.[112] In its echo of "there she was, however; there she was" of much earlier in the novel, readers can mark how their knowledge of Clarissa has grown,[113] yet in its echo of a key sentence in Clarissa's meditation on Septimus, "There he lay," readers are prompted to remain open to Clarissa, an other who cannot be fully known.[114]

Mrs. Dalloway and "The Doll's House," different in many ways, have in common their authors' abiding interest in exploring the varied kinds of hospitality that are possible. Moreover, through adroit use of point of view, they guide readers to welcome the other. Today, with 21.3 million refugees and nearly 34,000 people adding to that number each day, surely we hear Mansfield and Woolf, in their ceaseless grappling with the ethical dilemmas of the relation between self and other, speaking to us urgently.[115]

Notes

1 Katherine Mansfield to Virginia Woolf, December 27, 1920, in *The Collected Letters of Katherine Mansfield*, 5 vols., ed. Vincent O'Sullivan and Margaret Scott (Oxford: Clarendon Press, 1984–2008), 4:154. All subsequent letters from Mansfield are from this source.
2 Katherine Mansfield to Virginia Woolf, December 27, 1920, 4:154.
3 See Julian Pitt-Rivers, "The Stranger, the Guest and the Hostile Host: Introduction to the Study of the Laws of Hospitality," in *Contributions to Mediterranean Sociology: Mediterranean Rural Communities and Social Change*, ed. J. G. Peristiany (Paris: Mouton, 1968), 13–30.
4 Jacques Derrida, *Adieu to Emmanuel Levinas*, trans. Pascale-Anne Brault and Michael Naas (Stanford: Stanford University Press), 50. Limitations of space prevent me from explaining in detail the overlaps and distinctions of Levinas's and

Derrida's theories, but even a very general account of their views provides what I hope is a valuable guiding framework for my argument.

5   Anne Olivier Bell, ed., *The Diary of Virginia Woolf*, 5 vols. (New York: Harcourt, 1977–1984), 1:150.
6   Bell, *Diary of Virginia Woolf*, 1:243.
7   Bell, *Diary of Virginia Woolf*, 1:243.
8   Bell, *Diary of Virginia Woolf*, 1:291.
9   See Hermione Lee, *Virginia Woolf* (New York: Vintage-Random House, 1999), 381–95 and Angela Smith, *Katherine Mansfield & Virginia Woolf: A Public of Two* (Oxford: Clarendon-Oxford University Press, 2007).
10 Mansfield to Woolf,? June 24, 1917, 1:313.
11 Mansfield to Woolf,? June 24, 1917, 1:313.
12 Virginia Woolf to Vanessa Bell, June 27, 1917, in *The Letters of Virginia Woolf*, ed. Nigel Nicolson and Joanne Trautmann, 6 vols. (New York: Harcourt, 1975–1980), 2:159.
13 Mansfield to Woolf, c. August 23, 1917, 1:327.
14 Mansfield to Woolf, c. August 23, 1917, 1:327.
15 Mansfield to Woolf, c. November 10, 1918, 2:289; Mansfield to Woolf, August 13, 1919, 2:347.
16 Bell, *Diary of Virginia Woolf*, 2:61.
17 Bell, *Diary of Virginia Woolf*, 2:62.
18 Bell, *Diary of Virginia Woolf*, 2:45.
19 Bell, *Diary of Virginia Woolf*, 2:44.
20 Bell, *Diary of Virginia Woolf*, 1:58.
21 Bell, *Diary of Virginia Woolf*, 1:257.
22 Bell, *Diary of Virginia Woolf*, 2:226.
23 Patricia Moran, "The 'dream of roots and the mirage of the journey': Writing as Homeland in Katherine Mansfield," in *Katherine Mansfield & Continental Europe: Connections and Influences*, ed. Janka Kaščáková and Gerri Kimber (New York: Palgrave Macmillan, 2015), 202–18.
24 Margaret Scott, ed., *The Katherine Mansfield Notebooks*, 2 vols. (Minneapolis: University of Minnesota Press, 2002), 2:127.
25 Mansfield to John Middleton Murry, November 30, 1919, 3:127–28.
26 Janet Wilson, "'Where is Katherine?': Longing and (Un)belonging in the Works of Katherine Mansfield," in *Celebrating Katherine Mansfield: A Centenary Volume of Essays*, ed. Gerri Kimber and Janet Wilson (Houndmills: Palgrave Macmillan, 2011), 178–79; Andrew Gurr, *Writers in Exile: The Identity of Home in Modern Literature* (Brighton: Harvester Press, 1981), 15.
27 Scott, *Mansfield Notebooks*, 2:166.
28 Virginia Woolf, *A Room of One's Own* (1929; repr., San Diego: Harcourt, 1981), 6.

29 Virginia Woolf, "Old Bloomsbury," in *Moments of Being*, 2nd ed., ed. Jeanne Schulkind (San Diego: Harcourt, 1985), 182.
30 Woolf, "Old Bloomsbury," 181–201.
31 Mansfield to Ottoline Morrell, August 15, 1917, 1:326.
32 O'Sullivan and Scott note that Mansfield could be referring to the gossiping of Maynard Keynes and Clive Bell with Woolf or to comments made by Clive Bell and Desmond MacCarthy, which Woolf relayed to Mansfield. See Mansfield to Virginia Woolf, c. August 23, 1917, 1:327n1.
33 Mansfield to Woolf, c. August 23, 1917, 1:327.
34 Mansfield to Murry, June 1, 1918, 2:210.
35 Bell, *Diary of Virginia Woolf*, 1:58.
36 Mansfield to Woolf,? June 24, 1917, 1:313.
37 Katherine Mansfield, "Bliss," in *The Collected Works of Katherine Mansfield, The Collected Fiction*, ed. Gerri Kimber and Vincent O'Sullivan, 2 vols. (Edinburgh: Edinburgh University Press, 2012), 144.
38 Virginia Woolf, *Mrs. Dalloway* (1925; repr., New York: Harcourt, 1981), 77.
39 Woolf, *Mrs. Dalloway*, 131.
40 Derrida, *Emmanuel Levinas*, 15–16.
41 Mansfield, "Bliss," 2:142.
42 Mansfield, "Bliss," 2:142.
43 Mansfield, "Bliss," 2:143–44.
44 Mansfield, "Bliss," 2:142.
45 Mansfield, "Bliss," 2:147.
46 Katherine Mansfield, "A Cup of Tea," in *Collected Fiction*, ed. Kimber and O'Sullivan, 2:463.
47 Katherine Mansfield, "Prelude," in *Collected Fiction,* ed. Kimber and O'Sullivan, 2:58.
48 My use of the term "treachery" is inspired by James A. W. Heffernan's extensive study of hospitality, *Hospitality and Treachery in Western Literature* (New Haven: Yale, 2014). Heffernan includes a lengthy discussion of *Mrs. Dalloway* (305–24), a novel to be discussed later in this chapter, but engages negligibly with Levinas and Derrida.
49 Mansfield, "A Cup of Tea," 2:465.
50 Mansfield, "Bliss," 2:144.
51 Katherine Mansfield, "The Doll's House," in *Collected Fiction*, ed. Kimber and O'Sullivan, 2:416.
52 Mansfield, "The Doll's House," 2:416.
53 Mansfield, "The Doll's House," 2:416.
54 Mansfield, "The Doll's House," 2:417.
55 Mansfield, "The Doll's House," 2:416.

56 Mansfield, "The Doll's House," 2:416.
57 Mansfield, "The Doll's House," 2:417.
58 Mansfield, "The Doll's House," 2:417.
59 Mansfield, "The Doll's House," 2:417.
60 Mansfield, "The Doll's House," 2:417.
61 *Oxford English Dictionary*, 2nd ed. 20 vols. (Oxford: Oxford University Press, 1989), s.v. "Guy," sb.[2]
62 Mansfield, "The Doll's House," 2:419.
63 Mansfield, "The Doll's House," 2:419.
64 Mansfield, "The Doll's House," 2:419.
65 Mansfield, "The Doll's House," 2:419.
66 Emmanuel Levinas, *Totality and Infinity: An Essay on Exteriority*, trans. Alphonso Lingis (Pittsburgh: Duquesne University Press, 1969), 203.
67 Mansfield, "The Doll's House," 2:419.
68 Mansfield, "The Doll's House," 2:419.
69 Mansfield, "The Doll's House," 2:419.
70 Mansfield, "The Doll's House," 2:419.
71 Mansfield, "The Doll's House," 2:420.
72 Mansfield, "The Doll's House," 2:420.
73 Mansfield, "The Doll's House," 2:420.
74 Mansfield, "The Doll's House," 2:420.
75 Mansfield, "The Doll's House," 2:420.
76 Mansfield, "The Doll's House," 2:420.
77 Mansfield, "The Doll's House," 2:420.
78 Mansfield, "The Doll's House," 2:420.
79 Mansfield, "The Doll's House," 2:420.
80 Meghan Marie Hammond in *Empathy and the Psychology of Literary Modernism* notes, "In their ephemerality, [Mansfield's] character minds always leave our readerly desire to empathise frustrated" (Edinburgh: Edinburgh University Press, 2014), 91. I have tried to show the ethical work that readers can perform when thusly frustrated.
81 Mansfield to Dorothy Brett, October 11, 1917, 1:330.
82 Virginia Woolf, *To the Lighthouse* (1927; repr., San Diego: Harvest-Harcourt, 1981), 89, 95.
83 Woolf, *To the Lighthouse*, 92.
84 Woolf, *To the Lighthouse*, 92.
85 Woolf, *Mrs. Dalloway*, 110.
86 Woolf, *Mrs. Dalloway*, 108. For discussion of Lady Bruton's emigration scheme, see David Bradshaw, introduction to *Mrs. Dalloway*, by Virginia Woolf (Oxford: Oxford University Press, 2000), xxv–xvii, ProQuest ebrary.

87 Woolf, *Mrs. Dalloway*, 152.
88 Woolf, *To the Lighthouse*, 51. I thank Erika Baldt for prodding me to consider the ancient Greek allusion.
89 Hammond's exploration of Woolf's questioning and disrupting of empathy in her political writing and late novels adds to our understanding of Woolf's varying stances toward the relation between self and other, which constitute what I contend is Woolf's ceaseless questioning (*Empathy and Psychology* 148–75).
90 Woolf, *Mrs. Dalloway*, 183, 184.
91 Woolf, *Mrs. Dalloway*, 186.
92 Woolf, *Mrs. Dalloway*, 184.
93 Woolf, *Mrs. Dalloway*, 184.
94 Woolf, *Mrs. Dalloway*, 184.
95 Woolf, *Mrs. Dalloway*, 184.
96 Woolf, *Mrs. Dalloway*, 186.
97 Woolf, *Mrs. Dalloway*, 184.
98 Woolf, *Mrs. Dalloway*, 184.
99 Woolf, *Mrs. Dalloway*, 186.
100 Woolf, *Mrs. Dalloway*, 149.
101 Woolf, *Mrs. Dalloway*, 186.
102 Woolf, *Mrs. Dalloway*, 185.
103 Woolf, *Mrs. Dalloway*, 41, 48, 190.
104 Woolf, *Mrs. Dalloway*, 186.
105 Woolf, *Mrs. Dalloway*, 177.
106 Woolf, *Mrs. Dalloway*, 179.
107 Woolf, *Mrs. Dalloway*, 182.
108 Woolf, *Mrs. Dalloway*, 182.
109 Woolf, *Mrs. Dalloway*, 147.
110 Molly Hite explores *Mrs. Dalloway* as a "tonally indeterminate narrative" in "Tonal Cues and Uncertain Values: Affect and Ethics in *Mrs. Dalloway*," *Narrative* 18, no. 3 (2010): 249–75, *JSTOR*.
111 Woolf, *Mrs. Dalloway*, 62, 98.
112 Woolf, *Mrs. Dalloway*, 194.
113 Woolf, *Mrs. Dalloway*, 76.
114 Woolf, *Mrs. Dalloway*, 184. Annalee Edmondson offers a compelling discussion of Clarissa as both a model of responding ethically to others and a prod to readers' enacting her kind of response in "Narrativizing Characters in *Mrs. Dalloway*," *Journal of Modern Literature* 36, no.1 (2012), 17–36. *Project Muse*.
115 "Figures at a Glance," UNHCR, June 20, 2016, http://www.unhcr.org/en-us/figures-at-a-glance.html (accessed December 19, 2016).

A Critical Duet: Katherine Mansfield and Virginia Woolf Reviewing their Contemporaries

Sydney Janet Kaplan

Critical theories dating back to Matthew Arnold reflect concern over the relationship between the art object and the critic's task, whether the critic depends on the artist or whether the critic is a creative force herself without regard to the artist. Varying emphases on the art as product, on the artist as producer, on the relationship between reader and writer, and so on, all separate and draw boundaries around specific attributes considered "worthy" of discussion. Much always lies outside those boundaries. If we expand them, if we look at critical practice as a shifting field of relationships (outside a fixed pattern set by rules), we might find something else: something in constant flux, movement, and alteration, perhaps affected by nuances drawn from personal life and events as much as from purposeful written texts (such as books of literary theory, critical reviews, and theoretical overviews).

The related critical practices of Katherine Mansfield and Virginia Woolf are especially relevant to these concerns. Reading through their reviews of their contemporaries, we may discover how much the act of criticism is inescapably enmeshed in the life of the critic, in that critic's interaction with other people, and the intellectual/emotional atmosphere that surrounds the critical activity. I have thought about their interaction for a long time. In *Katherine Mansfield and the Origins of Modernist Fiction*, I focused much of my discussion of their critiques on both women's treatments of the novels of Dorothy Richardson and their mutual concerns over literary experimentation.[1] In *Circulating Genius*, I considered their "implicit critical dialogue" in connection with their competition as writers of fiction during John Middleton Murry's editorship of the *Athenaeum* between 1919 and 1921.[2] In this chapter, I expand my interest in that critical dialogue to the question of how personal connections with the authors under review might have affected their critical practice.

Before I do so, I should emphasize that both Mansfield and Woolf had come to book reviewing not primarily as professional critics but as practitioners of fiction. Nonetheless, it is important to situate their reviewing within the institutions of literary criticism of their day. Clearly, their reviews were not informed by the academic institution of criticism, which was still at an early stage of development. "Schools" of criticism were not yet as politically contested within university culture as they would become during the later decades of the twentieth century. In fact, one of Woolf's reviews in the *Athenaeum*, "The Anatomy of Fiction" on May 16, 1919, is a scathing attack on a book by an American professor who appeared to be trying to teach students how to read literature according to a precise method where "every work of art can be taken to pieces, and those pieces can be named and numbered, divided and subdivided, and given their order of precedence, like the internal organs of a frog."[3] Instead, Woolf's and Mansfield's "institution" was that of British journalism, and its politically contested positions were influenced by the ideological stances of individual editors and their financial backers.

Yet, frequently, more than ideology was involved. We must not forget how much personal connections counted in the "business" of book reviewing. Not only were reviewers often friends and acquaintances of the editors of the periodicals involved, but they often were asked to review books by writers who were also friends and acquaintances. For instance, Mansfield reviewed books in the *Athenaeum* by fourteen people she knew. These included Virginia Woolf (reviewed twice), Gilbert Cannan (also twice), and W. L. George (again, twice); also, she reviewed her own cousin Elizabeth von Arnim, H. M. Tomlinson, Frank Swinnerton, J. D. Beresford, Stephen Hudson (Sidney Schiff), and E. M. Forster. Such personal connections must, of necessity, increase the need to develop strategies for achieving the appearance of "objectivity." Nonetheless, she did not reject Murry's request to "give a leg up"[4] for Lawrence by reviewing *Sons and Lovers* (1913), responding with this double-edged remark: "I'll do that about Sons & Lovers & incidentally get a whack in a perlite one at the Bloomsberries."[5] (As it happened, Mansfield never wrote that review.)

The curiously incestuous nature of London book reviewing is noticeable in Murry's assignment of books for review. This is certainly apparent in the case of Mansfield's writing about Virginia Woolf's fiction, and although Woolf did not review Mansfield, she did struggle over Murry's request that she take on both his long poem *The Critic in Judgement* (1919) and T. S. Eliot's *Poems* (1919), which she had just published at the Hogarth Press. Her letter of June 30, 1919, to Phillip Morrell reveals her discomfort:

> The truth is that Murry asked me to do it, and I refused; then he insisted, and with the greatest labour in the world I began an article, but broke down. Leonard went on with it: and then we cobbled the two parts together hoping that no one would recognise either of us. It's rather important both for the Hogarth Press and for the Athenaeum that nobody should know this; so please keep the secret.[6]

Woolf's later explanation to Eliot may be somewhat disingenuous: "I have to confess that it was not I who reviewed your poems in the Athenaeum, but my husband. (I don't think I told Murry this). We felt awkward at reviewing our own publications, and agreed to share the guilt: he reviewed you, and I reviewed Murry."[7]

Every line of the "cobbled" review is ambiguous; its title alone suggests as much: "Is This Poetry?" Nonetheless, Woolf must not have seen it as negative. Six days before it was published, on June 20, 1919, she wrote in her diary with dismay about the June 12 anonymous review in *TLS*, entitled "Not Here, O Apollo," which was critical of both Murry and Eliot:

> A very severe review of Murry, a severe review of Eliot, appeared in the Lit. Sup. on Thursday. Considering their general slackness I don't see why they choose to come down so hard upon Murry; & I wish they hadn't. I attribute the extreme depression of him & Katherine at least partly to this. And I felt gorged & florid with my comparative success. Poor Murry pretended not to mind, but much like a small boy sticking it out that caning doesn't hurt. A poem is a very sensitive part to be beaten. But Katherine looks so ill & haggard that I suppose health may make a great part of her depression. She is going to San Remo for a year in September. Murry means to live alone in the country. I don't see how, all this being so, they can look forward to their future.

Woolf's overriding feeling of the pathos of Mansfield and Murry's situation brings this diary entry to its saddened close: "Anyhow I went off rather sombre, leaving them to their spare lonely meal, nothing seeming to grow or flourish round them; leafless trees."[8]

Mansfield had praised Woolf's *Kew Gardens* (1919) in her review on June 13th, the same day as Woolf's visit. Her reaction five months later to *Night and Day* (1919) was another matter. She was deeply uncomfortable about how to express her disappointment in it without damaging their friendship. She disliked the novel because it did not express the change in consciousness brought on by the

Great War. She exclaimed to Murry that "[w]e have to face our war—they won't. I believe [...] our whole strength depends upon our facing things. I mean facing them without any reservations or restraints."⁹ That credo underlies much of her reviewing for the *Athenaeum*.

That Woolf and Mansfield each came to their writing for the *Athenaeum* at different stages in their work as book reviewers is another important consideration. I have mentioned before how Murry's achievement at the *Athenaeum* was to make it into "a vehicle for the expression of a consolidating, Bloomsbury brand of modernism."¹⁰ Although Mansfield had much earlier reviewed books for *Rhythm*, by now, for both Murry and Mansfield, the exuberant antics of "The Two Tigers" were long in the past. Murry's biographer remarks that when Murry had begun to work with MI7 during the War, "it was good-bye to small magazines, country cottages, flittings: goodbye to Bohemia and poverty."¹¹ Ironically, Virginia Woolf, at exactly the same time that Murry was preparing his first issue of the *Athenaeum*, was reflecting upon her own growing sense of alienation from Bohemia (despite the fact that unlike Murry and Mansfield, she had never really lived that life herself). In a letter to her sister on March 23, 1919, she describes a ruckus at a café when

> a prostitute who was dining at the next table suddenly threw her glass on the floor and upset the mustard and walked out leaving her poor young man to look most uncomfortable. It was a very remarkable scene; and altogether I enjoyed myself very much. But its useless to pretend that I have any real connection with the Bohemian world any longer; I see that its my fate to be sucked under by the Bourgeois and made a sacrifice of two old family friends.¹²

Woolf took up her invitation to write for the *Athenaeum* enthusiastically. Unlike Mansfield, the designated reviewer of new fiction who would be assigned several books a week, Woolf would have much more freedom to pick and choose. In the same letter to Vanessa quoted above, Woolf conveys her initial delight in being involved in its production:

> It is rather fun about the Athenaeum, as every one is to write what they like, and Mrs [Humphry] Ward is to be exposed, and in time they hope to print imaginative prose by me—Murry has got a man called John Gordon, a very bad painter he says, to do art criticism; but I suggested that he'd much better get Duncan to do the important things at any rate—not that Duncan is exactly fluent in composition, but I don't see why he and I and you shouldn't maunder about in picture galleries, and what with his genius and your sublimity and my perfectly amazing gift of writing English we might turn out articles between us.¹³

Woolf would come to write seventeen articles for the *Athenaeum*, on diverse subjects ranging from reviews of books of poetry and prose, to biographies, memoirs, and literary history. Eventually, she even had a chance to write a description of her visit to an exhibition at the Royal Academy.[14] These diverse subjects gave her a chance to stretch her intellectual range, to learn more about many topics, and to develop theories about them. At the same time, she continued to review for the *Times Literary Supplement*, and about fifty unsigned pieces by her appeared there during the two years of the *Athenaeum*. These included some of her most famous essays, such as "Modern Novels" (which appeared on April 10, 1919, fifteen days before her first article in the *Athenaeum*), followed by "The Anatomy of Fiction," on May 16, and seven on the same novels that Mansfield reviewed for the *Athenaeum*. One of those novels is Frank Swinnerton's *September* (1919), which I will use to exemplify the differences between her approaches to it and those of Mansfield.

Woolf's high spirits during the spring of 1919 are evident in her journal entries, which are full of lively depictions of social encounters, conversations with her many friends, and pleasurable professional engagements related to the Hogarth Press. Her second novel was soon to be published and she comments happily on May 22, 1919:

> A few vegetable notes ought to prelude this page: the weather continues fine; the blue seems eternal; an occasional wind rises; we rock slightly; then steady ourselves, & ride on serenely.... I had a surfeit of praise for Kew Gardens— the best prose of the 20th century, surpassing Mark on the Wall, possessing transcendent virtues, save for one passage, between the women, & highly admired by Clive & Roger.[15]

Contrast this mood with Mansfield's journal entry on the very same day:

> *Wednesday* morning. Temp 100.2 Cough troublesome. Signs of blood persist until noonday. Severe pain in lung & feel very cold and nauseated. Shivered all the afternoon but temperature 101. Lung still very painful at each breath.[16]

On May 29, only a week after that journal entry, Mansfield and Murry hosted an *Athenaeum* party at Portland Villa, which Woolf was unable to attend. Mansfield later described the party to Lytton Strachey and mentioned that "Frank Swinnerton came too with whiskers—like an Irish terrier...."[17] Mansfield had known him since the *Rhythm* days. In his autobiography, Swinnerton describes how he became acquainted with her after she had reviewed (anonymously) his early novel *The Happy Family* (1912) in the *Saturday Westminster Gazette*.[18] He remarks that she had been "pleased with the study of a little girl which appeared in this book (she was a specialist, you remember, in little girls)," and afterward wrote to him "suggesting a meeting with herself and Middleton Murry."[19] That meeting soon took place at their flat in Chancery Lane, where he found Mansfield "enchanting" and remembered that he felt he "had never met so mentally-attractive a young woman." He began to contribute to *Rhythm* and its successor, *The Blue Review*, where he was scheduled to write the "Chronicle on English Literature" each month. After its demise, Swinnerton says he "did not hear again of Murry and Katherine Mansfield ... until after the War, when 'The Athenaeum' became for a time, under Murry's editorship, a really brilliant episode in literary journalism."[20] About that period, Swinnerton wrote of Mansfield:

> I still recall her with affectionate respect, not quite as a real woman, but as a being charmingly remote and tender, speaking chiefly of art, but thinking all the time of delicious secrets, with a half-smile upon her lips. This was true of her to the end; perhaps more true of post-War days at Hampstead, when she was very ill and silent, and liked a friend to sit quietly beside her and talk without requiring any answer.[21]

Mansfield's review of his novel *September* would appear on October 10, 1919, following Woolf's review of September 25 in *TLS*. (It's likely that Mansfield had not read Woolf's review, however; it appeared just about the time she was moving to Ospedaletti from San Remo.) Only a month before her own review appeared in the *Athenaeum*, Mansfield had written a warm letter to Swinnerton, thanking him for his essay on Jane Austen, which had appeared in two parts in the *Athenaeum* on September 5 and 19: "What a beautiful little article it is—Are you going to write more often for the paper? Will Murry persuade you? One of the great joys of being a writer (even though, God knows, I am only a beginner) is enjoying another man's work."[22] I can't help but feel that Mansfield's reading of Swinnerton's essay on Austen might have been an unconscious factor in her reference to Austen later in her review of Woolf's *Night and Day*. She might have taken in Swinnerton's observation that in reading Austen, it is a mistake to try to bring in "modern irreverence and experimentalism into a period which was not irreverent or experimental."[23]

Despite the warmth of her letter, the tone of her review of *September* is decidedly chilly: "Perhaps it is owing to the composure and deliberation of Mr. Swinnerton's style in this his new novel that we are sensible of a slight chill in the air long before Marion [sic] Sinclair [sic] discovers that she is in the September of her life."[24] Mansfield recounts the plot of the novel in some detail, but always with a pointed, ironic tone. For example, she quips that Marian "has been married for fifteen years to a wealthy City man whom she knows thoroughly well and is clever enough not to despise." Marian is

> Fond of flowers, enthusiastic over her bees, a good tennis-player, playing the piano with a sensitive touch, though without technical equipment enough for Chopin's Ballade in A Flat—does the author mean to be cruel or to be kind in thus describing her? We are never wholly certain, but having her thus framed and glazed, we are rather acutely conscious of his task when he proceeds to turn the lady into flesh and blood.[25]

Mansfield's readers might well be reminded here of the way Marian's talents seem to bear a faint resemblance to her own depiction of a rather similar woman, also over thirty, in the story she had written a year earlier: "Bliss" (1918). There, Bertha breathlessly sums up all the good things in her life: "Really—really—she had everything" with her "absolutely satisfactory house and garden," "books," "music," and a marriage in which she and her husband "were really good pals."[26] In fact, I wonder if Mansfield might also have sensed some inner-structural similarities between Swinnerton's description of a wife's discovery of her husband's duplicity and her own treatment of it in "Bliss." Both she and Swinnerton reveal that duplicity through imagery and moments of epiphanic awakening to the hidden meaning behind a gesture or remark. In *September*, it is the husband's use of a "silly name" for a cigarette that makes Marian aware that it is "a joke he has with another woman, and that he is being unfaithful to her."[27] That parallel continues with the later revelation that the young woman, Cherry Mant, who "is of the very nature of Spring" yet is also both "wild and treacherous—a little savage, trying to destroy her own flowers," fascinates Marian almost to the point of obsession.[28] Even if Cherry's temperament is the opposite of Pearl's in "Bliss," the situation itself is reminiscent.

Although Swinnerton's writing clearly lacks Mansfield's wit and precision, I found that when I read the novel itself, I actually became intrigued with his treatment of the ambiguous relationship between Marian and Cherry, especially in a scene where he creates a moment of silent connection between the two women as they walk out into the garden:

> The darkness closed upon them, warm and fragrant. The night was there, and the faint sounds of the trees were all they heard. There was no emotion between them, no love, no hate—only a suspense. Neither was in the least aware of the other's thoughts. Both were mysteries—Marian a mystery to Cherry; Cherry a mystery to both Marian and herself. Marian felt that a hundred years of life had made her old.[29]

There even is a moment when Swinnerton places Marian and Cherry standing together looking at the roses and Marian thinks of "today in perfection" and of "no word being spoken."[30] Mansfield, however, is impatient with Swinnerton's attempt to probe the complexities of Marian's conflicting feelings about Cherry:

> The ideas, emotions and suggestions that she evokes in Marion [sic] seem inexhaustible; she might be the first young woman whom the older woman had ever encountered. Every glance of hers is a surprise and a wonder, and when Marion discovers her locked in her husband's arms, her astonishment is not particular; it is all a part of her endless astonishment.[31]

Mansfield concentrates her attention on the way that each of Marian's actions elicits a "portrait of a lady." Extending that trope, Mansfield writes: "In her frame she could not be more convincing, but out of it—do such ladies ever escape? Do they not rather step into other frames?" She extends it further to the other characters by referring to "a whole succession of 'problem' portraits," which are "most carefully, most conscientiously painted, but we are not held." Mansfield claims that they all "have weathered the storm, and dawn finds them back again in the same harbour from which they put out—none the worse or the better for their mock voyage."[32] That shift to the analogy of the ship in the harbor might function as a prelude to her more elaborate construction of that same analogy two months later in her review of Woolf's *Night and Day*.

The last paragraph of Mansfield's review refers to *September* as a "study" without "expression": "And what do we mean exactly by that word 'expression'? Can we afford to leave it out of a page, of a paragraph—after Tchehov?"[33] That reference to Chekhov as her final thrust suggests two submerged elements in Mansfield's critique, the first being her adherence to the concept of a hierarchy of greatness in the arts. Here she resembles Murry, who wrote that the "function of true criticism is to establish a definite hierarchy among the great artists of the past, as well as to test the production of the present."[34] Of course, that "test" would undoubtedly fail *any* of the novels Mansfield reviewed for the *Athenaeum*. The second, and more deeply submerged element is her choice of Chekhov, a writer who was not a novelist, as her touchstone. Could it be that Chekhov is her unconscious substitution for herself: the writer who knew *how* to create "expression"?

Virginia Woolf did not need to consider any personal relationship with Frank Swinnerton when writing her review: she had none. I have been unable to find any evidence that the two of them ever met (although they would have if Woolf had attended the *Athenaeum* party on May 29). Of course she would have been aware of his considerable reputation as a novelist. He had already published eight other novels as well as critical studies of George Gissing and Robert Lewis Stevenson. She also might have been aware that he was an editor at Chatto and Windus, thereby making him a prominent figure in the publishing world. Unlike Mansfield, she does not try to measure his achievement against some figurehead "great" writer such as Chekhov. Instead, Woolf's interest focuses more on what the author is attempting to do and how successful is his attempt. As a novelist herself, Woolf was aware of a writer's struggle through the long, complicated process of creating complex characters that needed to change within the course of the story, as well as making that "story" reveal much about the society in which it takes place. She also had been forced to confront the frightening openness that the "baggy" shape of a novel presents to a novelist. Thus, she was more interested than Mansfield in the question of the *process* of development: not only of the characters within the story, but of the novelist's own development and that novelist's place in the ongoing movement of literary history. Consequently, she places *September* within the context of the trajectory of its author's evolution as a novelist.

Here, then, are the opening sentences of her review: "*September* is a better book than *Shops and Houses*. It is, indeed, a very able book. With candour and with sincerity Mr Swinnerton has applied his brain to a very difficult task."[35] Note Woolf's reference to the "brain" here. In her review of his novel *Shops and Houses* (1918) the previous year, she had emphasized its author's intelligence, remarking that "Mr Swinnerton takes up his position upon a little mound of intellectual honesty, from which he observes and according to which he judges."[36] Not surprisingly, she placed him "among the group of honest observers of contemporary life who filter their impressions sedulously and uncompromisingly through the intellect and suffer nothing to pass save what possesses meaning and solidity."[37] Now, with *September*, Woolf again pays attention to the intellect, this time in terms of how it functions in the strategies of its author's construction of plot and characters. Woolf points out that Swinnerton's construction of the character of Marian is "finally and logically outlined, because the intellect has had much to do with the shaping of it; and wherever Mr Swinnerton can use his brain he uses it to good effect." In contrast, she seems to feel that he is less successful with the character of Cherry, because although "the intellect is there … it is at the mercy of a thousand instincts." She continues:

> Once more we are reminded of the supreme difficulty of transferring the mind of one sex into that of the other. The mental changes which each woman produces in the other are credible for the most part, always interesting and often subtle.

> Yet it is impossible not to hear, as the close tense narrative proceeds, a sound as of the cutting of steps in ice.[38]

That last image, of "a sound as of the cutting of steps in ice," might remind us of Mansfield's reference to a chill in the air. But Woolf's comment on the "difficulty of transferring the mind of one sex into that of the other" should also remind us of her rapidly developing feminist concerns. She is clearly greatly interested in this male writer's attempt to penetrate women's minds. She draws attention to the fact that although this is a story about heterosexual relationships and the issue of infidelity, "[t]he relationship between the two women is the theme of the book; and as Mr Swinnerton has been at pains to endow each with character, and to make out from his own insight how such a relation might shape itself, the development is original enough to have an unusual air of truth."[39]

Woolf appears to appreciate Swinnerton's attempt and despite her hesitations brings her review to its conclusion on a positive note.

> It is easy enough to mark out the boundaries of Mr Swinnerton's talent—to say that his is a lucid rather than a beautiful mind, intellectual in its scope, rather than imaginative. But praise ought to have the last word and the weightiest. For among modern novelists very few would choose to make the fruit of the contest something so quiet and, until we give it a second look, so ordinary as the power which Marian Forster retrieved from the wreck of brighter hopes. Few would plan their story so consistently with that end in view. We read with the conviction that we are being asked to attend to a problem worth solving—a conviction so rare as by itself to prove that September is a novel of exceptional merit.[40]

What neither Woolf nor Mansfield considers in their reviews of *September* is the larger, sociocultural significance of its treatment of women's marital dissatisfaction. Swinnerton's novel, along with a number of others they reviewed, such as J. D. Beresford's *An Imperfect Mother* (1920), use the possibility of women's adultery to reveal how sexual incompatibility has become an issue of social concern that might finally be explored in fiction. (This trend will come to its most notorious climax in Lawrence's *Lady Chatterley's Lover*, nearly a decade later.) Feminist writers earlier in the century had taken up this concern, but the onus in such writing is more often on the male figure, who is either physically abusive, overbearing, or deceptive. Mansfield creates marital situations such as Linda Burnell's fear of sexuality and Bertha's suppressed "bliss," but in neither story does she describe a married woman in love with another man. Woolf, interestingly, does not focus at all on the theme of adultery. I wonder if the prevalence of that theme in novels written by men after the Great War reflects male anxieties over women's independence from them and their corresponding fears of the loss of masculinity. In these novels, the problems stem not from the husband's power and aggression, but from their failures as lovers and companions.

Marian develops a passion for Nigel, a man much younger than her, and Swinnerton emphasizes his masculine attributes and suggests Marian's secret arousal by him in the "fluttering of the breast that showed a heart throbbing fast under that tranquil demeanor."[41] Her reactions, though, to her husband's loss in a tennis game with Nigel evoke "some ghost of ancient love" for him and "Marian had a quick pity for him." And when Marion goes to sleep thinking about Nigel, she dreams instead of "Howard as he had been and as he was no longer."[42] This abrupt transition from longed-for lover to bored-with husband bears a certain similarity to Mansfield's handling of Bertha's transition from desire for Pearl to desire for her husband.

Perhaps the whole subject of adultery was particularly unsettling to Mansfield when she was writing her review of *September*. She had just begun to live in Ospedaletti and Murry had returned to their home in Hampstead. Whenever she was separated from him, her old fears about his attraction to other women began to torment her. Swinnerton's novel was touching upon matters that disturbed her greatly, unlike Woolf, whose sense of security in her marriage to Leonard allowed her more freedom to distance herself from the situation Swinnerton was exploring. Moreover, Woolf's interest in the relationship between the two women in the novel might have helped her to form more ideas about ways of probing the consciousness of female characters and propelled her toward a fuller development of one who also bears some resemblance to Marian Forster: Clarissa Dalloway. Woolf might well have appreciated how far Swinnerton was able to go in showing how Marian's thoughts were so much more complex than the "portrait of a lady" that Mansfield derided. Swinnerton describes "thoughts thronging her mind like characters in a dream. She was full of vibrations and responses to all these impressions of the day."[43] Woolf would go on to convey such "vibrations" and "impressions" and was able to avoid the problem she believed that Swinnerton could not completely solve: "the difficulty of transferring the mind of one sex into that of the other." Moreover she could go beyond the "boundaries" of Swinnerton's "talent," what she had referred to as "a lucid rather than a beautiful mind, intellectual in its scope, rather than imaginative."[44]

So could Mansfield. What Woolf referred to as the "difficulty of transferring the mind of one sex into that of the other" did not inhibit Mansfield from doing just that when she wrote her next story, "The Man Without a Temperament" (1920), only a few months after her review of *September*. Through exactly the right combination of memories, images, and external gestures, she conveys the consciousness of Robert Salesby, the husband of a gravely ill woman. The contrast between his inner life and his demeanor, in which his feelings are tightly suppressed, gives us a brilliant example of Mansfield's genius in creating "expression."

Notes

1   Sydney Janet Kaplan, *Katherine Mansfield and the Origins of Modernist Fiction* (Ithaca: Cornell University Press, 1991), 161–68.
2   Sydney Janet Kaplan, *Circulating Genius: John Middleton Murry, Katherine Mansfield and D. H. Lawrence* (Edinburgh: Edinburgh University Press, 2010), 109.
3   Virginia Woolf, "The Anatomy of Fiction," *Athenaeum* no. 4646 (May 16, 1919): 331.
4   John Middleton Murry to Katherine Mansfield, October 17, 1919, in *The Letters of John Middleton Murry to Katherine Mansfield*, ed. C.A. Hankin (London: Constable, 1983), 188.
5   Katherine Mansfield to John Middleton Murry, October 22, 1919, in *The Collected Letters of Katherine Mansfield*, 5 vols., ed. Vincent O'Sullivan and Margaret Scott (Oxford: Clarendon Press, 1988–2004), 3:42. All subsequent letters from Mansfield are from this source.
6   Virginia Woolf to Phillip Morrell, June 30, 1919, in *The Letters of Virginia Woolf, 1912-1922*, vol. 2, ed. Nigel Nicolson and Joanne Trautmann (New York: Harcourt Brace Jovanovich, 1976), 373. All subsequent letters from Woolf are from this source.
7   Virginia Woolf to T. S. Eliot, July 28, 1920, 437.
8   Anne Olivier Bell, ed., *The Diary of Virginia Woolf, 1915-1919*, vol. 1 (New York: Harcourt Brace Jovanovich, 1977), 281–82.
9   Mansfield to Murry, November 10, 1919, 3:82.
10 Kaplan, *Circulating Genius*, 104.
11 F. A. Lea, *John Middleton Murry* (New York: Oxford University Press, 1960), 54.
12 Virginia Woolf to Vanessa Bell, March 23, 1919, 341.
13 Woolf to Vanessa Bell, March 23, 1919, 341.
14 Virginia Woolf, "The Royal Academy," *Athenaeum* no. 4660 (August 22, 1919): 774–76.

15 Bell, *Diary of Virginia Woolf*, 275–76.
16 Margaret Scott, ed., *The Katherine Mansfield Notebooks*, vol. 2 (Minneapolis: University of Minnesota Press, 2002), 174.
17 Mansfield to Lytton Strachey, early June 1919, 2:321.
18 Mansfield had during that time anonymously reviewed Swinnerton's novel *The Happy Family* in the *Saturday Westminster Gazette* on September 21, 1912. The review is reprinted in Gerri Kimber and Angela Smith, eds., *The Collected Works of Katherine Mansfield: The Poetry and Critical Writings*, vol. 3 (Edinburgh: Edinburgh University Press, 2014), 435–36.
19 Frank Swinnerton, *Swinnerton: An Autobiography* (New York: Doubleday, 1936), 109–110.
20 Swinnerton, *Autobiography*, 111.
21 Swinnerton, *Autobiography*, 110–11.
22 Mansfield to Frank Swinnerton, September 8, 1919, 2:354.
23 Frank Swinnerton, "Jane Austen," *Athenaeum* no. 4664 (September 19, 1919): 906.
24 Katherine Mansfield, "Portraits and Passions," in *Collected Works*, ed. Kimber and Smith, 514.
25 Mansfield, "Portraits and Passions," 514.
26 Katherine Mansfield, "Bliss," in *The Collected Works of Katherine Mansfield: Collected Fiction, 1916-1922*, vol. 2, ed. Gerri Kimber and Vincent O'Sullivan (Edinburgh: Edinburgh University Press, 2013), 145.
27 Mansfield, "Portraits and Passions," 514.
28 Mansfield, "Portraits and Passions," 515.
29 Frank Swinnerton, *September* (New York: George H. Doran, 1919), 83.
30 Swinnerton, *September*, 91.
31 Mansfield, "Portraits and Passions," 515.
32 Mansfield, "Portraits and Passions," 516.
33 Mansfield, "Portraits and Passions," 516.
34 John Middleton Murry, *Aspects of Literature* (New York: Knopf, 1920), 14.
35 Virginia Woolf, "September," in *Contemporary Writers* (New York: Harcourt, 1965), 102.
36 Woolf, "September," 99.
37 Woolf, "September," 99.
38 Woolf, "September," 103.
39 Woolf, "September," 102.
40 Woolf, "September," 104.
41 Swinnerton, *September*, 68.
42 Swinnerton, *September*, 68.
43 Swinnerton, *September*, 89.
44 Woolf, "September," 103.

4

Katherine Mansfield and Aldous Huxley: A Blighted Friendship

Gerri Kimber

The relationship between Katherine Mansfield's husband John Middleton Murry and Aldous Huxley is well documented. David Goldie notes that "Murry began the post-war period with the critical world at his feet but ended it as something of a doormat,"[1] exemplified by Huxley's lampooning of Murry as the hypocritical character of Burlap in his novel *Point Counter Point* (1928). However, the connection between Mansfield and Huxley has always remained rather a footnote to the relationship between the two men. This essay seeks to redress such an imbalance. Huxley's initial acquaintance with Mansfield at Garsington led to dinners and private visits recorded by both parties, and to the fictionalizing of each other in their creative writing. What emerges is a difficult relationship, blighted almost from the start by the friendships—and enmities—of those around them.

Literary London was a small world in the 1910s and early 1920s, with Mansfield flitting in and out as her health permitted, before her untimely death in Fontainebleau from tuberculosis in January 1923, aged just 34. Many relationships were initiated and developed at Garsington, the Oxfordshire home of Lady Ottoline Morrell, where her encouragement and generosity toward frequently penniless young writers brought many of them together. As Carolyn Heilbrun notes, "Lytton Strachey and Aldous Huxley, for instance, were both undergraduates. She picked them out, according to her custom, because she thought they could contribute to the life of the spirit to which she aspired."[2] Leonard Woolf offers a clear picture of a youthful Huxley at Garsington:

This chapter is a longer version of an essay first published in *Aldous Huxley Annual: A Journal of Twentieth Century Thought and Beyond* 14 (2014): 163–78.

> The only distinguished women whom I ever saw at Garsington were Margot [Asquith], Katherine Mansfield, and Virginia; but there were always a galaxy of male stars, from ancient red giants like Yeats to new white dwarfs from Balliol and New College. [...] There for the first time I saw the young Aldous Huxley folding his long, grasshopper legs into a deckchair and listening entranced to a conversation which is unlike that of any other person I have talked with. I could never grow tired of listening to the curious erudition, intense speculative curiosity, deep intelligence which, directed by a gentle wit and charming character, made conversation an art.[3]

Michael Holroyd claims that for the young Huxley, Garsington "appeared as an Oriental palace from a story by Scheherezade,"[4] and Huxley himself wrote how it gave him "a complete mental reorientation."[5]

Early Garsington regulars were keen for Mansfield to be invited. Bertrand Russell wrote to Morrell: "I want to get to know Katherine Mansfield really well. She interests me mentally very much indeed—I think she has a very good mind, & I like her boundless curiosity."[6] Mansfield first invited herself in a letter to Morrell on June 27, 1916. Murry had already spent the previous Christmas there while Mansfield had been in Bandol in the South of France, and Garsington curiosity about her was evident, and "her exact relationship to the wispy figure of Middleton Murry was something one had to establish by tactful enquiry."[7] Their mutual friend, D.H Lawrence, already a regular visitor, had encouraged Morrell to befriend them both, a year before:

> Murry has a genuine side to his nature; so has Mrs. Murry. Don't mistrust them. They are valuable, I know.
>
> We must have some meetings at Garsington. Garsington must be the retreat where we come together and knit ourselves together. Garsington is wonderful for that. [...] We must draw together. Russell and I have really got somewhere. We must bring the Murrys in. Don't be doubtful of them [...].[8]

Morrell recorded this first visit to Garsington in July 1916, noting how Mansfield was "strangely dark in her black and white clothes." Her impression was that she regarded them all with a "novelist's eye, as potential material, and that she herself was being recorded as 'a grand lady patronizing artists for my own glory.'"[9] Around this time, Morrell is recorded as saying, "I asked Aldous Huxley [...] '*Did* Katherine Mansfield have any personality of her own?' And Aldous answered 'None.'"[10] Nevertheless, Morrell was fascinated by Mansfield's past—no doubt enhanced by the latter's infamous ability to embellish the truth—be it about her colonial upbringing in New Zealand, her education at Queen's College in Harley Street (where Ottoline's old friend John Cramb had been one of her tutors), or the few weeks she spent with a travelling opera company in the north of England. Lytton Strachey also recorded his impression of her on that visit: "an odd satirical woman behind a regular mask of a face […] very difficult to get at; one felt it would take years of patient burrowing, but that it might be worth while."[11] And here is Bertrand Russell again:

> Her talk was marvelous, much better than her writing, especially when she was telling of things she was going to write, but when she spoke about people she was envious, dark, and full of alarming penetration in discovering what they least wished known and whatever was bad in their characteristics.[12]

Huxley was also a visitor to Garsington at this time; in August he would go on to become a permanent resident on the estate for several months, working on the land alongside established conscientious objectors. After one visit he recorded how he "'spent most of the night talking with intelligent people'" and sleeping out on the roof in the company of "an artistic young woman in short hair and purple pyjamas."[13] Similar events would later be replicated in his first novel, *Crome Yellow* (1921). Neither Huxley nor Mansfield recorded what they thought of each other on this initial visit. Six years younger than Mansfield, Huxley was a precociously intelligent recent Oxford graduate, obtaining a first in English (an unusual subject for formal study at that time). He wrote to Morrell discussing his degree results on July 27, 1916: "About my schools—they published the list on the day I was last over at Garsington: they had the wit to give me a first. In the list published in the Sunday papers there was the most wonderful version of my name: viz 'Aldores Huxley'—which is most gloriously Spanish."[14]

However, a notorious episode involving Mansfield and an Indian friend of Huxley's would lead to a closer connection. On the night of August 30, 1916, at the Café Royal in London, Mansfield publicly defended a book of poems—*Amores* (1916)—written by Lawrence, which was being derided by a group of other diners, one of whom was a Bengali Muslim called Husyen Suhrawardy, whom Huxley had previously befriended and taken to Garsington. (The incident would later be used by Lawrence in chapter 28 of *Women in Love* [1920]: "Gudrun in the Pompadour.") Huxley, although not present, had received news of the episode by the next morning and had immediately written to Morrell, as had the artist Mark Gertler, who had been one of Mansfield's party. Morrell immediately forwarded Huxley's letter to Mansfield, fishing for more details; her response to Morrell: "Huxley's languid letter doesn't tempt me dreadfully to tell him—to satisfy even his 'very idlest curiosity' and 'merest inquisitiveness.'

I am afraid I am not young enough to dance to such small piping. Heavens, his letter makes me feel so old."[15] There is feigning on both sides here, and a certain shrewd jockeying for position with Morrell. Nevertheless, a friendship of sorts was developing, with Morrell frequently acting as a sounding board to the other two.

Christmas 1916 saw a large gathering at Garsington; a letter from Dora Carrington to her soldier brother in France listed the company:

> [T]he lady of Gower Street Katherine Mansfield and her melancholy spouse, Lytton, Brett, Aldous Huxley of Balliol (attached to Maria Nys and she to him) a lanky youth with one eye gamey who writes poetry, and is well versed in the literary accomplishments which the lads of Balliol do acquire.[16]

Mansfield was tasked with writing a play which the guests performed on Boxing Day. It was called *The Laurels* and a three-page fragment still exists. The cast list read as follows:

Lytton	—	Dr Keit
Carrington	—	his grandchild, Muriel Dash
Mansfield	—	Florence Kaziany
Aldous	—	Balliol Dodd
Maria	—	Jane
Murry	—	Ivan Tchek

It was a "kind of Ibsen-Russian play," as Carrington told her brother, "marvellously witty and good."[17] Or as Huxley told his brother Julian on December 29, 1916: "We performed a superb play invented by Katherine, improvising as we went along. It was a huge success, with Murry as a Dostoevsky character and Lytton as an incredibly wicked old grandfather."[18] Antony Alpers notes that no one but Mansfield would have been alert to the dark humor of the character she herself played, an unmarried mother whose name drew on Floryan Sobienowski, her Polish lover during her stay in Bavaria in 1909, and Kaziany, a woman violinist they had known together. The first few lines are as follows:

> (Act I Scene I. Breakfast room. Ivan enters, pours out a cup of coffee, lights a cigarette, stamps on the cigarette, says)
>
> IVAN: And so it goes on. (And walks out, wrapped in gloom. Enter JANE who clears away and resets the table etc., brushes away cigarette ash and goes to the door and calls)
>
> JANE: Miss Muriel.

MURIEL: (in the distance)   Just coming. (She comes in with a bird in a cage, takes off cover and hangs the bird in the window, saying) Now you can look out and sing and see the sun (sighs profoundly) shining on the land.
JANE: Mr Tchek has had his breakfast Miss. It's all ready for the master.
MURIEL: Oh, very well Jane. I'll call him. (Looks at Jane) What's the matter Jane? You've been crying.
JANE: (at table)   Oh, don't notice me, Miss Muriel. I'm nobody. I'm nothing.
MURIEL: (Shocked)   Whatever do you mean Jane? (Jane puts her hand over her eyes and sobs.)
MURIEL: (taking the hand away)   Poor Jane and you do look so dreadful. (Brightly) Tell me then [?]
JANE: Oh Miss if you knew what I feel about—It seems funny don't it Miss—things happen like that. When I saw 'is boots in the passage this morning—those black button ones with the brown tops—I felt I could bear it no longer. I felt quite wild Miss, in the kitchen jest now. Oh Mother what 'ave you been and gone and done. And it's not as though it's my fault Miss. That's what makes it so hard to bear.
MURIEL: Bewildering—what on earth are you talking about Jane?
JANE: Oh Miss—it's Mr Tchek—the Russian gentleman.
MURIEL: Are you in love with him Jane?
JANE: Oh Miss—
MURIEL: But whatever is there to cry about in that Jane? Oh Jane—you lucky girl. Just to be in love—isn't that enough? Oh how I envy you, how I envy you. I've nobody—nobody to be in love with except (she points) my canary, and there comes a time Jane (taking the cage) when even a canary isn't half enough. One seems somehow to want more. Oh Jane—
JANE: But you don't understand Miss. If I was like you, with my Pa and me Ma in a lovely double frame on the dressing table, it'd be alright. But there—I've got to tell somebody. (Beats her breast) I'm a love child, I am.
MURIEL: (Claps her hands) A love child, Jane? How too divine. What is it? How pretty it sounds. (dreamily) A love child.
JANE: (leaning towards her curiously) Do you mean to say you *don't know*, Miss? It means I haven't got no Father.
MURIEL: But oh, Jane, how perfect. Just like the Virgin Mary.[19]

Mansfield's acute ear for accents and her sense of humor are all present in this passage. Sadly, the section containing "Balliol Dodd's" lines no longer exists.

There are numerous records of meetings between Huxley and Mansfield during the height of their acquaintance in 1917, all divulged to Morrell. On February 6, Huxley wrote to her: "I should have liked to have come this weekend—with Katherine but I am going to see my sister at school"; and again on March 1: "I met Katherine in a bus yesterday and am going to see her tonight." On May 10, they spent the evening together:

> I dined with Katherine last night in her delightful rabbit hutch in Church Street and we proceeded to the second house at the Chelsea Palace, where there was a perfectly fabulous woman called Florrie singing a quite unbelievably wonderful song, of which the last lines of the refrain were:
> Talk about the West End with its wonderful sights.
> But O-o-o-oh! Those Arabian nights!
> And the whole of her mountainous body positively shook with the voluptuousness of the conception. Katherine was very delightful and amusing, a little less acting a part than usual.[20]

Murry and Mansfield were at this time living separately, their relationship in one of its phases of fluctuation, and Huxley visited Mansfield on more than one occasion at her studio flat in Chelsea. On June 16, Mansfield wrote to Morrell: "I want to make you laugh about my dinner with [...] Aldous & his khaki brother and French Polish Elliot [sic]."[21] Just a couple of weeks later on July 3, she was again writing to Morrell:

> Aldous came to see me last Wednesday. He told me more news in half an hour than I have heard for months. At present he seems to be a great social success and "incredible" things happen to him *at least* every evening. He spoke of the Isola Bella [a restaurant at 15 Frith Street, Soho] as though it were the rendezvous of Love and High Adventure [...] I felt my mind flutter over Aldous as if he were the London Mail. There was a paragraph about simply everybody.[22]

At the height of this friendship Mansfield wrote a dialogue piece for the *New Age*, on May 24, 1917, called "In Confidence" and uncollected until the Edinburgh edition of her complete fiction, published in 2012. It is her first pastiche of a thousand similar conversations overheard at Garsington:

> *(Five young gentlemen are having no end of an argument in a big, shadowy drawing-room. They are tremendously at their ease. One is playing with the ears and kissing the top of the head of a blue Persian cat, two are sitting on the floor hugging their knees, the fourth sprawls on a sofa, one leg doubled under him, cutting a French book with a jade paper-knife, and the fifth droops over the gleaming grand piano. Marigold is curled up in a black chair. Now and again she murmurs "How true that is" or "Do you really think so?" Isobel sits on the arm of her chair, smiling faintly.)*

4TH GENTLEMAN: But look here, all I wanted to say is that the lack of prudery in France merely seems to me to prove that the French do believe that man is *au fond* a rational animal. You don't dispute that, do you? I mean—well—damn it all! their literature's based on it. Isn't it?

2ND GENTLEMAN: And that, according to you, explains why they seek their inspiration, their very inspiration, in realism. Does it?

4TH GENTLEMAN (*superbly*):   Of course it does. Absolutely. How else are you going to explain it?

1ST GENTLEMAN: Then a nation that's "got prudery," as the Americans would say, is a nation that believes man is not a rational animal?

5TH GENTLEMAN (*very bitterly*):   There are things, say the English, which are not to be talked about. *Fermez la porte, s'il vous plaît.*

3RD GENTLEMAN (*greatly excited*):   But look here—half a minute—don't go too fast; this is damned interesting. Now we really are getting at something. If what you say is true, then prudery is a step towards real art—what? For what do we mean by prudery? Prudery is false shame, the negative to real shame, which again is, as it were, the negative to reverence. Reverence being the positive quality, the thing that great art's got to have—what?

5TH GENTLEMAN (*extremely bitterly*):   I heard a good bit of Bowery slang the other day. (*With a strong Yankee drawl.*) Put sand on your boots, kid; you're sliding.

4TH GENTLEMAN: Oh, shut up. If you don't want to talk, go and play croquet. Yes, that's what I was more or less driving at.

2ND GENTLEMAN: And that, according to you, explains why the English seek their inspiration, their very inspiration, in idealism, does it?

4TH GENTLEMAN: Precisely. And also why the English must of necessity beat the French at this art game all the time.

1ST GENTLEMAN: Therefore it's all a question of values—a sense of moralities....

3RD GENTLEMAN: And puts the stopper finally and irrevocably on old man Kant—what?[23]

Did no one at Garsington read the *New Age*? Perhaps not. It certainly anticipates similar conversations in *Crome Yellow* and other early Huxley novels. The piece was signed Katherine Mansfield and reads as though it was taken verbatim from any one of a thousand such Garsington exchanges.

Virginia Woolf's impression of Huxley at this time was recorded in a diary entry for November 19, 1917, following a trip to Garsington: "People strewn about in a sealingwax coloured room: Aldous Huxley toying with great round disks of ivory & green marble—the draughts of Garsington";[24] and again on

November 27, in a letter to her sister, Vanessa Bell: "There were endless young men from Oxford, and Brett and Lytton and Aldous Huxley who talks too much about his prose romances for my taste and falls into deep glooms."[25] And yet, for all the outward bonhomie in communications between Mansfield and Huxley at this time, a certain distrust prevailed. In December 1917, following a visit from Mansfield, Morrell wrote:

> I felt very doubtful about her and she left me with rather a feeling of distrust. Her curious, smooth unruffled face, like a Japanese mask. I am afraid she really dislikes me underneath and envies the comfort and comparative luxury of our home, and laughs at us all and thinks we are negligible [...] She is too dreadfully lacking in human kindness ever to be very sympathetic to me [...] She enjoys mocking and I recoil from it.[26]

At almost the same time, on December 11, 1917, Huxley was writing to Juliet Baillot of another visit to Mansfield:

> Last Sunday I looked in on Katherine [Mansfield] in her curious little kennel in Chelsea; all very mysterious, particularly when she suddenly gave a shout in the middle of our conversation and was answered by the sleepy voice of somebody who was in bed behind a curtain and whose presence I had never realised.[27]

By January 7, 1918, Mansfield's health had deteriorated (still at this time thought to be severe rheumatism), to the extent that doctors were advising her to urgently seek a warmer climate, and from this point onward, her relationships with people like Huxley, Morrell, and Woolf could be likened to flickering candles, which, one by one, were extinguished. There were other difficulties too. In August 1917, Murry had revealed to Mansfield that Morrell had fallen deeply in love with him (which she had not), and thus Mansfield was forced into a false relationship with her, outwardly friendly, inwardly wary, which Morrell had astutely picked up on. And once Mansfield had left for Bandol in the South of France in early 1918, Huxley would become more involved with Murry, when the latter, newly appointed as editor of the *Athenaeum*, offered both him and J.W.N. Sullivan assistant editorships in January 1919. From this point, Mansfield's fondness for Huxley would mutate into something less forgiving and more condemnatory.

Mansfield wrote her story "Bliss" in Bandol during the second half of February 1918, telling Murry on February 26, "You will again 'recognize' some of the people. *Eddie* of course is a fish out of the Garsington pond (which gives me joy) and Henry is touched with W. L. G [the novelist W. L. George]."[28] As noted first by Alpers: "The satire of arty London drawing-rooms is as clever and thin as that of Aldous Huxley, himself the model for Eddie."²⁹ A diary entry of Virginia Woolf's from March 9, 1918, describes Huxley at this time: "We had tea at the 17 Club. One room was crowded, & silent; at the end of the other Aldous Huxley & a young woman in grey velvet held what should have been a private conversation. A. has a deliberate & rather dandified way of speaking."³⁰ Mansfield mimics this dandified tone perfectly in her story "Bliss":

> The bell rang. It was lean, pale Eddie Warren (as usual) in a state of acute distress.
> "It is the right house, *isn't* it?" he pleaded.
> "Oh, I think so—I hope so," said Bertha brightly.
> "I have had such a *dreadful* experience with a taxi-man; he was *most* sinister. I couldn't get him to *stop*. The *more* I knocked and called the *faster* he went. And *in* the moonlight this *bizarre* figure with the *flattened* head *crouching* over the *lit-tle* wheel...."
> He shuddered, taking off an immense white silk scarf. Bertha noticed that his socks were white, too—most charming.
> "But how dreadful!" she cried.
> "Yes, it really was," said Eddie, following her into the drawing-room. "I saw myself *driving* through Eternity in a *timeless* taxi."³¹

In turn, Huxley would trace physical elements of Mansfield in the character of Anne in *Crome Yellow*:

> In her low deck-chair Anne was nearer to lying than to sitting. Her long, slender body reposed in an attitude of listless and indolent grace. [...H]er face had a pretty regularity that was almost doll-like. And indeed there were moments when she seemed nothing more than a doll; when the oval face [...] expressed nothing; when it was no more than a lazy mask of wax.³²

So many contemporaries of Mansfield noted her doll-like appearance and her mask-like face. The caricature was instantly recognizable.

Yet their characters were similar in many ways. Christopher Isherwood once wrote of Huxley:

> Fearless curiosity was one of Aldous's noblest characteristics, a function of his greatness as a human being. Little people are so afraid of what the neighbors will say if they ask Life unconventional questions. Aldous questioned unceasingly, and it never occurred to him to bother about the neighbors.³³

If you substitute the name, this quotation would fit Mansfield perfectly; the attributes described above—the fearless curiosity, the unconventionality, the questioning—are all hallmarks of her personality. One also senses that with

Huxley, Mansfield may have given too much of herself away. During their brief period of intimacy, secrets may have been divulged (perhaps relating to Rasputin in a previous quotation, who was in fact Floryan Sobieniowski, a Polish former lover of Mansfield's who would go on to blackmail her over letters he had kept since 1909). Mansfield had a habit of drawing people near and then bitterly regretting it. Frieda Lawrence was another friend whom she confided in at the start of their relationship in 1914 and remained wary of ever after. It was a pattern in her life, repeated with Virginia Woolf and even her own cousin, Elizabeth von Arnim, and to a certain extent, Morrell. In fact, Morrell had a similar personality trait. David Cecil recounts: "Even when her friendships did not actually involve love, they tended to get overheated to a point which ended in an explosion, followed by a breach. However, while they lasted, both love affairs and friendships were rapturous and fruitful."[34] Nearly ten years after Mansfield's death, Morrell would record in a letter to D'Arcy Cresswell on June 11, 1932:

> I have reread all Katherine Mansfield's Letters to me & I am overcome by this. They are adorable. I wish & wish & wish I could talk to her now. I have just written a little Sketch of her, for a Lady who is writing her Life; but my pen is made of lead; & hers was a radiant and many coloured feather.[35]

In the last long spell that Mansfield would spend in England following her return from Bandol in April 1918, Huxley was still a welcome guest at the Murrys' Hampstead home. In a letter to Woolf of May 5, 1919, Mansfield wrote: "Aldous came in later, lay upon the sofa, buried his head in a purple pillow and *groaned* over the hor-rible qual-ity of Smollett's coarseness. In the afternoon of the same day Lytton came to tea. I was excessively dull, but he was charming."[36] Is there almost a sense of one-upmanship in her description of these guests frequenting her home—both well known to the rather insecure Woolf? (Again, note her mimicry of Huxley's voice.) Ruth Mantz also notes how, "[a]s a guest at Portland Villas, [Huxley] sprawled on the drawing room 'stickleback' couch as he hoarded his impressions of Katherine as 'Mary Thriplow,' which he would […] evolve in his novel, 'Those Barren Leaves.'"[37] In the meantime, Huxley was settling to his editorial work at the *Athenaeum*; he wrote to Gidley Robinson on August 9, 1919: "the whole atmosphere […] is so delightfully remote, in its purely literary preoccupations, from the horrors of the present that it is in a way restful work."[38]

With her health deteriorating and tuberculosis now confirmed, in September 1919 Mansfield set off once more for the Mediterranean and would not return to England again except for a couple of brief visits. Murry initially accompanied her, returning to England in early October. With the *Athenaeum* rudderless for a short time, Huxley wrote to Morrell on October 3, 1919: "Sullivan and I are wondering when, if ever, Murry is going to return. No news of him: he was supposed to come back yesterday."[39] Mansfield was now reviewing several books a week for the *Athenaeum* and in her letters to Murry she commented on Huxley's contributions and role on the paper: "Sullivan & Huxley are different creatures—so *tightened up*";[40] "Huxley is very silly and young sometimes—& watery headed."[41] If only Sullivan and Huxley had known what was being said about them.... On January 5, 1920, Murry wrote to Mansfield: "What a joy it will be when you are back? You and I with our heads together—are the only editors of this paper. It's a mistake to have to let anyone else have control." In a more measured assessment of his assistant editors' capabilities than his wife, however, he continued: "They are splendid, Sullivan & Huxley, at their jobs—but outside them useless."[42]

In February 1920, Mansfield sent Murry a review of *Limbo*—a collection of stories and a play—by Huxley. (The review itself is unfortunately now lost.) Murry had commented on her review's rather scathing tone and she had responded: "I'm so sorry about Aldous. Do publish another review by another hand if you've a mind to. Ill [sic] understand absolutely—only I *could* not say more. Boge they were such BILGE."[43] There is evidence here of Mansfield's territorial positioning—after all, the short story was *her* literary patch. Murry obviously thought better of publishing the review and instead wrote the following three-line summary of Huxley's book, unsigned, in the issue for March 19, 1920: "A collection of short stories by one of the most distinguished writers of the younger generation, who is better known, and we think better inspired, as a poet."[44] As can be seen, the sting was not entirely removed.

Mansfield returned to England at the end of April 1920, and within a couple of days, called in at the *Athenaeum* offices. Her description of what she saw, written in a letter to Sydney and Violet Schiff, was scathing:

> I drove to the office of the Athenaeum & thought there at least there would be men I knew who responded who—were alive and cared about life and the paper and work and—The untidiness of John's desk [...] was my first crushing blow. There was over all the office a smell of stone and dust. Unthinkable disorder and ugliness. Old Massingham like a cat dipped in dough blinking in the doorway & asking whether the French were furious with [Lloyd] "George"—Huxley wavering like a candle who expected to go out with the next open door, poor silly old men with pins in their coat lapels, Tomlinson harking back to the mud in Flanders, Sullivan and E. M. Forster very vague, very frightened.[45]

The impression given is that of a poorly run, down-at-heel gentlemen's club, where a fastidious woman such as Mansfield would have been a fish out of water.

By mid-September 1920, Mansfield was back on the Riviera again, her health deteriorating further, though her attitude toward Huxley and Sullivan's capabilities had softened somewhat. Discussing a recent issue of the *Athenaeum* with Murry she wrote: "I thought Aldous v. good on Thomas—didn't you? And Old Sullivan was excellent. He has got a good firm touch with him—nowadays."[46] In fact, Huxley's review of Edward Thomas's *Collected Poems* had impressed her so much, she sent him a postcard. However, with Mansfield's health continuing to deteriorate, it finally became clear to Murry that he could not be separated from her anymore and they were now privately discussing his giving up the editorship. On November 21, 1920, Mansfield wrote to him: "We shall talk about all this when you come over. Youre [*sic*] not going to tell a soul about your giving up the paper till then—are you?"[47] Mansfield's criticism of Huxley's contributions was still evident: "Marginalia is utterly feeble. It had a moment, a little spurt, a few weeks ago but ever since then it has been dead as a nib."[48]

In December 1921, Mansfield innocently wrote to Morrell from Montana in Switzerland where she and Murry were now living: "Have you read Aldous' novel? I have seen it reviewed but that is all. Is it very good?"[49] The book in question was *Crome Yellow*, written during the seven months Huxley spent in Italy from March to September 1921 and published in November. She followed this query up a month later with a more vituperative comment, since by now, the book had become somewhat of a scandal in Garsington circles:

> I haven't seen Aldous book and I do not want to. The idea bores me so terribly and I won't waste time on it. The only reviewer who really realised its dullness was Rebecca West. She said just what was right—she shuddered at the silliness of it. But everybody else seems to puff him up. It gets very awkward if young men are forced to feed out of their friends inkpots in this way. In fact I confess it downright disgusts me [all *sic*].[50]

From 1920 to 1922, West wrote a series of review essays for the *New Statesman* called "Notes on Novels"; her review of *Crome Yellow* appeared on December 17, 1921. Ottoline was deeply hurt by the book, as Heilbrun notes:

> D. H. Lawrence and Aldous Huxley, two men she had been particularly fond of, had repaid her affection by publishing books, *Women in Love* and *Crome Yellow*,

which portrayed her and life at her home in unflattering terms. The result had been a quarrel with both; and though later she was to be reconciled to them, they never again became the friends they had been before.[51]

Miranda Seymour explains further:

> Huxley's *Crome Yellow* was a […] serious embarrassment. He had been almost an adopted son of the house at Garsington; Morrell cared a good deal less about any faint resemblance his Priscilla and Henry Wimbush might bear to herself and Philip than to the fact that the novel was crowded with caricatures of her friends and wartime guests. Gertler, Carrington, Brett, Russell, there they all were, recognizable and ludicrous. In the copy of the book which he sent her, Aldous wrote: "Ottoline Morrell—with apologies for having borrowed some of her architecture and trees"; his claims that the characters were pure invention were singularly unconvincing. [Morrell wrote (December 1921):] "It is simply photography and poor ragged photography at that."[52]

The character of Priscilla Wimbush—unquestionably based on Morrell—was indeed not really the point of the upset, but the fact that Morrell's houseguests had been so mercilessly satirized. Morrell complained to Huxley that she and her guests had been used as mere marionettes. Huxley responded: "mere marionettes, not you at all—mere marionettes—why should mere marionettes destroy a long & cherished friendship? Yours very affectionately Aldous Huxley."[53] But "mere marionettes" had destroyed it. And yet, as Ronald Sion notes, "Every writer has to reach into his or her bag of experiences from which to create both the plot and the characterizations fashioned in a work of fiction. And it was no different with Huxley."[54] It was certainly also no different with Mansfield. She quarried her childhood memories and fictionalized them mercilessly in story after story, sometimes not even bothering to disguise names. Her later life experiences were equally fictionalized and characters only lightly disguised. One thinks of Francis Carco in "Je ne parle pas français," her own parents and sisters in numerous stories, including "Prelude" and "At the Bay," the Trowell brothers in her unfinished novel *Juliet*, and of course Huxley as Eddie Warren in "Bliss"—the list is endless.

Crome Yellow, and Huxley's three novels which followed—*Antic Hay, Those Barren Leaves,* and *Point Counter Point*—"may be categorized as novels of social criticism wherein Huxley employs satire or comic criticism to castigate the multiple social failings of his age."[55] David Bradshaw notes that "at first glance *Crome Yellow* may appear to be Huxley's celebration of this doomed way of life," but that in fact at Crome, "civilized eccentricity has degenerated into the egocentric crotcheteering of the Wimbushes and their house party of fatuous ciphers."[56] J. B. Coates makes the point that

> The emotional drive behind these early works is Huxley's craving for fullness of experience. His heroes are men seeking for completeness in living or made wretched through their inability to attain it, while the characters who are the butt of his satire are departmentalized beings, only functioning with one part of their nature.[57]

Not everyone hated *Crome Yellow*; reviewing it in the *St. Paul Daily News* in America, F. Scott Fitzgerald declared it "the highest point so far attained by Anglo-Saxon sophistication."[58] But if the Garsington guests are satirized, where is Mansfield? Glimpses of her can be found in Anne, as noted previously: "uninhibited, hedonistic, sexually sophisticated."[59] The following passage (written on August 15, 1917), from Woolf to Morrell, offers further discernible echoes of *Crome Yellow*: "Katherine Mansfield describes your garden, the rose leaves drying in the sun, the pool, and long conversations between people wandering up and down in the moonlight."[60]

As noted earlier, Mansfield was renowned at Garsington for the tall stories she recounted about her youthful bohemian life and experiences. Garsington was an intellectually competitive hothouse where all the guests vied with each other to provide brilliant, scintillating conversation. Mansfield was more than equal to the game, and she was pretty too. Even the notoriously difficult-to-please Lytton Strachey was strongly attracted to her when he first knew her.[61] In a letter to Bunny Garnett on November 10, 1915, describing his first meeting with Mansfield at Brett's studio, he wrote: "Katherine Mansfield was also there, and took my fancy a good deal."[62] On October 3, 1919, he sent her fan mail:

> The Government tells one only to write letters that are necessary—so be it! This is the letter of a loyal subject, because I can *think* of nothing more necessary than to tell you how much I admire your Athenaeum reviews, and how grateful I am to you for such charming weekly titillations.... I should be very glad to hear any news of you—but I don't want to give trouble—only let me have a word or two some day.[63]

Like every other character in that hothouse, however, attraction and friendship vacillated, and Murry's posthumous recreation of Mansfield the writer encouraged dislike where once there had been friendliness. Michael Holroyd notes how in Strachey's library there was a copy of Katherine Mansfield's *Journal*, edited by Middleton Murry, which in September 1927, he described as quite shocking and incomprehensible. I see Murry lets out that it was written for publication—which no doubt explains a good deal. But why that foul-mouthed, virulent, brazen-faced broomstick of a creature should have got herself up as a pad of rose-scented cotton wool is beyond me.[64]

The alteration in tone from the earlier quote to the one above explains a good deal of how the relationships between this group of writers vacillated over the years.

Crome Yellow could in fact be read as a longer version of Mansfield's "Bliss," with equally ridiculous characters, relying heavily on Huxley's memories of the garden at Garsington. It is hard to justify Mansfield's personal harsh critique of it, except as platitudes delivered to someone—Morrell—with whom she wanted to remain on good terms. By the time the book was published in November 1921, she and Murry were living in Switzerland and no longer involved with the *Athenaeum*. There was no need for pretense. Of course, Huxley went on to represent Mansfield in two further books: with "his satiric version of 'Mary Thriplow,' would-be novelist—romantic sentimentalist, in *Those Barren Leaves*, and with a shifting of the caustic light in *Point Counter Point*, he gave a glimpse of the [...] past in which the shadowy 'Susan' had lived."[65] Indeed, the portrayal of Murry and Mansfield in *Point Counter Point* (1928) elicited this comment from Lawrence to Huxley in October 1928:

> I have read *Point Counter Point* with a heart sinking through my boot-soles and a rising admiration. I do think you've shown the truth, perhaps the last truth, about you and your generation, with really fine courage. It seems to me it would take ten times the courage to write *P. Counter P.* than it took to write *Lady C.*: and if the public knew *what* it was reading, it would throw a hundred stones at you, to one at me.[66]

After Mansfield's death, Huxley wrote a page-long critique of her fiction in "The Traveler's Eye View" from the essay collection *Along the Road* (1925). Though brief, it represents his longest discussion of Mansfield and work that exists. Dismissive on the whole, it contains a mild sting at the end of almost every sentence:

> Miss Mansfield's studies of interiors are like those brilliant paleontological reconstructions one sees in books of popular science—the ichthyosaurus in its native waters, pterodactyls fluttering and swooping the tepid tertiary sky—too excitingly romantic, in spite of their air of realism, to be quite genuine. [...] Each of Miss Mansfield's stories is a window into a lighted room. The glimpse of the inhabitants sipping their tea and punch is enormously exciting. But one knows nothing, when one has passed, of what they are really like. That is why,

however thrilling at a first reading, her stories do not wear. Chekhov's do; but then he had lived with his people, as well as looked at them through the window. The traveler's-eye view of men and women is not satisfying. A man might spend his life in trains and restaurants and know nothing of humanity at the end.[67]

The reference to Chekhov was a deliberate, below-the-belt punch, comparing Mansfield with the writer whom many people reading his essay would be aware was her greatest literary inspiration. By 1925, Murry had published three posthumous volumes of Mansfield's work: two volumes of stories, most incomplete or rejected for publication by Mansfield herself during her lifetime, and a volume of poetry. As Ian Gordon notes of Murry's editorial policy:

> He discarded her tough-mindedness; her shrewdness with money; her carefully kept accounts and balance sheets; her single-minded (on occasion, even ruthless) determination; her jealous bitchiness [...]. His selected and re-arranged material offered instead a romanticized, insubstantial persona who, he wrote, "seemed to adjust herself to life as a flower adjusts itself to the earth and sun."[68]

In addition, by now editor of the *Adelphi*, Murry had turned the journal into a hagiographical outpouring of unpublished Mansfield material, to the disgust of those who had known her. Lawrence, for example, was one of many who "took Murry to task in his role of propagandist of Katherine Mansfield. [... He] had not shrunk from denouncing the whole policy and atmosphere of the *Adelphi* in this particular matter, which [...] he had found repugnant."[69] Both Mansfield and an assessment of her fiction were therefore unfairly caught up in a literary war against Murry, and, by association, her reputation in England was blighted for many years.

With the passage of time, Huxley's viewpoint would soften and certain bridges would be rebuilt, as in this letter written to Murry on May 26, 1946:

> Thank you for your very friendly letter. I am glad you liked the pamphlet and glad too to have this opportunity for saying that I admire very much what you have done and for telling you that I am sorry for some of the things that I have done. That wonderful Chinese allegory, *Monkey*, which [Arthur] Waley translated a few years back, gives a very forceful account of that blessing and curse of cleverness, with which the Fairy Godmother, who is also the Wicked Fairy, endowed me, and with which, as a young man, I was in considerable measure identified. However, there is, let us hope, Evolution and a Descent of Man; and I have tried to drop the old tail and tricks, or at least to make use of them for better and less malicious purposes than in the past.[70]

This letter is a confession of sorts that his early satirical novels were in fact not as innocently produced as he had initially made them out to be. Indeed, Philip

Thody asserts that "so numerous were the [...] identifiable portraits, that the success of Huxley's first three novels was attributed by some people to a prurient curiosity about the bohemian goings-on in London café society."[71]

Toward the end of his life, Huxley was often asked to comment on his knowledge of Mansfield and Murry, especially after the latter's death in 1957. In a letter to Myrick Land on March 1, 1962, he wrote:

> Murry (and Catherine [sic] too) had a strange way of churning themselves, violently and indefatigably, in the hope of transforming a native inability to feel very strongly or continuously into a butter-pat of genuine emotion, true passion, unquestioning faith. (Read in this context Murry's novel, *The Things We Are*. It contains the most extraordinary passages, in which the hero (Murry) works up bogus Dostoevskyan passions out of nothing at all.)[72]

Again we see his resurfaced contempt for Murry clouding his judgment of Mansfield. Another of his assessments comes in a letter to Allan Crane, written on January 27, 1963:

> Yes, I knew Katherine Mansfield fairly well, and liked her stories. She was an unhappy woman, capable of acting any number of parts but uncertain of who, essentially, she was—a series of points and arcs on the circumference of a circle that was uncertain of the location of its centre.[73]

This is a measured appraisal, not unkind, but still colored by the connection to Murry and still only discussing Mansfield's personality and not her remarkable literary achievements.

Murry's star waned during the twentieth century, though in the past few years a reassessment of his life and work is evolving.[74] His literary ostracization was mainly a result of the overexposure of his dead wife's work and his aim to publish as much of her literary remains as the public could stomach. Murry's editorial stance remained more or less the same until his death in 1957. But as her husband's star has waned, so Mansfield's star has risen. Her contribution to modern literature as an innovator of the modernist short story is now widely recognized, and many of her stories are perceived as modernist masterpieces. It is clear from the evidence presented here that for a short time Huxley and Mansfield enjoyed a close friendship which would soon become tainted by the complexity of other relationships in their immediate circle. Nevertheless, it is to be hoped that future biographers of both writers will be encouraged to consider this friendship as more than a mere footnote and to engage more closely with their detailed depictions of each other in their creative output.

Notes

1. David Goldie, *A Critical Difference: T. S. Eliot and John Middleton Murry in English Literary Criticism, 1919-1928* (Oxford: Clarendon Press, 1998), 2.
2. Carolyn G. Heilbrun, *Lady Ottoline's Album* (London: Michael Joseph, 1976), 10.
3. Leonard Woolf, *Downhill all the Way: Autobiography,* vol. 2, 1911-1969 (London, Hogarth Press, 1967), 146-47.
4. Michael Holroyd, *Lytton Strachey* (London: Chatto & Windus, 1994), 330.
5. Holroyd, *Lytton Strachey*, 221.
6. Ray Monk, *Bertrand Russell: The Spirit of Solitude* (London: Jonathan Cape, 1996), 485.
7. Antony Alpers, *The Life of Katherine Mansfield* (London: Jonathan Cape, 1980), 209.
8. D. H. Lawrence to Aldous Huxley, June 1915, in *The Letters of D. H. Lawrence*, ed. Aldous Huxley (London: Heinemann, 1932), 239.
9. Miranda Seymour, *Ottoline Morrell: Life on a Grand Scale* (London: Hodder and Stoughton, 1998), 365.
10. Ruth Mantz, *Swing on the Garsington Gate* (unpublished book manuscript), Ruth Mantz Collection, Harry Ransom Humanities Research Center, University of Texas at Austin.
11. Holroyd, *Lytton Strachey*, 369.
12. Bertrand Russell, *Autobiography* (Abingdon: Routledge, 2010), 236.
13. Nicholas Murry, *Aldous Huxley: An English Intellectual* (London: Abacus, 2003), 75.
14. Aldous Huxley to Ottoline Morrell, July 27, 1916, in *Aldous Huxley: Selected Letters*, ed. James Sexton (Chicago: Ivan R. Dee, 2007), 30.
15. Katherine Mansfield to Ottoline Morrell, September 12, 1916, in *The Collected Letters of Katherine Mansfield*, 5 vols, ed. Vincent O'Sullivan and Margaret Scott (Oxford: Clarendon Press, 1984-2008), 1:280. All subsequent letters from Mansfield are from this source.
16. Alpers, *Life*, 225-26.
17. Alpers, *Life*, 227.
18. Aldous Huxley to Julian Huxley, December 29, 1916, in *Letters of Aldous Huxley*, ed. Grover Smith (London: Chatto & Windus, 1969), 118.
19. Katherine Mansfield, "The Laurels," in *The Collected Works of Katherine Mansfield, The Collected Fiction*, 2 vols., ed. Gerri Kimber and Vincent O'Sullivan (Edinburgh: Edinburgh University Press, 2012), 2:5-6.
20. Huxley to Morrell, May 10, 1917, in *Selected Letters*, ed. Sexton, 46; 48; 51.
21. Mansfield to Morrell, June 16, 1917, 1:310-11.
22. Mansfield to Morrell, July 3, 1917, 1:315.

23 Katherine Mansfield, "In Confidence," in *Collected Fiction,* ed. Kimber and O'Sullivan, 2:31–2.
24 Anne Olivier Bell, ed., *The Diary of Virginia Woolf,* 5 vols. (London: Hogarth Press, 1977–1984), 1:78.
25 Virginia Woolf to Vanessa Bell, November 27, 1917, in *The Question of Things Happening: The Letters of Virginia Woolf,* vol. 2, 1912–1922, ed. Nigel Nicolson (London: Hogarth, 1976), 198.
26 Robert Gathorne-Hardy, ed., *Ottoline at Garsington: Memoirs of Lady Ottoline Morrell 1915–1918* (London: Faber and Faber, 1974), 236–37.
27 Huxley to Juliet Baillot, December 11, 1917, in *Letters,* ed. Smith, 140.
28 Katherine Mansfield to John Middleton Murry, February 26, 1918, 2:97–98.
29 Alpers, *Life,* 274.
30 Bell, *Diary of Virginia Woolf,* 1:125.
31 Katherine Mansfield, "Bliss," in *Collected Fiction,* ed. Kimber and O'Sullivan, 2:146.
32 Aldous Huxley, *Crome Yellow* (London: Chatto & Windus, 1921), 16.
33 James Sexton, introduction to *Aldous Huxley: Selected Letters,* ed. James Sexton (Chicago: Ivan R. Dee, 2007), 10.
34 Heilbrun, *Album,* 4.
35 Ottoline Morrell to D'Arcy Cresswell, June 11, 1932, in *Dear Lady Ginger,* ed. Helen Shaw (London: Century, 1983), 40.
36 Mansfield to Virginia Woolf, May 5, 1919, 2:316.
37 Mantz, *Garsington Gate.*
38 Huxley to Gidley Robinson, August 9, 1919, in *Letters,* ed. Smith, 180.
39 Huxley to Morrell, October 3, 1919, in *Selected Letters,* ed. Sexton, 92.
40 Mansfield to Murry, October 22, 1919, 3:43.
41 Mansfield to Murry, January 7, 1920, 3:171.
42 John Middleton Murry to Katherine Mansfield, January 5, 1920, in *The Letters of John Middleton Murry to Katherine Mansfield,* ed. C. A. Hankin (London: Constable, 1983), 245.
43 Mansfield to Murry, c. February 22, 1920, 3:226.
44 Review by John Middleton Murry (unsigned) of Aldous Huxley's *Limbo,* in "List of New Books," *Athenaeum* 4690, no. 19 (March 1920): 384.
45 Mansfield to Sydney and Violet Schiff, May 4, 1920, 4:5.
46 Mansfield to Murry, September 27, 1920, 4:53.
47 Mansfield to Murry, November 21, 1920, 4:117.
48 Mansfield to Murry, December 5, 1920, 4:135.
49 Mansfield to Morrell, c. December 20, 1921, 4:345.
50 Mansfield to Morrell, c. January 24, 1922, 5:20.
51 Heilbrun, *Album,* 5.
52 Seymour, *Life on a Grand Scale,* 436–37.
53 Bell, *Diary of Virginia Woolf,* 2:180.

54 Ronald T. Sion, *Aldous Huxley and the Search for Meaning: A Study of the Eleven Novels* (Jefferson, NC: McFarland, 2010), 29.
55 Sion, *Huxley*, 10.
56 David Bradshaw, introduction to *Aldous Huxley Between the Wars: Essays and Letters*, ed. David Bradshaw (Chicago: Ivan R. Dee, 1994), 12–13.
57 J. B. Coates, *Ten Modern Prophets* (London: Frederick Muller, 1944), 39.
58 Bradshaw, *Huxley*, 17.
59 Jocelyn Brooke, *Aldous Huxley* (London: Longmans, Green & Co., 1968), 13.
60 Woolf to Ottoline Morrell, August 15, 1917, in *Question of Things,* ed. Nicolson, 174.
61 Holroyd, *Lytton Strachey*, 351.
62 Holroyd, *Lytton Strachey*, 351.
63 Holroyd, *Lytton Strachey*, 727.
64 Holroyd, *Lytton Strachey*, 573.
65 Mantz, *Garsington Gate*, 232.
66 Lawrence to Huxley, October 1928, in *Letters of D. H. Lawrence*, ed. Huxley, 757.
67 Aldous Huxley, "The Traveler's Eye View," in *Complete Essays*, vol. 1, 1920–1925 (Chicago: Ivan R. Dee, 2000), 435.
68 Ian A. Gordon, ed., *Katherine Mansfield: The Urewera Notebook* (Oxford: Oxford University Press, 1978), 16–17.
69 Catherine Carswell, *The Savage Pilgrimage: A Narrative of D. H. Lawrence* (London: Martin Secker, 1932), 207–8.
70 Huxley to John Middleton Murry, May 26, 1946, in *Letters*, ed. Smith, 544.
71 Philip Thody, *Aldous Huxley: A Biographical Introduction* (London: Studio Vista, 1973), 34–35.
72 Huxley to Myrick Land, March 1, 1962, in *Letters*, ed. Smith, 929.
73 Huxley to Allan Crane, January 27, 1963, in *Letters*, ed. Smith, 948.
74 See Sydney Janet Kaplan, *Circulating Genius: John Middleton Murry, Katherine Mansfield and D. H. Lawrence* (Edinburgh: Edinburgh University Press, 2010).

5

"Feuille d'Album": Katherine Mansfield's Prufrockian Encounter with T. S. Eliot

Janet Wilson

Katherine Mansfield and T. S. Eliot first met through their mutual friend Lady Ottoline Morrell at Garsington Manor on December 3, 1916, at a time when they were becoming acquainted with the Bloomsbury circle, developing friendships with Bertrand Russell and meeting guests like Aldous Huxley and Lytton Strachey.[1] Significant parallels between them have been pointed out, such as that they were almost exactly the same age—twenty-eight years old. They were also "colonial" émigrés from New Zealand and the United States, respectively, and as outsiders to the English literary elite they approached its literature and culture through continental intermediaries who wrote in another language: Mansfield through Chekhov and Eliot through Jules Laforgue,[2] although both were also influenced by Arthur Symons's book on symbolism.[3] They also had in common the fact that being foreigners they had a capacity for self-invention, including the act of being English, and could quickly articulate a sense of displacement. Not surprisingly, they both recognized in the other this talent for the theatrical, and both commented adversely on the other's use of mask and disguise as a source of irritation, creating a kind of negative symbiosis.[4] Their acquaintance was intermittent— they met rarely and probably not at all after about 1920—but references to each other appear in correspondence with John Middleton Murry and Vivien Eliot, as well as with friends and Bloomsberries such as Ezra Pound, Lady Ottoline Morrell, Virginia Woolf, Violet Schiff, and Dorothy Brett. The ripples of antagonism and open hostility on both sides that appeared around 1920—due seemingly to a sense of betrayal on her side and mistrust on his (and no doubt to professional rivalry)—raise questions that have never been

My thanks to C.K. Stead and Anna Smith for suggestions made during the writing of this article.

answered satisfactorily, including the question of their literary relations.[5] Can any artistic influence be defined, or was the relationship one of criticism and scrutiny, or a case of parallel development as their similarities suggest?[6] Until recently, such issues have come second to examining the complex web of emotions that underlay their fraught acquaintance, and the likelihood of a more intense literary engagement, especially on Mansfield's part, has only just begun to receive attention.[7]

This chapter argues that Katherine Mansfield was in fact inspired by Eliot's early poetry and that in particular his landmark modernist poem "The Love Song of J. Alfred Prufrock" (1915) provided her with a source of creative energy, one that goes deeper than the verbal echoes and scattered references to poems like "Rhapsody on a Windy Night" (published in a special war issue of *Blast* in July 1915) and "Conversation Galante" (1916), references that have already been identified in certain stories and poems as well as in letters and her journals. The most extended artistic encounter with Eliot as poet and man appears in Mansfield's story "An Album Leaf," first published in *New Age* in September 1917 and later revised and renamed "Feuille d'Album"; it can be traced to her fascination with Eliot's "Prufrock" which was published in *Prufrock and Other Observations* soon after they met.[8] Initially they seem to have been on friendly terms, and Mansfield wrote to Ottoline Morrell on June 24, 1917: "I liked him very much and did not feel he was an enemy"; the story's preoccupation with transformation suggests that her encounter both with the poem and its author had a stirring effect on her.[9]

That Mansfield saw herself early on as in dialogue with Eliot's imagination, stimulated by his way of looking at the world and his thoughts about art and aesthetics, is apparent from the details of her urban settings and landscapes that show traces of his thought patterns and turns of phrase. Fleeting glimpses of his style detectable in her writing smack of imitation.[10] Most famous is her description of the night scene near Hammersmith Bridge in London where she and Eliot walked along the riverside, having left together from a dinner party hosted by Eliot's friends, Mary and Jack Hutchinson. In the same letter to Ottoline Morrell she writes: "we walked past rows of little ugly houses hiding behind bitter smelling privet hedges: a great number of amorous black cats looped across the road, and high up in the sky there was a battered old moon."[11] C. K. Stead, who fictionalizes their encounter on that night in his novels *The Secret History of Modernism* (2001) and *Mansfield: A Novel* (2004)—the latter opens with an imaginative reconstruction of their conversation[12]—comments that this arresting visual account of the cityscape seems to owe more to Eliot's poetry than to real life,[13] notably to "Conversation Galante," for Mansfield's "battered old moon" recalls

Eliot's description of "an old battered lantern hung aloft" (ln. 4).[14] Further verbal echoes of Eliot's early poems have been identified in other texts dating from this period: both her poem "Night-Scented Stock," which Mansfield sent to Lady Ottoline Morrell in 1917,[15] and the dialogue "The Common Round," written and published in the *New Age* in May 1917 and later revised as "Pictures," carry verbal traces of "Preludes" (1915) and "Rhapsody on a Windy Night (published in *Blast* in 1915)."[16] Sydney Janet Kaplan notes Prufrockian echoes in representations of the city life that dominates the character of Ada Moss in "Pictures" and that the "grey crabs all the way down the street" (referring to washerwoman on the steps) recalls the "ragged claws" in Eliot's poem; amorous cats also make an appearance in her satirical story, "Bliss" (1918).[17] Similar allusions appear in "Feuille d'Album," which notes, "Among the flowers the old women scuttled side to side like crabs," crabs being Mansfield's metonym for the movements of working-class women.[18] But I suggest that her encounter with "Prufrock" in "Feuille d'Album" goes much further than superficial allusions to and mimicry of Eliot's work, especially in the story's involvement with proletarian, urban life, its response to the poem's preoccupations with unfulfilled longing and sexual inhibition, and its engagement with Eliot's images and metaphors of extreme emotional diffidence.

Mansfield's acquaintance with Eliot's early masterpiece can be dated to June 3, 1917, a few days before the dinner party that she and Eliot attended at the Hutchinsons, when she read "Prufrock" aloud to the assembled company at Garsington in what was apparently the first public reading by a woman.[19] In the words of Roger Fry, who brought with him copies of *Prufrock and Other Observations* to distribute to the guests, it "caused a stir, much discussion, some perplexity."[20] For Mansfield, it clearly struck a chord, undoubtedly as a key "modern" poetic text, for this term of approbation appears in letters written several years later, suggesting that the poem stayed with her. In March 1921, she wrote to Sydney Waterlow, "I think that's what I want modern poetry to be. I even have a feeling […] that Johnny Keats would have admired it"; then in August 1922 she declared to Violet Schiff that it was by "far and away the most interesting and best modern poem—It stays in one's memory as a work of art."[21] Echoes of the poem appear in a journal entry of August 1919 in which she laments the meagerness of her output: "Is that all, […] that is not what I meant at all."[22] As Stead comments, this image of her own lapsed creativity, "hovering on the brink of stories but unable to press forward and write them," comes directly from Eliot's protagonist's words.[23] That "Feuille d'Album" took shape as a response to Eliot's verse might be inferred from the fact that it was among the few stories she wrote after her Garsington reading of "Prufrock" in June 1917 and may indeed have been the first new one.[24] In the intervening months Mansfield had completed and revised *The Aloe* which she sent in October to Virginia and Leonard Woolf for publication by the Hogarth Press under the new name of *Prelude*.

It is therefore worth asking whether "Prufrock" was to Mansfield's mind exempt from the criticism that she levied in a letter to Virginia Woolf in 1919 about the aridity of Eliot's verse, saying that "the poems *look* delightful but I confess I think them unspeakably dreary. How one could write so absolutely without emotion—."[25] Certainly "Prufrock" would have engaged her interest then because of the representation of voice through dramatic monologue at a time—May to June 1917—when she was experimenting with mime and dialogue, as in "The Common Round," "The Black Cap," and "Two Tuppenny Ones, Please."[26] Such negative comments, therefore, might be read in terms of her more general attack on the masculine tenor of much modernist writing, especially its conceits of artifice and sterility, as typified by her image of those "dark young men—so proud of their plumes and their black and silver cloaks."[27] Mansfield's views of Eliot by 1919, however, point to the growing ideological and artistic polarization between her and Murry and Eliot and others, as both she and Murry became convinced of the poetic importance of Romantic artists like Keats; this later developed into a debate between Murry and Eliot on the relative merits of Romanticism and Classicism. But by 1918, Mansfield and Murry were already at odds with Bloomsbury, and their relationship with Lady Ottoline's Garsington circle was also deteriorating.[28]

"Feuille d'Album," therefore, belongs to this brief period of her first encounter with Eliot and these literary circles and reflects the creative energy that was unleashed when, in a positive frame of mind, she entered into dialogue with his work. In this light, Mansfield's comment to Virginia Woolf made in 1919, "I don't think he is a poet—Prufrock is after all a short story,"[29] may be read as a form of artistic license or slippage; that is, as less a criticism of Eliot than an indirect allusion to the narrative potential of "Prufrock" that evidently inspired her story.

* * *

In the reading that follows, "Feuille d'Album" is interpreted as Mansfield's literary encounter with Eliot's persona of "The Love Song of J. Alfred Prufrock," a kind of "writing back" to his representations of masculinity, gendered relations, and the psychological hesitation in thought, speech, and action for which his poem is known. Mansfield's narrator displays an acute awareness about the complexities of male inhibition and lightly shifts the focus of Eliot's memorable portrait of male disempowerment onto the women he avoids, then playfully, in a shift toward fantasy, restores a sense of potential happiness and release from his locked-in state of selfhood. Furthermore, Mansfield's story, unlike Eliot's poem, identifies empathetically with its protagonist's dilemma and imagines a cityscape capable of transformation, contrasting Eliot's depictions of male heroism in decline, urban wastelands, or the collapse of civilization.[30] Reinforcing her tone of light-hearted irreverence is Mansfield's setting in Paris, home of creative energy and of youthful romance and folly, such as in stories like "The Little Governess" and "Something Childish but Very Natural." For Mansfield, Paris was a mecca for her writing, because as she noted, "All my observation is so *detailed*, as it always is when I get to France."[31]

Mansfield's female riposte, as the story may be described, opens with comments by various women on the "impossible" nature of her protagonist, a young artist called Ian French, a prototype of Prufrock with his sexual ambiguity, hesitation, and resistance to any overtures for social engagement. He remains detached from human relationships and impervious to the women's blandishments; but in the second half of the story, which represents his desire and dreams through free indirect discourse, he demonstrates the beginnings of self-agency through the dramatic sensation of falling in love, a reprieve that Eliot never grants to his hero. But the witty denouement can be seen as a repositioning of the eccentric, neurotic elements of Eliot's Prufrock in a vision of absurdist possibility. Mansfield's hero addresses the woman with whom he has fallen in love through a mix of a plausible social gesture and the unreal: "'Excuse me, Mademoiselle, you dropped this.' And he handed her an egg."[32] Unlike Prufrock's stuttering hesitation, Mansfield's comic joke confirms that words can be uttered and overtures made to the opposite sex, although the reality they point to is phenomenologically impossible. In 1917, then, she may have been writing indirectly and allusively—as a gesture—in order to communicate beyond the real-life limits of her relationship with Eliot, not just as a witty amplification of his vision of the individual's inability to signify and view of life as artifice. That is, the story might be read as a metaphor for their delicately balanced personal relations which even then were being undermined as Eliot penned his satire, "Eeldrop and Appleplex," largely targeting Mansfield. If there is any such correspondence between life and art, then the position of the woman in Mansfield's story as the passive object of the hero's gaze—lacking in voice and unable to see him within her line of vision—suggests a strategic reverse mirroring within the narrative frame of the role of the artist/creator.

In order to approach these speculations, one must consider the ambivalence of Mansfield's responses to Eliot the man, evinced in correspondence from about 1919, a period when both Mansfield and Murry were identifying with the poetic and ideological values of Romanticism rather than wholeheartedly embracing modernism. The earlier feeling of exhilaration in Eliot's company seems to have given way to a more skeptical attitude to which this aesthetic preference might correspond; that is, Mansfield now singles out Eliot's ponderousness and social awkwardness in company, seeing this as a pose or performance, perhaps identified with Prufrock who says: "there will be time/To prepare a face to meet the faces that you meet" (lns. 26–27).[33] By 1921 her attraction to him was mixed with reservations as she confided to Sydney Waterlow: "Hes a rare delightful being—isn't he? That's what I always feel, even when the bluff oppresses me."[34] Writing to Brett the following year, she adds, "He suffers from feelings of powerlessness. He knows it. He feels weak. It is all disguise. That slow manner, that hesitation, sidelong glances, and so on are *painful*."[35] The idea of bluff and its phonic counterpart "buff" (as in the game, Blindman's Bluff, which was originally called buff—in the sense of pushing or nudging the person wearing the blindfold) are useful in considering Mansfield's suspicion of counterfeit and disguise in Eliot's manner, for they provide a metaphor for her gender-sensitive approach; that is, in writing "Feuille d'Album" as a response to Eliot's modernist statement as articulated in "Prufrock," she plays with Eliot's bluff (exterior/guise) to present an alternative. Namely she hints, in the form of a buff or nudge, that his poem's underlying message—the hesitation about speech, the questioning of the self, and relatedness to others—can be displaced with a vision of art/life as rooted in natural forces and enhanced by spiritual wonder, even though her story's comic, absurd ending undercuts any idea of transcendence. In other words, she answers Prufrock's central quest for a voice with which to propose to a woman, daring to contradict the poem's main premise that this is impossible.[36]

Specific details in "Feuille d'Album" are reminiscent of Eliot the man, suggesting Mansfield saw in Prufrock's identity features of his creator. Eliot's presence in his own writing evokes a comment from her on his essay on Ben Jonson, and Mansfield's perception corresponds to the critical consensus about the sources of "Prufrock's" shifting subjectivity.[37] Marjorie Perloff, for example, says that Prufrock "cannot be separated from the poet who has invented him," while Elizabeth Scheider also comments that the protagonist is a "hybrid of the poet's self and Laforgue."[38] But there are also elements of Mansfield's own personality in the story's elevation of art as a guiding principle of life, which for her replaced religion as the highest sources of truth and value; her idealized portrait of the artist figure, Ian French, displays aspects of her own personality such as her fastidious control over her domestic surroundings. For the first time since "An Indiscreet Journey," written in 1915, and by contrast to other stories of 1917 such as "Mr Reginald Peacock's Day," "The Common Round," and "A Dill Pickle," all set in London, Mansfield returns to France, specifically Paris. This alternative cityscape allows her a vital distance from the metropolitan setting of America, where Eliot's text is set, and London, usually her preferred location for stories written then. Further, the aerial positioning of the narrator from the artist's studio at the top of the building where the protagonist lives, and the panoramic view of the cityscape, presented through cinematic panning shots, convey the sense of freedom and lightheartedness that Mansfield associated with the French cultural and social milieu; but the setting is also a reminder that Eliot went to Paris in 1910 to study philosophy (Bergson and Laforgue) at the Sorbonne. Paris as location is further reinforced by the name of her excruciatingly shy and gauche protagonist, Ian French, which recalls her nickname for Eliot as "French Polish Eliott."[39] A famous artist, described as "very clever,"[40] Ian French's buried emotions are glimpsed through images of cultural and artistic value that Mansfield herself subscribed to and would identify with an artist like Eliot. The contents of his studio are arranged to form the pattern of a "still life"; this fusion of art and life and the sequestering of his studio kept "as neat as a pin,"[41] from all who wish to enter, recalls the fin de siècle, Wildean, art for art's sake aesthetics which she originally embraced. Finally the fact that the girl Ian falls in love with in his fantasy "was the only other person alive who was just his age,"[42] is possibly a coded reference to Eliot's closeness in age to Mansfield (with only ten days' difference between them).

The story's opening defines character traits of Ian French that recall Prufrock's capacity to perplex and puzzle because of his inability to give voice to his intentions as in "It is impossible to say just what I mean" (ln. 104): "He really was an impossible person. Too shy altogether. With absolutely nothing to say for himself."[43] Mansfield continues by playing with the language of blushing to suggest that in addition to signaling self-consciousness the blush belongs to a performance designed to elicit erotic, tender attention. French's blushes of embarrassment signal his endearing boyishness and unattainability: "How could one resist him? Oh, one's heart was wrung at the sight. And as if that were not enough there was his trick of blushing.... Whenever the waiter came near him he turned crimson—." Further, blushing encapsulates the maladroit gesture at the climax when "more crimson than ever" he handed her the egg.[44] The third person narrator voices the suspicion that French's facial changes in reddening are part of a masquerade, stating finally, "It can't all be as innocent as it looks!"[45] These flourishes and the layered, knowing commentary can be read as a further expansion of the monologue of Prufrock whose inhibition and tongue-tied state stem from anxiety about how he will be perceived, mainly by women.

Mansfield may have studied Eliot's technique, adapted from Jules Laforgue, of using judgments made by others—either overheard or imagined—as a means of inhibiting the speaker,[46] for although there is no insight into the enigmatic Ian French's point of view, the opening report of three different female admirers consists of such judgments about the impossibility of any intimacy with him. The focus on the female response recalls the alternative title Eliot considered for the poem—"Prufrock among the Women"[47]—and the mystery of the artist, as they see it, recalls the poem's refrain: "In the room women come and go/ talking of Michelangelo" (lns. 13–14; 35–36). French's resistance to their various overtures—to mothering, to a nightlife, to physical intimacy—and his refusal to come alive emotionally and sexually, provokes their threefold choric response, "hopeless."[48]

If the story opens by playing on the "bluff" of Ian French's presence—the women see him as inarticulate and emotionally detached—then the second half constitutes the "buff," the nudge toward another angle of vision, an alternative view of life. Prufrock's extreme self-consciousness, being tongue-tied and unable to formulate "some overwhelming question" as he wanders "half deserted streets" (lns. 10; 4), and his procrastination are wittily hinted at in the printed notice, "GET UP AT ONCE," which hangs on French's bedroom wall.[49] But Mansfield's protagonist then begins to depart from the Eliot's character traits as the story's urban setting leads into a narrative momentum that will culminate in his proposal. The transformation in mood and style (from social realism to fantasy) in "Feuille d'Album" begins with the narrator's ringing announcement: "Really there was no need for him to go out,"[50] implying that psychological change occurs through attunement to the inner voice, not social engagement. Ian French's vision occurs in response to the revivification and transfiguration of the natural world: "It had been raining—the first real spring rain of the year had fallen—a bright spangle hung on everything and the air smelled of buds and moist earth."[51] Anne Mounic points out that the opening of the "two wings of windows"[52] of the girl's house opposite implies a miraculous soaring of the imagination following the rain soaking the earth, while the daffodils the girl carries, the sight of which catapults him into love, also convey a sense of wonder.[53] Mansfield is showing that through the transformative powers of the imagination, art can become a way of living life, not a substitute for it.[54] A kind of resurrection is suggested by these images of romance, but in an antirealist move the perspective switches from the hero to the woman he loves who sees only a "hollow in the air"[55] where he might have been, suggesting the spell under which he has fallen is the work of art or magic. This is reinforced by an image that in Eliot-like fashion, like the fog imaged as a cat in "Prufrock" (lns. 15–22), balloons away from its referent and assumes a life of its own;[56] in being pierced in love, his heart, imaged as a weapon or spear, plunges down from his window and finds its destination in the flower pot of daffodils below. In the story's ending, therefore, the irresolvable dilemma of Prufrock, who could never bring himself to propose to a woman, who sees himself as no more than a "pair of ragged claws," and who suffers cosmic distress at the fear of being laughed at, has been transformed into Ian French's sudden discovery of his voice through "an extended joke."[57] Prufrock's chronic dithering, hesitation, and prevarication—"Should I, after cake and tea and ices/Have the strength to force this moment to its crisis?" and "And would it have been worth it, after all?" (lns. 79–80; 87)—find an answer in French's comic statement, as he seizes his chance to make the woman's acquaintance, by claiming, implausibly, to return an egg she supposedly had dropped.

* * *

To examine the Eliot-Mansfield relationship from the other side is to discover, in C. K. Stead's words, "something typically dark and Eliotic."[58] When Eliot met Mansfield, he would have been primed by Bloomsbury gossip to see her as impenetrable, masklike, but he also knew of her, as Scofield Thayer wrote to him, as "England's latest short story prima donna."[59] Mansfield at that stage had only published one slim volume, *In a German Pension* (1911), although she was writing extensively for little magazines like the *New Age* and *Rhythm*. Her arrival as a supreme writer of short fiction lay in the future, but she had made a name with the publication of her masterpiece, the long story *Prelude* in 1917, the second volume in the Hogarth Press, and Eliot, who had not yet met the Woolfs but who was their choice for publication number three, was jealous of this modest success.[60] It is therefore perhaps not surprising that when Ezra Pound solicited him for a contribution to *The Little Review* Eliot should produce, in what is his only piece of prose fiction, a satire on Mansfield.[61] The attack appears in Part II of "Eeldrop and Appleplex," written and published in September 1917, ironically around the same time Mansfield was writing "Feuille d'Album." Eliot's protagonists Eeldrop (alias Eliot) and Appleplex (a version of Apollinax, Eliot's name for Bertrand Russell, with whom Vivien Eliot was then having an adulterous affair) are close friends whose philosophical positions differ: Eeldrop is "a sceptic, with a taste for mysticism," and Appleplex "a materialist with a leaning towards skepticism."[62] In Part II their conversation dwells entirely on the character and activities of Scheherazade (alias Edith), a name which Carole Seymour-Jones says was inspired by fin de siècle sexuality and decadence and which would have invoked the image of Nijinsky dancing the Golden Slave in the Ballet Russes production of Rimsky-Korsakov's ballet in London in 1912.[63] For Mansfield, it would have been associated with "Sumurûn," the dramatic production adapted from the story in the *Arabian Nights* about a slave girl, which played to full houses in London's Coliseum for six weeks in January 1911 and about which she wrote a creative response.[64] Two recent studies of Eliot and his wife argue for different contenders for the real-life counterpart to Scheherazade: Vivien Eliot and Mansfield:[65] commonplace gossip about both women and Bertrand Russell had been circulating in the Bloomsbury circle.[66] But Eliot in fact acknowledges the libelous attack on Mansfield in a letter to Ezra Pound of 1935.[67] Close scrutiny identifies features of Mansfield's life and character, notably the phrase "what is called her impenetrable mask" probably echoes Lytton Strachey's observation that she had "a passive mask of a face."[68] Appleplex's defense of Eeldrop's charge of her "passion for experience," that she has a "shrewd observation," recalls Russell's comment about Mansfield as being "full of alarming penetration,"[69] while the observation about "her sarcasm at the expense of her friends" may be an allusion to Mansfield's capacity for the cutting phrase. Eeldrop's malicious critique of Scheherazade as artist also rings true of Mansfield: she is too conscious of how she presents herself and too rational, "her experience […] already digested by reason"; she uses herself as the material for her art unlike the "true artist" who "disintegrates or solidifies" when separated from his work, and who lives by instinct.[70] Underlying this is the judgment that Edith/Scheherazade is not as great an artist as she and others think, a view that matches Eliot's doubts about Mansfield's talents. Finally are the facts of Scheherazade's personal life: she "married a celebrated billiard professional in San Francisco after an acquaintance of twelve hours, lived with him for two days, joined a musical comedy chorus, and was divorced in Nevada."[71] These details in the satire recall Mansfield's brief marriage to George Bowden which lasted for just one night in 1909, after which she left with her lover, Garnett Trowell, for Liverpool, joining the chorus of the Moody-Manners Opera Company, as well as her idea about getting a divorce in America in 1912.[72]

Whether Mansfield knew of this satire, which Eliot refused to have reprinted, or saw herself as a target, is not known.[73] Relations with the Eliots declined upon Mansfield's first meeting Vivien at a dinner at the Murrys on May 14, 1920: her dislike of Vivien, and distaste at Eliot's solicitousness toward her, were palpable. She wrote to her wealthy American friends, Sydney and Violet Schiff:

> The Elliots [*sic*] have dined with us tonight. They are just gone—and the whole room is *quivering* […] Mrs E's voice rises "Oh don't commiserate with Tom; he's *quite* happy." I know its extravagant; I know […] I ought to have seen more—but I dislike her so *immensely*. She really repels me. She makes me shiver with apprehension....[74]

Indicative of her sentiment about Eliot is her announcement of his place in her affections: "I am so fond of Elliott. […] But this teashop creature …",[75] her violent reaction to Vivien, though, suggests that she considered his marriage to her a betrayal of some sort. To make matters worse, Vivien told her she had previously visited the Murrys' flat, and Murry, in explaining the circumstances of the meeting, implied an attraction between them. Mansfield concludes bitterly, speaking of both Vivien and Murry: "I feel as tho' Ive been stabbed."[76]

Mansfield's "deep sympathy" for Eliot remained, as evidenced in a letter to Violet Schiff in October 1921: "Poor Eliot sounds tired to death. […]—as though he were being tortured."[77] Although Eliot's satire in "Eeldrop and Appleplex" suggests he was from the beginning more foe than friend, his critical attitude may not have registered with Mansfield until 1920. In this year Eliot denounced her in a letter to Ezra Pound—"I believe her to be a dangerous WOMAN"[78]—while Vivien's highly strung fears and anxieties led her to see Mansfield as predatory and untrustworthy. These signs of dislike had developed into what seems like irrational hatred by 1922 when Eliot's new journal, *Criterion*, was thought to be at financial risk. Mansfield had met Lady Rothermere, one of the journal's financial backers, when both were staying at Gurdjieff's Institute for the Harmonious Development of Man, and the latter claimed that she was the most intelligent woman she had ever met. The Eliots and Pound feared that Mansfield might influence their patron negatively in favor of Eliot's rival, John Middleton Murry and his journal the *Athenaeum*, especially as Lady

Rothermere's response to the first issue of the *Criterion* had been negative on account of its dullness. Vivien attacked Mansfield in hyperbolic terms, writing to Pound on November 2, 1922:

> She [Lady R.] is unhinged—one of those beastly raving women who are the most dangerous. She is now in that asylum for the insane called La Prieuré where she does religious dances naked with Katherine Mansfield. "K.M.", she says in every letter—"*is the most intelligent woman* I have *ever* met." K. M. is pouring poison in her ear (of course) for K. M. hates T. more than anyone.[79]

Eliot, not to be outdone by his wife, denounced Mansfield even more vehemently to Pound five days later: "[she] is not simply the most intelligent woman Lady R. has ever met. She is simply one of the most persistent and thick skinned toadies and one of the vulgarest women Lady R. has ever met and is also a sentimental crank."[80]

* * *

Both "Feuille d'Album" and its successor, "A Dill Pickle," according to C. K. Stead, show "the subtlety, refinement and cleverness of Mansfield at her best"; he argues that these stories with their continental settings represent the beginning of a new departure in her work.[81] Her awareness of psychological distance in "Feuille d'Album" as well as her appropriation of some of the stylistic innovations of "Prufrock" anticipate later developments: the dark, metropolitan humor of "Je ne parle pas pas français," for example, with its handling of metaphor, metonymy, and image as well as the experimentation with cinematic technique. Neither Mansfield's borrowings nor her critical engagement with Eliot's developments in literary modernism, however, quite explain the hostilities of the Eliot-Mansfield relationship after 1920. The fact that Eliot labeled her a "thick skinned [...] toady" suggests that, even apart from the crisis over Lady Rothermere's loyalties, he perceived her as false and inauthentic, perhaps in reaction to the many masks that she wore. His own Prufrock-like mask of being inarticulate, awkward, and shy was not only densely consistent, by contrast, but comprised a significant part of his personality then. Lady Ottoline, for example, spoke of him as "dull, dull, dull. He never moves his lips and he speaks in an even and monotonous voice."[82] Significantly, Mansfield's own comment about him in 1922, that "he is too serious about himself, even a little bit absurd [...] he wants kindly laughing at and setting free,"[83] is corroborated by another woman who knew him well. Mary Hutchinson had a long-term close friendship with Eliot but found him a silent and tongue-tied companion. Speaking in ways reminiscent of the women who talk of Ian French in "Feuille d'Album," she commented in her diary: "Had I seen clearly, I could have been bolder, perhaps, stimulated his imagination, perhaps, given him experience, perhaps."[84] Mansfield's masks and guises, by contrast, never seemed to match with a "real" self at this time of her life. Eliot, in presenting himself to the world through his "bluff," may have become trapped in his own projected images of her bluff or disguises, so they both existed in a kind of counter-transference with each other.

"An Album Leaf" was revised and published in *Bliss and Other Stories* in 1920 with its French title "Feuille D'Album." It is unlikely that Eliot ever read it as a comment on his own life, yet he probably read the later story, "The Escape," published in the *Athenaeum* in July 1921, a story about a crisis in a dysfunctional marriage which, in the view of C. K. Stead, is in all probability about Eliot and Vivien, even though Mansfield wrote to Violet Schiff that the story was written for her and that it included "your tree."[85] If the Eliots read this story, then this might explain why Vivien wrote to Eliot three weeks later asking him to intervene with Sydney Schiff: "*Write to Schiff* […]. Must not let him fall into K. M.'s hands."[86] It may be another reason why Eliot remained unforgiving of Mansfield. The article he promised Murry he would write on her work after her death never appeared; he may have given up the intention to "deal with" her "inflated reputation," as he wrote to Richard Aldington.[87] In his lectures published as *After Strange Gods*, however, he criticized her story "Bliss" for its lack of "moral and social ramifications," adding that her skill was in handling the "*minimum* material" and that this limitedness makes the writing "feminine."[88] These terms were swiftly taken up by other male critics such as H. E. Bates[89] and later Frank Sargeson, preeminent New Zealand story writer in the 1930s.[90] Sargeson used these adjectives to launch an assault on Mansfield's posthumous reputation which led her to be relegated to the margins of the New Zealand national literary tradition as it developed through the mid- to late twentieth century, just as she was by the time of her death on the periphery of Bloomsbury and hence considered in the eyes of most critics as being tangential to mainstream modernism.

Notes

1   Antony Alpers, *The Life of Katherine Mansfield* (London: Jonathan Cape, 1980), 410.

2   C. K. Stead, "Katherine Mansfield and T. S. Eliot: A Double Centenary," in *Answering to the Language: Essays on Modern Writers* (Auckland: Auckland University Press, 1989), 149–50; Robert Crawford, *Young Eliot: From St Louis to The Wasteland* (London: Jonathan Cape, 2015), 267.
3   Sydney Janet Kaplan, *Katherine Mansfield and the Origins of Modernist Fiction* (Ithaca: Cornell University Press, 1991), 76.
4   She wrote of him, "it's all disguise." Katherine Mansfield to Dorothy Brett, February 26, 1922, in *The Collected Letters of Katherine Mansfield*, ed. Vincent O'Sullivan and Margaret Scott, 5 vols. (Oxford: Clarendon Press, 1984–2008), 5:75. All subsequent letters from Mansfield are from this source; Eliot's prose piece, "Eeldrop and Appleplex" (1917), published in two parts in *The Little Review*, targets "Scheherazade," possibly Mansfield, as "perfectly impenetrable" and mask-like. See T. S. Eliot, "Eeldrop and Appleplex" in *The Complete Prose of T. S. Eliot: The Critical Edition: Apprentice Years, 1905-1918*, ed. Jewel Spears Brooker and Ronald Schuchard (Baltimore: The Johns Hopkins University Press, 2014), 525–32. Project MUSE, https://muse.jhu.edu/chapter/1211122 (accessed December 20, 2016).
5   C. K. Stead, "Battle of the Wasps," *London Review of Books* 33, no. 5 (March 3, 2011): 19–21.
6   Kaplan, *Origins of Modernist Fiction*, 76.
7   See Sue Thomas, "Revisiting Katherine Mansfield: Virginia Woolf and the Aesthetics of Respectability," *English Studies: A Journal of English Language and Literature* 94, no. 1 (2013), 64–82; C. K. Stead, "Katherine Mansfield and the Fictions of Continental Europe," in *Katherine Mansfield and Continental Europe: Connections and Influences*, ed. Janka Kaščáková and Gerri Kimber (London: Palgrave, 2015), 236–51.
8   The poem was first published in *Poetry* (Chicago) in 1915 and in England in *Prufrock and Other Observations* by the Egoist Press in June 1917. See *The Poems of T. S. Eliot: Collected and Uncollected Poems*, vol. 1, ed. Christopher Ricks and Jim McCue (Baltimore: The Johns Hopkins University Press, 2015), 368. All future references to Eliot's poems will be to this edition with line numbers indicated in textual citations.
9   Katherine Mansfield to Ottoline Morrell, June 24, 1917, 1:312.
10 Alpers, *Life*, 244. Alpers makes this observation of Mansfield's letter to Ottoline Morrell, June 16, 1917, 1:311.
11 Mansfield to Morrell, June 24, 1917, 1:312.
12 C. K. Stead, *The Secret History of Modernism* (London: Harvill Press, 2001), 159–61; *Mansfield: A Novel* (London: Harvill Press, 2004), 1–11.
13 Stead, "Battle of the Wasps," 19.
14 T. S. Eliot, "Conversation Galante," 1:27.
15 See *The Collected Works of Katherine Mansfield: Poetry and Critical Writings*, vol. 3, ed. Gerri Kimber and Angela Smith (Edinburgh: Edinburgh University Press, 2014), 110–12.

16 Sue Thomas, "Revisiting Katherine Mansfield," 66–67, 69.
17 Kaplan, *Origins of Modernist Fiction*, 76–77.
18 Katherine Mansfield, "Feuille d'Album," in *The Collected Works of Katherine Mansfield: The Collected Fiction*, 2 vols., ed. Gerri Kimber and Vincent O'Sullivan (Edinburgh University Press, 2012), 2:94. Verbal correspondences suggest certain phrases have been adapted from the poem. Consider, for example:

> "Prufrock":   "I am Lazarus, come from the dead,/Come back to tell you all, I shall tell you all—" (lns. 94–95)
> "Feuille d'Album":   "but that was all. […] those far-seeing women were quite right. It wasn't all." (2:94; 2:95);
> "Prufrock":   "Arms that lie along a table, or wrap about a shawl." (ln 67)
> "Feuille d'Album":   "the concierge […] wrapped up in a filthy shawl" (2:94)
> "Prufrock":   "Is it perfume from a dress/That makes me so digress?" (lns. 65–66)
> "Feuille d'Album":   "She […] leaned over him so that he might smell the enchanting perfume of her hair" (2:94).

19 Crawford, *Young Eliot*, 278.
20 Clive Bell, *Old Friends: personal recollections* (London: Chatto and Windus, 1956), 122; Mansfield, *Letters* 1:313n4; Alpers, *Life*, 239.
21 Katherine Mansfield to Sydney Waterlow, late March 1921, 4:201–2; Katherine Mansfield to Violet Schiff, August 24, 1922, 5:256.
22 Margaret Scott, ed., *The Katherine Mansfield Notebooks*, 2 vols. (Canterbury New Zealand: Lincoln University Press and Daphne Brasell Associates, 1997), 2:83.
23 Stead, "Katherine Mansfield and T. S. Eliot," 154.
24 The exact date of composition of "Feuille d'Album" is not known, but as previously noted, it appeared in *New Age* in September 1917.
25 Mansfield to Woolf, c. May 12, 1919, 2:318. The Hogarth Press published Eliot's *Poems* on May 12th (2:318n1).
26 Alpers, *Life*, 238–39.
27 Mansfield to Woolf, c. May 12, 1919, 2:318.
28 Sydney Janet Kaplan, *Circulating Genius: John Middleton Murry, Katherine Mansfield, and D.H. Lawrence* (Edinburgh: Edinburgh University Press, 2010), 20, 86–87.
29 Mansfield to Woolf, c. May 12, 1919, 2:318.
30 Kaplan, *Origins of Modernist Fiction*, 75.
31 Katherine Mansfield to S. S. Koteliansky, November 19, 1915, 1:199–200.
32 Mansfield, "Feuille d'Album," 2:97.
33 T. S. Eliot, "The Love Song of J. Alfred Prufrock," 5–9.
34 Mansfield to Waterlow, late March 1921, 4:201.
35 Katherine Mansfield to Dorothy Brett, February 26, 1922, 5:75.
36 Elizabeth W. Scheider, *T. S. Eliot: The Pattern in the Carpet* (Los Angeles: UCLA Press, 1975), 30.

37 Katherine Mansfield to John Middleton Murry, November 19, 1919, 3:104.
38 Marjorie Perloff, *Twenty-First Century Modernism: The New Poetics* (Oxford: Blackwell, 2002), 24; Scheider, *The Pattern in the Carpet*, 24.
39 Katherine Mansfield to Ottoline Morrell, June 16, 1917, 1:311.
40 Mansfield, "Feuille d'Album," 2:95.
41 Mansfield, "Feuille d'Album," 2:95. On Mansfield's views of still life, that one must gather "round bright fruits [...] and become them, as it were," see her letter to Dorothy Brett, October 11, 1917, 1:330.
42 Mansfield, "Feuille d'Album," 2:95.
43 Mansfield, "Feuille d'Album," 2:93.
44 Mansfield, "Feuille d'Album," 2:93, 2:97.
45 Mansfield, "Feuille d'Album," 2:94.
46 Crawford, *Young Eliot*, 125
47 Crawford, *Young Eliot*, 160.
48 Mansfield, "Feuille d'Album," 2:93–94.
49 Mansfield, "Feuille d'Album," 2:95.
50 Mansfield, "Feuille d'Album," 2:94–95.
51 Mansfield, "Feuille d'Album," 2:95.
52 Mansfield, "Feuille d'Album," 2:95.
53 Anne Mounic, "'And he handed her an egg': The Art of Memory in 'Feuille d'Album', Katherine Mansfield and Proust," *Katherine Mansfield Studies* 1 (2009): 42–43.
54 See Keith Gregor, "Blissful Thinking: Katherine Mansfield and the En-gendering of Modernist Fiction," *Cuadernos de Filologia Inglesa* 611 (1997): 59–78 (65).
55 Mansfield, "Feuille d'Album," 2:95.
56 Perloff, *Twenty-First Century Modernism*, 25.
57 Andrew Gurr, *Writers in Exile: The Identity of Home in Modern Literature* (London: Harvester Press, 1981), 41–44.
58 Stead, "Katherine Mansfield and T. S. Eliot," 158.
59 Stead, "Battle of the Wasps," 19.
60 Carole Seymour-Jones, *Painted Shadow: The Life of Vivien Eliot* (London: Robinson, 2001), 194; Lyndall Gordon, *T. S. Eliot: An Imperfect Life*, 2nd ed. (London: Vintage, 1998), 106.
61 Eliot, "Eeldrop and Appleplex," 531n1.
62 Eliot, "Eeldrop and Appleplex," 525–26.
63 Seymour-Jones, *Painted Shadow*, 194.
64 Katherine Mansfield, "Sumurûn: An Impression of Leopoldine Konstantin," in *Collected Works*, ed. Kimber and Smith, 3:386–87.
65 Seymour-Jones argues that Vivien is the prime target but concedes that Katherine Mansfield may also have been a source (194); see Gordon, *An Imperfect Life*, 106.

66 See Seymour-Jones, *Painted Shadow*, 195; Alpers, *Life*, 233.
67 T. S. Eliot to Ezra Pound, August 13, 1935, YCAL MSS 43, Box 15, Folder 666. The Pound Papers, The Yale Collection of American Literature, Beinecke Rare Book and Manuscript Library, Yale University.
68 Eliot, "Eeldrop and Appleplex," 530; Alpers, *Life*, 210, 248.
69 Eliot, "Eeldrop and Appleplex," 530; Alpers, *Life*, 234.
70 Eliot, "Eeldrop and Appleplex," 530–31.
71 Eliot, "Eeldrop and Appleplex," 529.
72 Alpers, *Life*, 85–92, 145.
73 Eliot, "Eeldrop and Appleplex," 532n3. By 1935 Eliot saw it as a piece of juvenilia.
74 Katherine Mansfield to Sydney and Violet Schiff, May 14, 1920, 4:11.
75 Mansfield to Sydney and Violet Schiff, May 14, 1920, 4:11.
76 Mansfield to Sydney and Violet Schiff, May 14, 1920, 4:11.
77 Mansfield to Sydney and Violet Schiff, May 14, 1920, 4:11; Mansfield to Violet Schiff, October 24, 1921, 4:303.
78 T. S. Eliot to Ezra Pound, July 3, 1920, in *The Letters of T. S. Eliot,* vol. 1, rev. ed., ed. Valerie Eliot and Hugh Haughton (London: Faber, 2009), 473. All subsequent letters from T. S. and Vivien Eliot are from this source.
79 Vivien Eliot to Ezra Pound, November 2, 1922, 770; Crawford, *Young Eliot,* 416–20.
80 T. S. Eliot to Pound, November 7, 1922, 775.
81 Stead, "Katherine Mansfield and the Fictions of Continental Europe," 239.
82 Crawford, *Young Eliot*, 253.
83 Mansfield to Brett, February 26, 1922, 5:75.
84 Crawford, *Young Eliot*, 267.
85 Stead, "Katherine Mansfield and the Fictions of Continental Europe," 246–47. Stead suggests that the "hollow man" of Mansfield's story might have provided Eliot with the title "The Hollow Men" for his poem, written several years later (247).
86 Vivien Eliot to T. S. Eliot, August 16, 1920, 492.
87 Claire Tomalin, *Katherine Mansfield; A Secret Life* (London: Penguin, 1988), 240–41; Stead, "Katherine Mansfield and T. S. Eliot," 158.
88 T. S. Eliot, *After Strange Gods* (London 1934), 35–36. See Pamela Dunbar, "What does Bertha Want: A Re-reading of Katherine Mansfield's 'Bliss,'" in *Essays on Katherine Mansfield*, ed. Rhoda B. Nathan (New York: R. K. Hall, 1993), 128.
89 See Gregor, "Blissful Thinking," 66–67.
90 Frank Sargeson, "Katherine Mansfield," in *Conversation in a Train and Other Critical Writing*, ed. Kevin Cunningham (Auckland and Oxford: Christine Cole Catley, 1983), 29, 173; see Janet Wilson, "The 'Burden' of the Feminine: Frank Sargeson's Encounter with Katherine Mansfield," in *Katherine Mansfield and Her Legacy*, ed. Sarah Ailwood and Melinda Harvey (Edinburgh: Edinburgh University Press, 2015), 207–18.

6

"Memorials of the Dead": Walter de la Mare, Katherine Mansfield, and the Literary Afterlife

Jenny McDonnell

Katherine Mansfield once described Walter de la Mare as a figure who "haunts me here—not a persistent or substantial ghost but as one who shares my (our) joy in the *silent world*."[1] It seems a fitting description of a man who has only made fleeting appearances in studies of Mansfield to date. Although the two writers crossed paths in various ways, their personal and professional relationship has garnered relatively little critical interest since it was first given serious consideration by J. Lawrence Mitchell in a 1993 essay.[2] Yet the pairing of Mansfield and de la Mare remains an intriguing one. In the decade or so in which they knew one another, they shared publishers and editors as well as common friends and acquaintances that provide links to members of the Bloomsbury set and other groups. Indeed, the networks with which both were associated often intersect in ways that are appropriate for two writers at work within the complex literary marketplace of the early twentieth century. This essay explores the encounters between Mansfield and de la Mare within this broader context, before ultimately reappraising de la Mare's role in Mansfield's literary afterlife.

Toward the end of her life, Mansfield had anticipated the possibility that her unpublished writings might eventually be made public after her death, and she ostensibly took steps to exert some control over this in a series of documents written five months before she died. However, the instructions she outlined in a letter to John Middleton Murry dated August 7, 1922, and in a formal will a week

---

I would like to acknowledge the following for granting permission to quote from published and unpublished work by Walter de la Mare and Katherine Mansfield: the Literary Trustees of Walter de la Mare and the Society of Authors as their representative; the Society of Authors as the Literary Representative of the Estate of Katherine Mansfield; Oxford University Press; and the Newberry Library, Chicago (Special Collections). Thanks also to the librarians who provided assistance in accessing material that aided in the research of this essay, in particular Peter Attwell (Alexander Turnbull Library); Allison DeArcangelis (Newberry Library Special Collections); Lisa Kenny (British Library); and Curtis Small (University of Delaware Library Special Collections).

later were ultimately ambiguous, and articulated the same kinds of conflicted attitudes to the publication of her writing that had shaped her entire career. As I have argued in *Katherine Mansfield and the Modernist Marketplace*, Mansfield's writing was consistently influenced by "both her ambition to be an author and her anxiety about […] the editorial, critical and reading publics that influenced her professional development."[3] Her directions for the posthumous treatment of her writing were equally equivocal, simultaneously seeking and resisting the publication of at least some of her remaining manuscripts. In her letter to Murry, for example, she advised him "to do what you like" with the manuscripts while also asking him to "destroy all letters you do not wish to keep and all papers."[4] Likewise, in her will she stated that he should "publish as little as possible and tear up and burn as much as possible."[5] Despite her apparent reservations, then, in requesting that he publish "as little as possible," it is arguable that Mansfield allowed for the likelihood that he might publish some of the vast body of uncollected and unfinished work that she left behind.

In the wake of Mansfield's death, of course, Murry went on to preserve and publish a huge range of material, including editions of her letters, journals, critical writings, poetry, and stories. The first examples appeared in the pages of his newly established paper *The Adelphi* shortly after her death, while the first posthumous edition of her stories was published in June 1923. Like her previous two collections, *The Doves' Nest and Other Stories* was published under the Constable imprint. Whereas both *Bliss* and *The Garden Party* had been dedicated to Murry, however, *The Doves' Nest* instead featured an inscription to Walter de la Mare.[6]

In a way, the dedication of *The Doves' Nest* to de la Mare made it "a more precious book-gift" than the modest bequest that Mansfield had outlined in her will,[7] in which she included him in a list of people (among them A. R. Orage and D. H. Lawrence) to whom she wished to bequeath a book from her library. This in itself is evidence that she held him in high esteem, as is further suggested throughout her correspondence. Perhaps surprisingly for such prolific letter-writers, however, there seems to be a relative paucity of surviving letters between Mansfield and de la Mare. Just one letter from Mansfield is included in the five-volume *Collected Letters* (although two more are cited in Theresa Whistler's biography of Walter de la Mare), while a total of five letters from de la Mare can be found in the Newberry Library's Mansfield papers.[8] Nevertheless, Mansfield makes frequent affectionate references to de la Mare in letters to Murry in particular. In October 1920, for example, she warmly recalls a visit he once paid, accompanied by his wife and daughter: "I love Delamare [*sic*] love the man who came to tea—with his wife sitting there by the fire and dark, young, lovely Florence."⁹ Similarly, in a letter to Ottoline Morrell the following year, she calls him "one of the people whom I have most enjoyed meeting in Life," and a journal entry from January 20, 1922, states that she has just written to tell him "how much I thought of him. [...] I can truly say I think of W. J. D. [de la Mare], Tchekhov, [S. S.] Koteliansky, HMT [H. M. Tomlinson] and Orage every day. They are part of my life."¹⁰

Her fondness for the man was further complemented by her admiration of his writing, and she frequently quotes from and recommends his work to friends and family, citing the short story "The Three Mulla-Mulgars" and the poems "An Epitaph" and "Awake" as particular favorites.¹¹ Shortly before her death, she even asked Murry to buy a copy of his collection *Down-Adown-Derry: A Book of Fairy Poems* as a Christmas present for her sister Jeanne.¹² In addition to admiring de la Mare's poetry and fiction, she commented on his non-fiction work, albeit not always in positive terms, once describing a *Times Literary Supplement* article he wrote on Thomas Hardy as "superficial."¹³ By contrast, when she recognized de la Mare's work in an anonymous review in 1915, she asked Murry to pass on a compliment about the piece: "there is a review of *Mother Goose* under the title Nursery Rhymes in the Lit. Sup. for December 9th which is one of the most delightful reviews I ever read. If de la Mare wrote it & you see him please say how enchanting I thought it was."¹⁴ Later, she would come to seek de la Mare's good opinion of her own writing more and more. Writing to Murry about "The Lady's Maid" in December 1920, for example, she claimed "[t]*his* one I'd like you and de la Mare to like—other people don't matter."¹⁵ A few months later, when "At the Bay" appeared in the *London Mercury*, she asserts that "Tommy [H. M. Tomlinson] & DeLamare [*sic*] are the people Id [*sic*] *like* to please" while expressing an anxiety about how her work might be received: "Its [*sic*] just a queer feeling—after one has dropped a pebble in. Will there be a ripple or not?"¹⁶ Evidently, de la Mare became an important imagined audience for Mansfield. The feeling was clearly mutual, and among their surviving letters, one of the topics that recurs most is his 1921 novel *Memoirs of a Midget*. A misaddressed letter in which Mansfield purportedly outlined in detail her response to the novel never reached de la Mare, but she told him in a follow-up letter that "it seems to me impossible you should not know how much I loved Miss M."¹⁷ After her death, he still hoped that the missing letter might be traced, asking Murry to forward it to him should he come across it.¹⁸

Mansfield's letters and journal entries about de la Mare provide clear glimpses into her regard for the older writer, then, but the two seem to have met in person very rarely. Their acquaintance can be dated back to Mansfield's time at *Rhythm*, the magazine initially cofounded and coedited by Murry and Michael Sadleir in 1911, and eventually coedited by Murry and Mansfield until 1913. As Mitchell outlines, Murry most likely provided the initial point of contact,[19] and around this time he was also employed as a reviewer for the *Westminster Gazette*, with which de la Mare was long associated (not least through his relationship with the paper's literary editor Naomi Royde-Smith). Murry and de la Mare ultimately maintained a working and personal friendship for quite some time, and indeed, it was under Murry's editorship that the latter published an anonymous review of *Bliss and Other Stories* in the *Athenaeum* in January 1921.[20]

In addition to Murry, Mansfield and de la Mare shared other important professional contacts, including for a time the same publisher (Constable & Co.) and the same agent (J. B. Pinker). Furthermore, in the later stages of her career, Mansfield's work increasingly appeared in papers to which de la Mare also contributed, such as the *London Mercury* and the *Westminster Gazette* (for which he began writing literary reviews in 1909); the latter in particular is identified by S. P. Rosenbaum as one of the papers "in which Bloomsbury did not publish."[21] At the same time, de la Mare's working relationship with Murry aided him in making contributions to the *Athenaeum* alongside the likes of Virginia Woolf, E. M. Forster, and other representatives of Bloomsbury. These appearances in a diverse selection of periodicals and papers are in part illustrative of the ways in which both Mansfield and de la Mare traversed different literary networks during the time of their association.

Furthermore, the two writers maintained important links with members of the Bloomsbury group at various points throughout their careers, and both were visitors to Ottoline Morrell's manor at Garsington. It is arguable, nevertheless, that they remained relative outsiders. Roger Robinson has described Mansfield as "the literary colonial who was never quite accepted in Bloomsbury, the woman author publishing suspiciously popular stories on the fringes of a rather male Modernism."[22] Therefore, it is perhaps unsurprising that she should have been drawn to de la Mare, a man whose work might also be regarded as "suspiciously popular," specializing as he did in supernatural stories and children's verse.

He was also frequently associated with the Georgian movement, appearing in all five of the increasingly maligned anthologies of Georgian poetry that were edited by Edward Marsh and produced by Harold Monro's Poetry Workshop between 1912 and 1922. The movement ultimately came to gain a reputation as "a travesty of true artistic integrity because it was dominated by the middle-class, insular, mass-produced sensibilities it was written for,"[23] as Peter Howarth discusses in *British Poetry in the Age of Modernism* in reference to T. S. Eliot's critiques of the anthologies. Likewise, Peter Childs notes that "the expression 'Georgian poetry' has almost become a term of abuse."[24] However, de la Mare himself escaped criticism in Murry's infamous review of *Georgian Poetry IV*, first published in the *Athenaeum* in December 1919.[25] As Whistler notes, de la Mare "did not write the committed poetry Murry hoped young English writers would turn to, but Murry continued to feel him unassailable in the achievement peculiar to his own gift."[26] Moreover, he had already begun to establish a name for himself prior to his association with the Georgians, and his critical and commercial reputation was not solely tied to his (at times reluctant) affiliation with the movement.[27] This reluctance is apparent in his description of himself as "rather an old bird to be chirping in the new nest" in response to Marsh's suggestion that eight of his poems should be included in the fourth volume.[28]

Just as de la Mare defies easy categorization as a Georgian poet, Mansfield's practice of the short story form ultimately positioned her in the interstices between the "literary" and the "popular." As I have argued elsewhere, the short story's "combination of popular appeal and experimental attributes" eventually proved beneficial to her "as she sought to carve out a position for herself that could be marked by both commercial viability and literary credibility."[29] In fact, by the end of her career, as she became increasingly adept at capitalizing on her perceived "popular" tendencies, she had begun to explore new avenues of publication that largely saw her sever links with the *Athenaeum* (while Murry was still in place as editor), and also with Bloomsbury. After her experience of publishing *Prelude* at the Hogarth Press, she expressly ruled out working with Virginia and Leonard Woolf again, telling Murry in November 1919 that "I don't want the Woolfs to have any of my new work."[30] Indeed, Mansfield's increased affection for de la Mare toward the end of her life seems to have coincided quite closely with a growing discomfort about her previous associations with the Bloomsbury group in particular. She made this explicit in a February 1921 letter to Ottoline Morrell, in which she writes that "I read J. M. M's letters from Clive [Bell] and Co. & they horrify me. Did one know all the wrong people? Is that why nobody remains? Not a soul remains to me—not one—except Delamare [sic] whom I never knew when I was there [in England]."[31]

Given Mansfield's stated respect for de la Mare in the final years of her life, the pair may in fact be regarded as forming a "public of two,"[32] a term borrowed from

Virginia Woolf's famous description of her relationship with her younger friend and rival. As I suggest in *Katherine Mansfield and the Modernist Marketplace*, "these 'publics of two' punctuate [Mansfield's] career—with Beatrice Hastings, Woolf and Murry in particular—[but] they cannot be read in isolation from the wider circles and audiences with which she was associated."[33] Indeed, they emerged within a number of broader modernist and early twentieth-century literary networks that have been undergoing substantial critical reappraisal in recent years.[34] The landscape of the literary marketplace throughout the early twentieth century is replete with points of convergence across positions often considered mutually exclusive—literary and popular; modernist and Georgian; "the intellectuals and the masses"—which frequently reveal that these apparently monolithic classifications and groupings are actually far more fluid entities.[35] Indeed, as has already been noted, the "modernist" Mansfield and the "Georgian" de la Mare often populated the pages of the same publications—little magazines, literary periodicals, and newspapers—in ways that resist any such straightforward divisions into self-contained, distinct factions.

As Faith Binckes has argued in her compelling study of *Rhythm*, "when looked at up close, periodicals tend to reveal the tangled skeins that make up the fabric of modernism."[36] The Georgians, for example, may have been "subsequently placed well beyond the modernist pale," but Binckes makes a convincing case for understanding them as one of a number of "volatile intersecting networks, the interests of which […] often—but not always—overlapped."[37] By reading their work in the other contexts in which it was first produced and marketed (that is, not just in the anthologies that came to be so heavily criticized), Binckes argues that it is possible "to disaggregate the image of Georgianism as a twee, tweedy school of nature poetry," and instead emphasizes the ways in which it "was a construction mediated through a series of specific textual configurations."[38] In turn, this also provides an immediate context for Mansfield's working relationship with de la Mare, which was associated with a period of transition and mutability from the very start.

Mansfield's earliest encounters with de la Mare came at a time when *Rhythm* encountered severe financial difficulty (with Murry in particular facing bankruptcy charges). It subsequently underwent an organizational change, and was briefly repackaged as *The Blue Review*, funded by Edward Marsh and coedited by Wilfrid Wilson Gibson. Prior to this, other Georgian writers had contributed work throughout *Rhythm*'s run, among them Gibson himself, as well as Gilbert Cannan and John Drinkwater. In fact, de la Mare's involvement with the paper overlapped entirely with the transition from one incarnation to the other. Two poems—"The Changeling" and "The Mocking Fairy"—appeared in the final two issues of *Rhythm* in February and March 1913, respectively; the publication of "The Song of the Mad Prince" followed in the first issue of *The Blue Review* in May of the same year.[39] The final issue of *Rhythm* also featured an advertisement for the first volume of *Georgian Poetry*, as well as D. H. Lawrence's review of the same volume, to which he had himself contributed. Whistler notes that de la Mare played a pivotal role in the latter's involvement with the anthology at this juncture, suggesting that Lawrence considered him "a kind of unofficial agent in England." She indicates further that de la Mare mediated between Lawrence and Edward Marsh about the inclusion of the poem "Snapdragon" in the volume.[40] Once again, the publication of de la Mare and Lawrence side by side (in both *Rhythm* and in the first volume of *Georgian Poetry*) reveals the kinds of convergences previously noted. Although Georgian poetic conventions were soon to fall out of critical favor, it is nevertheless arguable, as Rennie Parker suggests, that "in many ways, the early Georgians *were* the modernists […], alongside *Des Imagistes* as anthologized by Ezra Pound. Pound wanted to wake up British art and 'make it new,' unconcerned that this was also the aim of Edward Marsh and Harold Monro."[41]

Of the Georgian poets that were published in *The Blue Review*, Rupert Brooke merits particular consideration within the context of the present discussion, not least because of his additional associations with both Bloomsbury and de la Mare. The Cambridge-educated Brooke remained friends with many members of the Bloomsbury group (including Virginia Woolf and James Strachey), and was at the forefront of the Georgian movement in its early stages through his involvement with *Rhythm*, *The Blue Review*, and the anthology. Binckes dates his association with *Rhythm* "from at least October 1912. By January 1913 he understood himself to be at the organizational centre of the publication."[42] This coincided with a reduction in Mansfield's practical editorial role in the journal, as she became increasingly alienated within the new lineup. Indeed, Antony Alpers detects a note of sexism in the assignment that she was given at the time to write on "dress," which ultimately remained uncompleted.[43]

There may well be further evidence of marginalization in a 1913 letter (cited by Angela Smith) that Brooke wrote to Edward Marsh in which he quips that Mansfield "really ought to remember she's a lidy [sic]." Smith sees the deliberate misspelling of "lady" as possibly "mocking Mansfield's accent" and suggests that the letter presents "[v]ulgarity and colonial provenance […] with an unspoken assumption that they will be linked in the mind of the recipient."[44]

If so, Brooke's comments might be interpreted as an example of the kinds of snobbery that Mansfield often detected within Bloomsbury, and from which she would eventually try to distance herself. Nevertheless, she later felt haunted by Brooke after his death, writing in May 1915 that she had dreamed of him the previous night: "[T]oday as I left the house he was standing at the door, with a rucksack on his back & his broad hat shading his face."[45] In fact, both writers were ultimately subjected to similar kinds of posthumous mythologizing, and for Frank O'Connor, for example, Mansfield's work was "obscured by her legend, as the work of Rupert Brooke has been."[46] Curiously, de la Mare was to play a role in the afterlife of each.

Brooke's death in the First World War (together with the death of Edward Thomas two years later) contributed greatly to the changing critical fortunes of the Georgian poetry movement, in which the "innovatory, affirmative minor rebels" of the prewar years gave way to "reactionary and sentimental escapists."[47] Yet his death had an inverse effect on Brooke's own commercial success. Bolstered by the emergence of hagiographic depictions of the poet, the posthumous sales of his writing soon increased exponentially. De la Mare was one of Brooke's initial eulogizers when he published a piece about him in the *Westminster Gazette* shortly after his death, which Whistler praises for its insight, and for "actually [prophesying] the myth: 'Once in a way Nature is as jealous of the individual as of the type. She gave Rupert Brooke youth, and may be, in these hyper-enlightened days, in so doing grafted a legend.'"[48] Brooke's successful posthumous career was ultimately set to have a huge material impact on de la Mare, when he was named as a beneficiary (along with Gibson and Lascelles Abercrombie) in Brooke's will, which stated that any money from the sale of his writings should be divided equally between all three. This was eventually to prove extremely profitable, and together with the Civil List pension he was granted in 1915, helped ease some of the financial pressures de la Mare had previously faced, freeing him from a reliance on other sources of income that at times proved wearing;[49] this had included a stint as a reader for Heinemann between 1911 and 1914.

In light of the impact that Brooke's popularity had on de la Mare's own career, it is interesting to note that he returned to two related themes—of the fate of an author's posthumous reputation, and of the potential for others to profit from their writing—in two ghost stories, "A Revenant" and "The Green Room." The first of these, "A Revenant" (dated 1935), explores questions about the role of criticism in interpreting an author's life and work, in particular in the wake of his/her death. The story presents a lecturer, Professor Monk, tasked with giving a talk (one that he "had delivered at least half a dozen times, and always with a modest satisfaction") on a favorite topic of his, Edgar Allan Poe, another writer whose myth threatens to distract from his work.[50] The story itself "was first written and delivered as a *lecture*,"[51] as Whistler notes, and in part it offers a metafictional commentary on the business of criticism and lecture-writing, two activities in which de la Mare was frequently employed. The story recounts Monk's delivery of his address and is punctuated throughout by the character's internal commentary on the lecture. Throughout, he remains distracted by the presence of a mysterious latecomer, "a solitary figure who was standing (almost like a statue in its niche)" in a doorway at the end of the room.[52] The figure—a ghostly version of Poe himself—finally approaches Monk in the closing pages of the story to critique what he has heard, telling him "[i]t needs [...] little courage to attack and stigmatise the dead. [...] Provided, of course, you are confident that dead he will remain."[53] In this way, the story explores the ethical implications of a literary afterlife that endures beyond the physical death of the author.

Another dead author surfaces in de la Mare's earlier story, "The Green Room" (dated 1925), in which Alan, "a young man of ample leisure and moderate means," frequently browses the shelves of Mr. Elliott's bookshop, which is stocked with old volumes: "'Look not too closely on us,' they seemed to cry. 'What are we all but memorials of the dead? And we too are swiftly journeying towards the dust.'"[54] An encounter with a ghostly female figure in the rooms that adjoin the shop soon leads to his discovery of "a square black American cloth-bound exercise book with *E. F.* cut out with a clumsy penknife at one of the top corners."[55] The notebook contains a photograph of the mysterious figure, as well as "verses, interlarded with occasional passages in prose, and a day or a date here and there, and all set down apparently just as it had taken the writer's fancy."[56] As he reads this disordered volume, Alan decides to undertake the task of editing and publishing the poems contained within, planning a private edition of the poems of "E. F."; once this is produced, though, the ghostly figure returns to have her say "by bringing the plaster ceiling down upon the newly-minted volumes."[57] Like Poe in "A Revenant," then, the unidentified author of these poems stubbornly refuses to stay dead, and returns to challenge Alan's attempts at taking control of her writing after her death.

When "The Green Room" was published in 1925, John Middleton Murry had already begun the process of publishing posthumous editions of Mansfield's writing. However suggestive the story might seem, though, the critic should, of course, be wary of presuming to speak on behalf of a dead writer by assuming any deliberate echo between the ghostly figure in "The Green Room" and the real-life case of Katherine Mansfield, without sufficient evidence. Nevertheless, it is certainly worth noting a link to Mansfield's own writing at a thematic level here, as she also addressed the subject of the literary afterlife, for example, in the letter to Murry previously discussed. This is further evident in her late story, "The Canary," in which she utilized her favored symbol for the professional writer (the caged bird) in order to contemplate what might endure after his/her death.[58] Mansfield simultaneously resisted and invited this kind of literary afterlife for her writing, but in the years that followed her death, her image itself was also subject to multiple revisions and rewrites, from Murry's construction of her as a childlike innocent to the many fictionalized and dramatized reinterpretations of her life and writing that have proven consistently popular.[59] Indeed, de la Mare himself became associated with the Katherine Mansfield industry that emerged after her death, but his involvement is more complex than has previously been acknowledged.

De la Mare has often been identified as having played a role in memorializing Mansfield in print, with the composition and publication of a poem that bears her name (or initials) as a title. In terms that echo Robin Hyde's 1938 description of the poem as "her obituary," for example, Mitchell refers to it as an elegy "written in direct response to the death of Katherine Mansfield."[60] In fact, the poem was originally titled "Horse in a Field (To Katherine Mansfield)" and was first published (as Kathleen Jones also notes) *before* Mansfield's death.[61] A letter held in the Newberry Library shows that de la Mare wrote to Mansfield on January 15, 1922, asking her permission for him to publish it, but noting: "I have been a little dubious about the printing of it, lest you should prefer not."[62] The poem was subsequently published in the *Saturday Westminster Gazette* on January 28, 1922, one week before Mansfield herself was set to make an appearance in the same newspaper with the first installment of "The Garden Party."[63] The following year, "Horse in a Field (To Katherine Mansfield)" was reprinted (alongside an actual obituary by Sylvia Lynd) in the renamed *Weekly Westminster Gazette* on January 20, 1923.[64] Over time, the poem underwent various revisions when it came to be collected and reprinted further; some minor changes were made to the wording, and the title eventually became "To K. M." (under which title it appeared in the third volume of *Katherine Mansfield Studies*, for example).[65] In this way, later reprints saw the erasure of the original title in favor of the parenthetical dedication, which may have helped transform the poem into a more overt memorial to Mansfield. However, the origin of the poem is indicative of a mutually supportive working relationship between two *living* writers.

It was initially inspired by a conversation in which, as Kathleen Jones describes, Mansfield and de la Mare played "an old riddle game where each has to contribute a line from a given image, and then develop it, batting lines between them."[66] Whistler presents the encounter (at Mansfield's Hampstead house, "The Elephant") as follows: "Katherine relaxed into her happiest and gentlest self, and de la Mare proposed one of his favourite mental games: 'Supposing I just say "Horse in a field"—what do you *see*?' Later on, ill and alone at Menton, Katherine reminded him by letter of this talk, and of the small chestnut horse *she* had seen."[67] These accounts of the context in which the poem was composed suggest that the subtitle "To Katherine Mansfield" may in fact have been more reflective of the collaborative process that inspired it. Rather than a funereal tribute, then, the closing lines emphasize a subject who is very much alive:

> This then the horse that I see: swift as the wind;
> That none may master or mount; and none may bind;
> But she, his Mistress; cloaked, and at throat that gem—
> Dark head, dark eyes, slim shoulder…
>
> God speed, K. M. (l.48-52)[68]

Moreover, its original appearance in such close proximity to the publication of "The Garden Party" in the same paper in 1922 further locates the poem as part of an encounter between two contemporaries at work within the literary marketplace.

During Mansfield's lifetime, de la Mare twice gave public expression to his admiration for her, in both his anonymous review of *Bliss* and in "Horse in a Field (To Katherine Mansfield)." By contrast, Mansfield's reciprocal esteem for de la Mare was only made public after her death, in different editions of her letters and notebooks, as well as the dedication in *The Doves' Nest*. As Mitchell suggests, it is uncertain whether the latter was an editorial decision on Murry's part or Mansfield's.[69] Interestingly, though, in a letter held in the University of Delaware, de la Mare specifically directed his gratitude to the now-dead Mansfield; writing to Murry on March 3, 1923, he asks to see a copy of the forthcoming collection of stories, and states: "I can't say what I feel about the dedication; but I send her my love."[70] Since he was already aware of her death at this stage, his comments may well imply that he interpreted the gesture as Mansfield's, one way or another.

Moreover, Mansfield's notebooks reveal that she had previously intended to dedicate a story to de la Mare. Notebook 25 includes a draft and fair copy of an unfinished piece entitled "By Moonlight"; the fair copy is explicitly headed, "To: W. J. D. [Walter John de la Mare]."[71] The fragment is of particular note in its depiction of the protagonist Laura wandering through her family home at night, which renders the ordinarily familiar space *unheimlich*:

> How much bigger the house felt at night, thought Laura. [...] Big—big and empty. No, not empty, exactly, but awfully strange. [...] [S]he had an idea that some one on the top landing was looking down at her. Someone had suddenly appeared from nowhere and with a brilliant round white face was staring! [...] What nonsense. It was the moon shining through the top landing window.[72]

There are echoes here with other Mansfield stories—for example, with young Kezia's leave-taking of another space rendered unfamiliar by the removal of the Burnell family from their old home in "Prelude." But these uncanny moments also resonate with the work of Walter de la Mare, both in his supernatural tales and in his poetry. Indeed, Peter Howarth's reappraisal of his verse in *British Poetry in the Age of Modernism* insists that the "peculiar ability to transform the most intimate and familiar matter into something disturbing—disturbing precisely because it is already familiar—[...] is central to de la Mare's work."[73] In light of this, Mansfield's decision to dedicate the haunting "By Moonlight" to de la Mare seems especially appropriate. In its depiction of a young protagonist who explores a familiar space made strange by the light of the moon, it offers further support for Mitchell's description of the pair as "kindred spirits, equally responsive to the sights and sounds of the natural world, equally interested in dreams and in the realm of childhood."[74] In this way, the piece contains echoes of the "silent world" that Mansfield felt she shared with de la Mare.

For a contemporary reader, "By Moonlight" is also significant (and arguably makes the familiar unfamiliar) because of the ways in which it resonates with the more famous "The Garden Party" by repeating a number of characters and motifs (including another rendition of the song "This Life Is Weary") as well as introducing a new character (Francie). It is one of several surviving fragments that suggests Mansfield may have intended to develop the Sheridan stories into a longer series, and she outlined a plan to do so in her notebooks in May 1922.[75] This ultimately never came to fruition, and "By Moonlight" was not published in Mansfield's lifetime, rendering her planned dedication of the work to de la Mare as another tribute to him that—like *The Doves' Nest*—only came to light in the wake of her death.

Mansfield's posthumous career began in earnest with the publication of *The Doves' Nest* in June 1923, and de le Mare's name became inextricably linked with her literary afterlife at the same time. However, their working relationship saw them encounter one another as colleagues who moved within diverse networks that included the Georgian poets and the Bloomsbury Group, and who shared the pages of a range of literary and popular journals and papers. This was the context in which they produced their work and their tributes to one another, all of which ultimately now endure in different ways as "memorials of the dead."

Notes

1. Katherine Mansfield to John Middleton Murry, October 18, 1920, in *The Collected Letters of Katherine Mansfield*, 5 vols., eds. Vincent O'Sullivan and Margaret Scott (Oxford: Clarendon Press, 1984–2008), 4:75. All subsequent letters from Mansfield are from this source unless otherwise indicated, and are quoted by permission of Oxford University Press. Emphasis in original.
2. J. Lawrence Mitchell, "Katherine Mansfield and 'The Man Who Came to Tea,'" *Journal of Modern Literature* 18, no. 1 (Winter 1992), 147–55.
3. Jenny McDonnell, *Katherine Mansfield and the Modernist Marketplace: At the Mercy of the Public* (Basingstoke: Palgrave Macmillan, 2010), 168. For a discussion of Mansfield's posthumous career in particular, see 168–73.
4. Mansfield to Murry, August 7, 1922, 5:234–35.
5. KM's will, dated August 14, 1922. Cited in *Collected Letters* 5:235n1.
6. B. J. Kirkpatrick, *A Bibliography of Katherine Mansfield* (Oxford: Oxford University Press, 1989), 17; 22; 26.
7. Mitchell, "The Man," 153. Mitchell also notes that it is unclear whether de la Mare ever received the book.
8. Whistler quotes two uncollected letters from Mansfield to de la Mare, one dated May 2, 1921 and the other postmarked January 21, 1922 (Theresa Whistler, Imagination of the Heart: The Life of Walter de la Mare (London: Duckworth, 1993), 306, 307.). De la Mare's letters to Mansfield are held in the Katherine Mansfield Papers—Additions (Box 7, folders 66–70), The Newberry Library, Chicago.
9. Mansfield to Murry, October 12, 1920, 4:67.
10. Mansfield to Ottoline Morrell, December 27, 1921, 4:356; Margaret Scott, ed., *The Katherine Mansfield Notebooks*, vol. 2 (Canterbury and Wellington, NZ: Lincoln University Press and Daphne Brasell Associates, Ltd., 1997), 318. This entry in Mansfield's notebook would seem to tally with the second letter cited by Whistler in note 8 above.

11 See Mansfield to Ida Baker, February 24, 1922, 5:74; to Elizabeth, Countess Russell, October 23, 1921, 4:301; and to Ottoline Morrell, c. January 24, 1922, 5:21.
12 Mansfield to Murry, December 17–20, 1922, 5:337.
13 Mansfield to Murry, December 3, 1919, 3:132.
14 Mansfield to Murry, December 12–13, 1915, 1:210.
15 Mansfield to Murry, December 6, 1920, 4:136. Emphasis in original.
16 Mansfield to Murry, May 9, 1921, 4:218. Emphasis in original.
17 Mansfield to Walter de la Mare, May 6, 1922, 5:168.
18 Unpublished letter from Walter de la Mare to John Middleton Murry, March 2, 1923. MSS 182, Walter de la Mare Letters to John Middleton Murry, Special Collections, University of Delaware Library, Newark, Delaware.
19 Mitchell, "The Man," 148. Whistler describes de la Mare's delight at their first meeting in early 1913 (*Imagination of the Heart*, 212–13).
20 Unsigned (Walter de la Mare) review of *Bliss and Other Stories*, *Athenaeum*, no. 4734 (January 21, 1921): 67. Reprinted in *The Critical Response to Katherine Mansfield*, ed. Jan Pilditch (Westport, CT & London: Greenwood Press, 1996), 2–4.
21 S. P. Rosenbaum, *Georgian Bloomsbury: The Early Literary History of the Bloomsbury Group 1910–1914*, vol. 3 (Basingstoke: Palgrave, 2003), 144.
22 Roger Robinson, Introduction to *Katherine Mansfield: In From the Margin*, ed. Roger Robinson (Louisiana: Louisiana State University Press, 1994), 1.
23 Peter Howarth, *British Poetry in the Age of Modernism* (Cambridge: Cambridge University Press, 2005), 10.
24 Peter Childs, *The Twentieth Century in Poetry: A Critical Survey* (London and New York: Routledge, 1999), 26.
25 John Middleton Murry, "The Condition of English Poetry," *Athenaeum* no. 4675 (December 5, 1919), 1283–85. Reprinted as "The Present Condition of English Poetry" in John Middleton Murry, *Aspects of Literature* (New York: Knopf, 1920), 139–49.
26 Whistler, *Imagination of the Heart*, 299.
27 Whistler, *Imagination of the Heart*, 207.
28 Whistler, *Imagination of the Heart*, 299.
29 McDonnell, *Modernist Marketplace*, 11.
30 Mansfield to Murry, November 26 and 27, 1919, 3:122.
31 Mansfield to Ottoline Morrell, February 2, 1921, 4:171.
32 Anne Oliver Bell and Andrew McNeillie, eds., *The Diary of Virginia Woolf*, 5 vols. (London: Hogarth, 1977–1984), 1:222.
33 McDonnell, *Modernist Marketplace*, 13.
34 See for example Faith Binckes, *Modernism, Magazines, and the British Avant-Garde: Reading Rhythm 1910–1914* (Oxford: Oxford University Press, 2010); Mark S. Morrisson, *The Public Face of Modernism: Little Magazines, Audience, and Reception*

1905–1920 (Madison: University of Wisconsin Press, 2001); Lawrence Rainey, *Institutions of Modernism: Literary Elites and Public Culture* (New Haven, CT and London: Yale University Press, 1998).

35 The phrase "intellectuals and the masses" is borrowed from John Carey, *The Intellectuals and the Masses: Pride and Prejudice among the Literary Intelligentsia, 1880–1939* (London: Faber, 1992).
36 Binckes, *Reading Rhythm*, 11.
37 Binckes, *Reading Rhythm*, 14; 170.
38 Binckes, *Reading Rhythm*, 197.
39 Walter de la Mare, "The Changeling," *Rhythm* 2, no. 13 (February 1913): 381; "The Mocking Fairy," *Rhythm* 2, no. 14 (March 1913): 446; "The Song of the Mad Prince," *The Blue Review* 1, no. 1 (May 1913): 1.
40 Whistler, *Imagination of the Heart*, 194.
41 Rennie Parker, *The Georgian Poets: Abercrombie, Brooke, Drinkwater, Gibson and Thomas* (Plymouth: Northcote House, 1999), 81. Emphasis in original.
42 Binckes, *Reading Rhythm*, 4.
43 Antony Alpers, *The Life of Katherine Mansfield* (New York: Viking, 1980), 157. For a more comprehensive discussion of Mansfield's involvement with both *Rhythm* and *The Blue Review*, see McDonnell, *Modernist Marketplace*, 46–76.
44 Angela Smith, *Katherine Mansfield: A Literary Life* (Basingstoke: Palgrave, 2000), 2.
45 Mansfield to Murry, c. May 13, 1915, 1:186. This draft letter is also included in Scott, *Mansfield Notebooks*, 2:13.
46 Frank O'Connor, *The Lonely Voice: A Study of the Short Story* (Cork: Cork City Council, 2003), 85.
47 Childs, *Twentieth Century*, 29.
48 Whistler, *Imagination of the Heart*, 248.
49 For an account of Brooke's bequest and its material impact on de la Mare, see Whistler, *Imagination of the Heart*, 248–53.
50 Walter de la Mare, "A Revenant," in *Strangers and Pilgrims: Tales by Walter de la Mare*, ed. Mark Valentine (Leyburn, North Yorkshire: Tartarus Press, 2007): 427. For a discussion of Poe's influence on de la Mare, see Burton R. Pollin, "The Pathway of Edgar Allan Poe Traced in the Works of Walter de la Mare," *English Literature in Transition, 1880–1920* 42, no. 1 (1999): 39–69.
51 Whistler, *Imagination of the Heart*, 151. Emphasis in original.
52 De la Mare, "Revenant," 429.
53 De la Mare, "Revenant," 447.
54 Walter de la Mare, "The Green Room," in Valentine, *Strangers and Pilgrims*, 186, 198.
55 Walter de la Mare, "The Green Room," 199.
56 Walter de la Mare, "The Green Room," 201.

57 Whistler, *Imagination of the Heart*, 353.
58 Katherine Mansfield, "The Canary," *Nation & the Athenaeum* 33, no. 3 (April 21, 1923): 84. For a discussion of the way in which the story reflects authorial anxieties, see McDonnell, *Modernist Marketplace*, 163–67.
59 For more on the topic of the posthumous rewritings of Katherine Mansfield, see Laura Marcus, *Katherine Mansfield's Afterlives*, ed. Gerri Kimber (Bath: Katherine Mansfield Society Publications, 2014).
60 Robin Hyde, "New Zealand Authoresses," in *Disputed Ground: Robin Hyde, Journalist*, ed. Gillian Boddy and Jacqueline Matthews (Wellington: Victoria University Press, 1991): 206; Mitchell, "The Man," 148.
61 Kathleen Jones, *Katherine Mansfield: The Story-Teller* (Edinburgh: Edinburgh University Press, 2010), 488n34.
62 Unpublished letter from Walter de la Mare to Katherine Mansfield, January 15, 1922. Katherine Mansfield Papers—Additions (Box 7, folders 66–70), The Newberry Library, Chicago.
63 Walter de la Mare, "Horse in a Field (To Katherine Mansfield)," *Saturday Westminster Gazette* (January 28, 1922): 10. "The Garden-Party" (the title of which was hyphenated for its initial publication) was serialized in three parts between February 4 and 18, 1922, during which time the newspaper underwent a name change from the *Saturday Westminster Gazette* to the *Weekly Westminster Gazette*.
64 Walter de la Mare, "Horse in a Field (To Katherine Mansfield)," *Weekly Westminster Gazette* (January 20, 1923): 12–13.
65 Walter de la Mare, "To K.M.," *Katherine Mansfield Studies* 3 (2011): 107–8.
66 Jones, *Story-teller*, 361.
67 Whistler, *Imagination of the Heart*, 306. Emphasis in original. Whistler is referring here to the letter of May 2, 1921, cited in note 8 above.
68 De la Mare, "Horse in a Field (To Katherine Mansfield)," *Saturday Westminster Gazette*, 10.
69 Mitchell, "The Man," 153.
70 Unpublished letter from Walter de la Mare to John Middleton Murry, March 2, 1923. MSS 182, Walter de la Mare Letters to John Middleton Murry, Special Collections, University of Delaware Library, Newark, Delaware.
71 Scott, *Mansfield Notebooks*, 2:221–26. This piece should be distinguished from a sketch, also entitled "By Moonlight," which formed the third part of "Tales of a Courtyard," a collection of Russian pastiches published in *Rhythm*. See Katherine Mansfield, "Tales of a Courtyard," *Rhythm* 2, no. 7 (August 1912): 99–105.
72 Scott, *Mansfield Notebooks*, 2:225.
73 Howarth, *British Poetry*, 113.
74 Mitchell, "The Man," 151.
75 Scott, *Mansfield Notebooks*, 2:292–93.

7

Mansfield and Dunning: An "important and shadowy" Friendship

Erika Baldt

In his essay on the final year of Katherine Mansfield's life, Vincent O'Sullivan refers to the friendship between Mansfield and Millar Dunning as "important and shadowy."[1] Indeed, from contemporary reports, it would seem that it was more one of shades, in the Greek sense. Dunning's wife Bill claimed to be able to channel Mansfield's spirit after her death,[2] and Virginia Woolf wrote in her diary in March 1923 that Dorothy Brett, inspired by what Woolf called Dunning's "jargon," reported "contact" with Mansfield's ghost.[3] While both then and now such reports must be taken with a grain of salt (both Bill Dunning and Brett seem to have had more than platonic feelings for John Middleton Murry, and used communion with his wife's shade as a kind of bonding exercise),[4] nevertheless, there was, as O'Sullivan suggests, a certain kinship between Mansfield and Dunning, though little is known of the latter.

Most accounts of Dunning describe him as either a "mystic"[5] or a "practising Yogi."[6] However, he was also, like Mansfield, a transplant from New Zealand who wrote for *The New Age* and attended Ottoline Morrell's Garsington parties, where he and Mansfield met around 1917.[7] Although Mansfield claimed in a letter to Murry in 1922 that "I dont *feel* influenced by Youspensky or Dunning. I merely feel Ive heard ideas like my ideas, but bigger ones, far more definite ones,"[8] I would argue not only that her work shares surprising parallels to Dunning's in both the content and form, but, more importantly, that she *was* influenced by his lifestyle in a way that colored the final years of her life.

In an undated journal entry of around 1920, Mansfield acknowledges that Dunning helped her see her own writing differently: "He made the Casetta story plainer: I saw how it could be made to 'fit.'"[9] Yet even before they had ever met, echoes can be found of each in the other's work. Three of Dunning's "sketches" of English life from his single published book, *The Earth Spirit* of 1920—"Red Lion Square," "An English Village," and "London"—function similarly to Mansfield's *In a German Pension* (1911) stories, employing a perspective that Jeffrey Meyers refers to as an "outsider in a hostile world"[10] in an attempt to reveal the hypocrisy of a society priding itself on its civility and order. Describing the tranquil beauty of the eponymous English Village, Dunning writes,

> But how shall one interpret it and give it a truthful reading—pierce the overhanging veil of obscurity—peer beneath and see the living reality, coherent and intelligible? All is so dumb, so inarticulate—these fields, these trees and gardens, these cottages and old churches. What is their tale and the nature of the spirit that pervades them and rules the lives of those who live among them? In it all there is something suggested which is not apparent—something deeper down, whose grimness all this beauty cannot hide.[11]

The grim "spirit" the narrator describes pervades both the natural and the man-made environments, subjugating those who live within it. The narrator himself, like Orpheus returned from the Underworld, is the sole observer of this death in life, able to identify the "reality" that others cannot comprehend. In "London" he makes a similar claim that a serene façade conceals a sinister, even "monstrous" side:

> Men and women sit out in the evening. Together thus, they seem to make themselves one with the all-pervading spirit of peace—for what can appeal more to our sense of the picturesque and seemly than a group of fellow-beings resting in the shadows that succeed the day.
>
> But thus it is that following the easier way we accept the more obvious reality, and pass over that which lurks beneath. Tradition would have us cry: "God's in his heaven, all's well with the world," while we, to uphold tradition, greet every seeming scene of tranquility with applause, hold it fast in our memories for evidence, and being satisfied pass on, although we have but witnessed the manifestation of a well-being so rare that we have long ceased to recognise it as the proper heritage of man; or if we recognise it as such, then only to take it as signifying a state of permanence which does not exist—a delusion nevertheless which enables us to go our way unhaunted by a truth too uncomely, too monstrous, to find itself at home in the delicate tenements of our unpractised minds.[12]

Here, the focus is on the inhabitants rather than the environment. While the observer this time is more inclusive, using the first person point of view to situate himself within the group of men and women described engaging in what at first seems to be an idyllic pastime, he still attempts to reveal the contrast between the "picturesque and seemly," the "tranquility" of the surface, and the shocking "truth" beneath. Again, too, the issue is put in terms of otherworldly shades, although this time the inhabitants choose to remain "unhaunted," preferring the "obvious reality" to a more difficult break with "tradition" that would result in freedom from "delusion."

Yet while Dunning is firm in his insistence in both pieces that there is "something" hidden which haunts the average citizen, it is never entirely clear what that "something" is. "Tradition," the word Dunning employs in "London," can encompass many beliefs and ideas, some of which Dunning attempts to address elsewhere. In a letter to the editor of *The New Age* in 1915, for example, Dunning speaks out against both the feminist movement and the First World War, claiming in regard to what he refers to as women's "short-sightedness," that

> No better example will ever be afforded the world than the characteristics of the feminist movement itself, and the attitude women generally have taken towards this war—terrible enough in all conscience. But, theoretically, and too often, too, practically, women are adding the most distasteful and discordant note of all. Listen where you will and you will hear the unreasoned, the unqualified scream—"run no risks, crush them, crush them, though you sink your own souls in hell."[13]

The war itself is "terrible enough," but worse, according to Dunning, is what he interprets as women's, specifically feminists', support for it. Here, too, he employs imagery of the Underworld, as he suggests that the crusade against the enemy effectively condemns its supporters' spirits to hell. It would not be difficult to imagine, then, that the "grimness" of which Dunning writes a few years later in his English sketches is a reference to the War and its aftermath. However, even in this early attempt to identify more explicitly what he considers the truth beneath the veil, Dunning seemingly failed to make his meaning clear. Responses to his letter in a subsequent issue of *The New Age* criticize its vagueness, with one writer claiming Dunning's missive was "a little obscure in the meaning intended"[14] and another describing Dunning's diction as "scarcely intelligible."[15] Yet, though Dunning's attempts to articulate his specific grievances may not have succeeded, his statement in "Sanatana Dharma" of 1919 more effectively conveys his pervading mistrust, suggested in the sketches for *The Earth Spirit*, of any and all social constructions: "We are […] a people of darkness, ingrained in the ways of darkness, and to any other way altogether estranged."[16] Dunning seems to suggest that anything created by humans, whether it be in a country village or city square, is an illusion that only serves to separate the individual from true knowledge.

Mansfield, too, addresses the illusory nature of "tradition" and appearances, but she does so with a much lighter touch than Dunning. For whereas Dunning's observer claims to see the truth beneath the facade, the narrator of the stories collected in *In a German Pension* refuses to comment explicitly on the absurdity of the goings on around her, using sarcasm and wit to hint at the shared "delusion," which in the case of Mansfield's stories refers to bourgeois European attitudes that Dunning attempts to expose. Several of the stories in the collection address just the situation Dunning describes, "a group of fellow-beings resting," in this case taking a "cure" in a German spa town that, while unnamed, is modeled on Bad Wörishofen, where Mansfield herself spent several months in 1909.[17] In each, though, Mansfield highlights the "uncomely" impulses that ripple the serene surface of communal life. A seemingly innocuous discussion of food in "Germans at Meat," for example, devolves quickly when the non-German narrator reveals she does not know her husband's favorite food: "'No wonder there is a repetition in England of that dreadful state of things in Paris,' said the Widow, folding her dinner napkin. 'How can a woman expect to keep her husband if she does not know his favourite food after three years?'"[18] Pleasantries are dropped as the Widow turns the narrator into a symbol of all that is wrong with English society. Rather than confront the social stereotypes, however, the narrator extricates herself from the situation, stating, "I closed the door after me,"[19] as if literally closing off what Dunning calls the "delicate tenements" of both her own and the others' minds from the unpleasant truth.

Indeed, many of the stories end similarly with a single glib or ironic statement that is meant to amuse the reader while showing in a humorous way that the narrator, much like Dunning's observer, perceives the "truth" of each situation but refuses to say it outright. Both "The Baron" and "The Sister of the Baroness" describe the fuss that is made over unremarkable individuals whose only claim to fame is seeming to have been born into the aristocracy. In the former story, the Baron on whom the narrator turns her attention has cultivated an air of mystery to the other guests at the pension; they derive great pleasure in anticipating when and how he will deign to break his habitual silence. The narrator, however, discovers that there is no romance to the Baron's routine, although she does not reveal the reason for his aloof behavior ("I sit alone that I may eat more,"[20] she learns), choosing instead to accept the largesse bestowed upon her by the other guests for her perceived closeness to this important personage. The story ends with the Baron's departure and a single ironic comment: "Sic transit gloria German mundi."[21] "The Sister of the Baroness" is similar, as the pension guests fawn over a woman who is believed to be part of the aristocracy but in fact turns out to be the equivalent of a nanny. After the true Baroness reveals that the young woman in question is her dressmaker's daughter, the story concludes with the words, "Tableau grandissimo!"[22] In each case, the remarks serve to undermine the importance placed by the other pension guests on class, nationality, and status, without addressing it directly. In fact, further distance is created by the use of foreign languages: while W. H. New suggests that phrases such as these invite readers "to share the narrator's superior judgment of the circumstances of the story,"[23] they are nonetheless neither in English, the language of the narrator, and, presumably, the reader, nor are they in German, the language of the individuals facing judgment. While the phrases themselves are not so uncommon, they are purposely opaque, as readers can only fully "share" the joke and the judgment if they are familiar with Latin or Italian. Thus, while Dunning's pieces may have been unintentionally vague in their critique of the mass's seemingly sinister preference for "obvious reality," Mansfield playfully adds another layer to purposely confound the "truthful reading" that the former would have us make of the individuals and beliefs described .

However, there are striking similarities between Dunning's "Red Lion Square" and Mansfield's "Tales of a Courtyard," published in *Rhythm* in August 1912. The first of Dunning's three English sketches, "Red Lion Square," employs many of the same images that Mansfield introduced in the 1912 story and refined in 1918's "Bliss." While Mansfield's "Tales of a Courtyard" comprises three different "tales" connected loosely by the lives of the three Russian students whose window looks out onto the courtyard, Dunning's sketch takes the form of a composition of "so many things, all of which find a niche within the frame of this winter's night"[24] and the more obvious frame of the village or city square.[25] Both texts are a series of vignettes juxtaposing human lives with the natural world. As in the *German Pension* stories, though, Mansfield's tone is lighter, more hopeful at the beginning of the first of the three "tales," entitled "Early Spring": "The chestnut tree grows in the middle of the court. There is a stone bench round it where the children chatter and scuffle by day and where the old people sit in the evening time, very quiet and close, counting the stars shining through the leaves as though the chestnut tree were their own fruit tree growing in a moonshiny orchard."[26] The courtyard becomes a gathering place for its inhabitants, the chestnut tree a beacon of hope. Yet while Mansfield focuses on new life, Dunning's scene is winter, the subject death:

> The trees remain. They are bare of their leaves. One is gnarled and leans for support. Another is large. Its branches are limned against the pink of the mist and against the black wall of the church. But the grass is wet, and all within the iron fence is desolate. No one paces the glistening paths. The grass only is green, and the box hedge and shrubs that cling close to the earth. They surround the dead fountain. They crowd up and peer over the sides, asking for reasons why. Why should the fountain be still—the sky so tearful and they so full of winter pain?[27]

Mansfield's courtyard scene is on the cusp of spring, while Dunning's square suffers in "winter pain." Though there is color in the scene, the green of the grass and the pink of the mist cannot diminish the pervading mood of desolation. It is as if the square is the "truth" Dunning suggests hides beneath the aforementioned English village's tranquil veil, the "grimness all this beauty cannot hide."

Also, the trees take on human characteristics, as one "leans for support" on its fellow, and the shrubs "crowd," "peer," and ask silent questions. The buildings, too, are personified, adding to the supernatural effect:

> All around, high unlighted windows look into the square, down through the lighted mist, to the leafless trees below. And the buildings that contain the unlighted windows are sentient things and they sense their way into every region of the world and into every manner of life. They follow the beings who shut their doors in the evening, follow them to their homes and seek them in their dreams and hold them through the night.[28]

The text explicitly states that the buildings are "sentient things," their windows eye-like and their gaze as inescapable as that of their inhabitants.

Surprisingly, though, this voyeuristic image also appears in Mansfield's story, for even while the initial description of the scene creates an optimistic opening to the tale, the inhabitants of the courtyard so enchanted by the chestnut tree soon betray the fact that they are only behaving "*like* people preparing for something pleasant" (my italics);[29] the tone soon shifts to one almost as dark as Dunning's. All is not as it seems as it becomes clear that the three Russian students, who also have a room facing the courtyard, are excluded from their neighbors' collective experience, which is relayed in the first person plural. Though "*we* shouted and laughed"[30] and "*we* preened ourselves like birds,"[31] "*they* were scarcely ever seen, except behind the window" (my italics).[32] In fact, it is on this very window that their neighbors fixate as a sign of the students' difference: "We had not seen them all through the winter. To-day their window was closed. A coat hung across it. The sleeves of the coat must have been pinned to the walls. It looked very strange as though trying to shield the room from our view. It made us angry."[33] The inanimate object becomes the focus of the neighbors' anger as they imbue it with qualities they perceive in the students: impropriety and a lack of respect for appearances. Some of their ire, however, may be a projection, a result of their envy of the others' seeming imperviousness to a hostile world that would, as Dunning puts it, "follow them to their homes and seek them in their dreams."[34]

This resentment of the students' self-imposed isolation and their disregard for the opinions of others is what leads to the morbid conclusion of the first tale. Just as the girl at the close of Dunning's piece "runs the gauntlet in the rain, and the youths chase her, and they laugh,"[35] the female Russian student in "Early Spring" finally exits her flat, exposing herself to the prying eyes of her neighbors:

> She blinked and peered at the light like a little animal. When she saw the people leaning from the windows she drew back—just for a moment, then she set her lips and walked out of the shadow. She looked at nobody. She kept her dark eyes fixed on the chestnut tree and the shining buds. And at the sight of her we leaned out, laughed, shook and screamed with laughter, holding our sides. Dead—were they! God in Heaven, that was good! The swine—they'd take some killing. "Look at her. There she goes!" And we jeered and pointed at the swollen distorted body of the girl moving through the sunlight.[36]

With her "swollen distorted body," it is as if the girl is already dead, rather than, as Meyers suggests, pregnant,[37] a grim foreshadowing of what may be to come, much like in Dunning's text in which the "topless trees," "dead leaves," and "grinding [...] music"[38] suggest a bitter end for the girl running a similar "gauntlet" of a menacing crowd. In both, the laughter of the crowd provides a sinister soundtrack while nature offers no solace from the cruelty of man.

Mansfield further develops this contrast between nature and humans' perceptions of it in "Bliss," as the protagonist Bertha Young interprets "the lovely pear tree with its wide open blossoms as a symbol of her own life."[39] An early indication, though, of the flaws in Bertha's perception, are the cats that infiltrate the garden in which the tree stands: "A grey cat, dragging its belly, crept across the lawn, and a black one, its shadow, trailed after. The sight of them, so intent and so quick, gave Bertha a curious shiver."[40] The image again finds an echo in Dunning: "Beyond the fountain the grass spreads around and up to the roots of the trees. And in the shadows and in the light strange creatures move about— big-headed cats, black and grey."[41] The cats in "Red Lion Square" contribute, like witches' familiars, to the otherworldly atmosphere of death and decay, while in "Bliss" they signal Bertha's subconscious misgivings about her life. She remains, however, fixated on the pear tree, ignoring the signs that the loveliness of the "wide open blossoms" is merely a projection of her own longing. Like the Russian girl in "Tales of a Courtyard," who "kept her dark eyes fixed on the chestnut tree and the shining buds" as she negotiates the jeering crowd,[42] Bertha looks to her pear tree for support after discovering her husband's affair with her friend, Pearl Fulton. This time, however, there is no hint of what is to come: "'Oh, what is going to happen now?' she cried. But the pear tree was as lovely as ever and as full of flower and as still."[43]

Looking at these texts side by side, it becomes clearer, perhaps, why Mansfield claimed that she did not "*feel* influenced" by Dunning: based on the timeline of the publication of their work, the opposite may have actually been more accurate—that Dunning's sketches were influenced by Mansfield. Indeed, Mansfield had moved well beyond the style and the attitude of these early stories by the time she met Dunning. In fact, when it was proposed that *In a German Pension* be republished, Mansfield was adamant that the stories were no longer representative of her work. Writing to Murry in 1920 she is scathing in her assessment of her own earlier stories: "I would not for a moment entertain republishing the pension. Its positively *juvenile* and besides that its not what I mean: its a lie."[44] Whereas Dunning's sketches are preoccupied with exposing a "truth" that has long been hidden, Mansfield came to see her own stories as "a lie." The fact remains, however, that Mansfield acknowledged a debt to Dunning in her comments about "the Casetta story." It seems, though, that it is only when Dunning's writing seems to come from the point of view of the "practising Yogi" that Mansfield's later life and work seem to join up with his as she attempts to find an equanimity that was lacking in her early work.

As she became more invested in attaining "that real living simple truthful *full* life I dream of,"[45] Mansfield came to see Dunning as a kindred spirit, someone that could ease the way to such a goal for both herself and Murry. As early as 1920, Mansfield wrote in her journal that "D[unning] has the secret of my recovery and of J's awakening."[46] She hoped that a stronger connection with Dunning might ease Murry, whom she believed had "rather a horror of anything at all … Eastern,"[47] into an understanding or at least acceptance of her decision to find a new treatment for her tuberculosis at Gurdjieff's institute at Fontainebleau, a decision that Sydney Janet Kaplan notes left Murry "shocked and dismayed."[48] Though Kaplan and O'Sullivan both note that, actually, Murry had more of an interest in Eastern ideas than Mansfield gave him credit for, [49] she nevertheless attempted to build up support for Dunning's ideas to fortify the bridge between herself and her estranged husband, writing to him of a meeting she attended in London in which the couple's friend J. W. N. Sullivan was swept up in Dunning's "wave of mysticism":

> Ask Sullivan about it when you see him in the country. He liked Orage and he found a very great similarity between his ideas and Dunnings. In fact the more we talked the more apparent were the resemblances. This pleased me for I felt that you would accept what Dunning believed and like that you and I would find ourselves interested equally in these things.[50]

Mansfield seems to have placed a considerable amount of faith in Dunning as a mediator for her cause. Somehow, Dunning was a figure that Murry would "accept"—after all, Murry had included him in a list of "nice people," along with Sullivan, Brett, and "Tom" Eliot, in a letter to Mansfield of 1920[51]—and who might succeed in interesting Murry in "these things" where she felt she herself had failed.

What Mansfield actually wanted Murry to accept was her giving up on traditional medicine and her embrace of what, for lack of a better word, might be called an "Eastern" spiritual philosophy. In a letter that she drafted in her journal in October 1922 but never sent to Murry, Mansfield attempts to articulate what it is she is after, and what so far had been missing from her search for health:

> Now, Katherine, what do you mean by health? And what do you want it for? Answer: By health I mean the power to live a full, adult, living breathing life in close contact [with] what I love—the earth and the wonders thereof, the sea, the sun. All that we mean when we speak of the external world. I want to enter into it, to be part of it, to live in it, to learn from it, to lose all that is superficial and acquired in me and to become a conscious, direct human being. I want, by understanding myself, to understand others. I want to be all that I am capable of becoming so that I may be—(and here I have stopped and waited and waited and it's no good—there's only one phrase that will do) *a child of the sun*. About helping others, about carrying a light and so on it seems false to say a single word. Let it be at that. *A child of the sun*.[52]

According to this description, the "health" she seeks is as much spiritual as it is physical. She acknowledges, though, that such a definition may be outside the realm of Murry's understanding, and, again, she calls on Dunning to mediate for her, closing by suggesting to Murry that "Suppose if this worries you, you show it to Dunning? I trust Dunning in spite of my thinking he did not really solve your problem. Let him see that, too. He will understand."[53] What is interesting here is that Mansfield does not idealize Dunning—there is skepticism of his methods—and yet her respect for the man himself is clear. She trusts him not only with her husband's fragile psyche, but with her own honest beliefs. Indeed, truth and honesty, the ability to be "real" were the very things Mansfield sought, as she wrote to Murry just before her death: "if I were allowed one single cry to God that cry would be *I want to be REAL.*"[54]

Through Dunning, it seems Murry was able to grasp, however lightly, Mansfield's intentions. In response to her letter he wrote, "like you I'm learning *how* unreal I am. (By the way, Dunning has lent me a deeply interesting Eastern book on this, called *Raja Yoga*: it's absorbing and very exciting. It makes me feel that I want to lose no time, to go terribly fast to the goal. But that, I know, is all wrong. There's no way of going fast.)"[55] While Murry's enthusiasm for this "deeply interesting Eastern book" is not necessarily as convincing as he would have hoped—he referred to it in a previous letter as "Rama Yoga"[56]—it nonetheless indicates an attempt, with the help of Dunning, to understand Mansfield's new perspective. In the book, described on its title page as "being lectures by the Swami Vivekananda with Patanjali's aphorisms, commentaries and a glossary of terms,"[57] Vivekananda suggests that clearing away extraneous external distractions and learning to know oneself is the only true knowledge: "The power of attention of mind, when properly guided, and directed towards the internal world, will analyse the mind, and illumine facts for us. The powers of the mind are like rays of light being dissipated; when they are concentrated, they illumine everything. This is the only source of knowledge that we have."[58] The focus on rays of light and illumination recalls Mansfield's desire to be a "child of the sun," and the process of concentration here described is like that which she sought to understand in an earlier journal entry of 1921 in which she recognized her own need to focus her attention internally:

> There seems to be some bad old pride in my heart; a root of it that puts out a thick shoot on the slightest provocation... This interferes very much with work. One can't be calm, clear, good as one must be while it goes on. [...] Calm yourself. Clear yourself. And anything that I write in this mood will be no good; it will be full of *sediment*. [...] One must learn, one must practise to *forget* oneself.[59]

Here Mansfield seems to be describing just such a focusing of the mind—a clearing away of the "sediment" and a movement from the external world to the internal. Dunning himself wrote in "Sanatana Dharma," which translates to the "Great Way" or path to wisdom, that such a process is "the highest endeavour of which the living spirit is capable […] an active renunciation of all of which we are so miserably proud—of our enduring certainty and inaccessible completeness, of all that for which and by which we seem to live."[60] Both Dunning and Mansfield identify "pride" and living for others' approval as stopping blocks to achieving clarity. As Mansfield had said, it is not that Dunning necessarily influenced her, but that they each articulated similar approaches to life.

It is when Dunning's writing focuses on this kind of awakening, rather than the hard and fast truth of his English sketches, that his work comes into alignment with Mansfield's more mature stories. His "Three Vignettes" of January 1919 bears striking similarities to the opening of Mansfield's "At the Bay" (1921): "Morning breaks through a haze of clambering mists and routs from nook and cranny the last lurking remnants of reluctant night. Throughout the night mists have rolled from field to field caressing the slumbering earth, and now, except where they fall to the river, only the higher trees and the spire of an old church stand clearly above."[61] This scene of awakening, of mists and the sea, is reminiscent of Mansfield's story: "Very early morning. The sun was not yet risen, and the whole of Crescent Bay was hidden under a white sea-mist. The big bush-covered hills at the back were smothered. You could not see where they ended and the paddocks and bungalows began."[62] Both descriptions set the scene for a similar awakening of consciousness of the individuals within the landscape. Dunning writes,

> thus we have won a truly stimulating experience, unlocking the way to our latent being and enabling it to grow and harmonise with the beauty and serenity which has stirred it to life. We become possessed of the freedom and the expanse of the soul, and are already in sight of that scintillating horizon which releases our thoughts from the bondage of commonplace inheritance. Life falls within the sphere of our comprehension and the ways of men are not impossible to understand. Sorrow is not without joy, nor living without reward.[63]

The expanse of the sea inspires the expanse of the soul, and those attuned to it can achieve a "comprehension" of life as a whole. Mansfield offers a similar awakening to Jonathan Trout in "At the Bay":

> At that moment an immense wave lifted Jonathan, rode past him, and broke along the beach with a joyful sound. What a beauty! And now there came another. That was the way to live—carelessly, recklessly, spending oneself. […] To take things easy, not to fight against the ebb and flow of life, but to give way

to it—that was what was needed. It was this tension that was all wrong. To live—to live! And the perfect morning, so fresh and fair, basking in the light, as though laughing at its own beauty, seemed to whisper "Why not?"[64]

Yet while Jonathan does experience the harmony with nature that Dunning describes, it is short lived, as he quickly catches a chill and considers the moment "spoilt."[65] For while Jonathan claims to want to accept "the ebb and flow of life," he comes to this realization while riding the crest of "an immense wave" that soon brings his consciousness crashing back to earth. As Vivekananda puts it in *Raja Yoga*, it is only when one achieves the "complete *suppression* of the waves in the ocean of the mind" that "the glory of the soul, untrammelled by the distractions of the mind, or the motions of [the] body, will shine in its full effulgence" (my italics).[66] Jonathan Trout's change in attitude is an indication of his inability to fully "give way" to life and can be seen as a reflection of Mansfield's own beliefs that she herself had not yet achieved the clarity that she sought.

Yet Dunning seems to have an answer for this attitude as well. In "The Subconscious Influence of Nature" of March 1919, Dunning writes of the potentially negative effect of nature, claiming that "In respect to trees [...] at least some people will have experienced their curious influence and their power under certain circumstances to force on the human spirit a mood startlingly like that of the vegetable itself" and that such feelings can "give rise to a multitude of self-estranging, almost non-human, thoughts [...] from which state there is no such speedy escape."[67] Though, as in many of his pieces, the impression created here verges on the Gothic and seems to have more in common with Edgar Allan Poe than Mansfield, we can still find within it hints of Linda Burnell and her fascination with the aloe in "Prelude" (1917): "Looking at it from below she could see the long sharp thorns that edged the aloe leaves, and at the sight of them her heart grew hard.... She particularly liked the long sharp thorns.... Nobody would dare to come near the ship or to follow after."[68] The plant certainly exerts what Dunning refers to as a "curious influence" on Linda, and while meditating on its sharp thorns she is overcome by a new understanding of what she considers the hopelessness of her life—a husband and children who are "killing" her:[69] "How absurd life was—it was laughable, simply laughable. And why this mania of hers to keep alive at all?"[70] While Dunning suggests that the way to resist these outward, "self-estranging" influences is to cultivate inner resources, Mansfield's stories show how difficult such a process can be, as her characters struggle with reconciling the demands of the external world with their internal desires.

Yet despite these divergent paths, both Dunning and Mansfield attempt to take readers on a similar journey in terms of the form of their writing. Dunning's "The Subconscious Influence of Nature" becomes a guided meditation through a landscape of the writer's creation, beginning, "Take, for example, the following scene and its possible effect. It is a hill-side slope which leads down to the sea."[71] Dunning walks the reader through the landscape with such cues as "here, near at hand, the sea is oval-shaped and wide" and ending with "nor would it be difficult to imagine a graduated series of scenes, each one growing less fearful, until at last we arrived at one altogether idyllic."[72] The journey he describes ends in an "altogether idyllic" scene, mirroring the process of meditation explained in *Raja Yoga*, the ultimate end of which is "the full blaze of illumination, the perception of the Self."[73] Mansfield attempts to create a similar visualization for her readers in "At the Bay," writing to Dorothy Brett in 1921 that

> Ive wandered about all sorts of places—in and out. I hope it is good. It is as good as I can do and all my heart and soul is in it—every single bit. […] I have tried to make it as familiar to "you" as it is to me. You know the marigolds? You know those pools in the rocks? You know the mousetrap on the wash house window sill? And, too, one tries to go deep—to speak to the secret self we all have—to acknowledge that.[74]

Both suggest that by taking the reader into a landscape—making one "see" the external—one can then turn the view inward to the "secret self," what Dunning describes in "Sanatana Dharma" as "piercing the veil of our own entirety and realising ever so dimly the living truth which lies beyond."[75]

Though Katherine Mansfield hardly knew him, Millar Dunning's interpretation of a "living truth" offered her a glimpse of the health and wholeness that had preoccupied so much of her adult life. For all of her letters to Murry, full of slightly patronizing praise for his having found Dunning ("Your little house and way of life sounds so nice. I am very very glad that you feel Dunning is your friend"),[76] Mansfield's best and seemingly most honest endorsement of him comes in a one-off mention of him to Ida Baker. In a letter in which Mansfield seems to be attempting to set LM up with a distraction in her absence, she suggests that she find Dunning: "I think it would be very well worth while for you to know Dunning. I am sure Dunning knows how to *live*."[77] That there was someone who knew how to "live" and who could share his secrets with those she loved seemed to make Mansfield's final days easier. Like Hermes, "the solemn guide of the dead […] who led the souls down to their last home,"[78] Dunning even attended Mansfield's funeral in Fontainebleau,[79] shepherding her to the last. In the end, it was through Dunning's "shadowy" friendship that "a beginning [became] possible. A small fire [was] lighted, a glimmer of its light [was] seen,"[80] and Mansfield found the "real Hope—not half-Hope"[81] she sought.

Notes

1. Vincent O'Sullivan, "Signing Off: Katherine Mansfield's Last Year," in *Celebrating Katherine Mansfield*, ed. Gerri Kimber and Janet Wilson (New York: Palgrave Macmillan, 2011), 15.
2. Kathleen Jones, *Katherine Mansfield: The Story-Teller* (Edinburgh: Edinburgh University Press, 2010), 42.
3. Anne Olivier Bell, ed. *The Diary of Virginia Woolf, 1920–1924*, vol. 2 (1978; repr., San Diego: Harcourt Brace & Company, 1980), 238.
4. Jones, *Story-Teller*, 42. Jones suggests that Murry's friends interpreted his relationships with other women, such as Bill Dunning, Mansfield's friend Vere Bartrick-Baker, and Frieda Lawrence as "John […] seeking to make contact with this dead wife" (42).
5. Margaret Scott, ed., *The Katherine Mansfield Notebooks*, vol. 2 (1997; repr., Minneapolis: University of Minnesota Press, 2002), 194. While Scott's footnote identifying Dunning in the *Notebooks* describes him as "Miller [sic] Dunning, an English mystic interested in yoga," his provenance is incorrect.
6. Bell, *Diary of Virginia Woolf,* 237n1.
7. O'Sullivan, "Signing Off," 14–15.
8. Katherine Mansfield to John Middleton Murry, October 4, 1922, in *The Collected Letters of Katherine Mansfield*, 5 vols., ed. Vincent O'Sullivan and Margaret Scott (Oxford: Clarendon Press, 1984–2008), 5:285. All subsequent letters from Mansfield are from this source; spelling and grammar original in this and following references.
9. Scott, *Mansfield Notebooks,* 194.
10. Jeffrey Meyers, *Katherine Mansfield: A Darker View* (1978; repr., New York: Cooper Square Press, 2002), 50.
11. Millar Dunning, "An English Village," in *The Earth Spirit: Symbolical and Other Pieces* (London: Grant Richards, 1920), 46.
12. Millar Dunning, "London," in *Earth Spirit*, 56–57.
13. Millar Dunning, "Women and War," *The New Age* 16, no. 10 (January 7, 1915): 261.
14. D. Q., "Women and War," *The New Age* 16, no. 12 (January 21, 1915): 323.
15. "One of the 'Half-Thinking Beings,'" "Women and War," *The New Age* 16, no. 12 (January 21, 1915): 323.

16 Millar Dunning, "Sanatana Dharma," *The New Age* 25, no. 23 (October 2, 1919): 381.
17 Antony Alpers, *The Life of Katherine Mansfield* (1980; repr., Oxford: Oxford University Press, 1982), 95.
18 Katherine Mansfield, "Germans at Meat," in *The Collected Works of Katherine Mansfield, The Collected Fiction*, 2 vols., ed. Gerri Kimber and Vincent O'Sullivan (Edinburgh: Edinburgh University Press, 2012), 1:167.
19 Mansfield, "Germans at Meat," 1:167.
20 Katherine Mansfield, "The Baron," in *Collected Fiction,* ed. Kimber and O'Sullivan, 1:175.
21 Mansfield, "The Baron," 1:175.
22 Katherine Mansfield, "The Sister of the Baroness," in *Collected Fiction*, ed. Kimber and O'Sullivan, 1:193.
23 W. H. New, *Reading Mansfield and Metaphors of Form* (Montreal & Kingston: McGill-Queen's University Press, 1999), 76.
24 Millar Dunning, "Red Lion Square," in *Earth Spirit*, 45.
25 Although it is not explicitly identified as such, Red Lion Square in London has an interesting history that seems to inform the dark mood Dunning creates in the sketch: Oliver Cromwell and two of his associates were believed to have been buried there and are said to haunt it still. See both Edward Walford, "Red Lion Square and neighbourhood," in *Old and New London*, vol. 4 (London: Cassell, Petter & Galpin, 1878), 545–53, and Peter Underwood, *Haunted London* (Stroud: Amberley Publishing, 2013), n.p. James Stuart also claimed in 1771 that the architecture of the square itself formed "a *memento mori*, more powerful to me than a death's head and cross marrow bones." James Stuart, *Critical Observations on the Buildings and Improvements of London* (London: J. Dodsley, 1771), 13.
26 Katherine Mansfield, "Tales of a Courtyard," in *Collected Fiction*, ed. Kimber and O'Sullivan, 1:280.
27 Dunning, "Red Lion Square," 42–43.
28 Dunning, "Red Lion Square," 40.
29 Mansfield, "Tales of a Courtyard," 1:280.
30 Mansfield, "Tales of a Courtyard," 1:280.
31 Mansfield, "Tales of a Courtyard," 1:281.
32 Mansfield, "Tales of a Courtyard," 1:281.
33 Mansfield, "Tales of a Courtyard," 1:281.
34 Dunning, "Red Lion Square," 40.
35 Dunning, "Red Lion Square," 45.
36 Mansfield, "Tales of a Courtyard," 1:281.
37 Meyers, *A Darker View*, 50.
38 Dunning, "Red Lion Square," 45.

39 Katherine Mansfield, "Bliss," in *Collected Fiction*, ed. Kimber and O'Sullivan, 2:145.
40 Mansfield, "Bliss," 2:145.
41 Dunning, "Red Lion Square," 43.
42 Mansfield, "Tales of a Courtyard," 1:281.
43 Mansfield, "Bliss," 2:152.
44 Mansfield to Murry, February 4, 1920, 3:206.
45 Mansfield to Murry, October 21, 1922, 5:305.
46 Scott, *Mansfield Notebooks*, 194.
47 Mansfield to Murry, December 9, 1922, 5:332.
48 Sydney Janet Kaplan, *Circulating Genius: John Middleton Murry, Katherine Mansfield and D. H. Lawrence* (Edinburgh: Edinburgh University Press, 2010), 167.
49 Kaplan, *Circulating Genius*, 168. Kaplan notes that Murry "was actually beginning to look beyond the framework of rationalism for emotional support in the midst of this present crisis, such as reading about Yoga" (168). As O'Sullivan puts it, Murry "had carried what might be called a cautious enthusiasm for mysticism, yoga and the vague attractions of 'eastern thought'" ("Signing Off," 14).
50 Mansfield to Murry, September 19, 1922, 5:267.
51 John Middleton Murry to Katherine Mansfield, April 19, 1920, in *The Letters of John Middleton Murry to Katherine Mansfield*, ed. C. A. Hankin (London: Constable, 1983), 315–16. All subsequent letters from Murry are from this source.
52 Scott, *Mansfield Notebooks*, 287. Underline in original.
53 Scott, *Mansfield Notebooks*, 287.
54 Mansfield to Murry, December 26, 1922, 5:341.
55 Murry to Mansfield, December 31, 1922, 367–68. Italics in original.
56 Murry to Mansfield, December 17, 1922, 366.
57 Swami Vivekananda, *Raja Yoga* (New York: Brentano's, 1920). Vivekananda travelled and lectured in the United States and Europe during the last decade of the nineteenth century, spreading "spiritual wisdom" from India. See Gwilym Beckerlegge, "The Early Spread of Vedanta Societies: An Example of 'Imported Localism,'" *Numen* 51, no. 3 (2004): 298.
58 Vivekananda, *Raja Yoga*, 6–7.
59 Scott, *Mansfield Notebooks,* 296. Underline in original.
60 Dunning, "Sanatana Dharma," 381.
61 Millar Dunning, "Three Vignettes," *The New Age* 24, no. 12 (January 23, 1919): 194.
62 Katherine Mansfield, "At the Bay" in *Collected Fiction*, ed. Kimber and O'Sullivan, 2:342.
63 Dunning, "Three Vignettes," 194.
64 Mansfield, "At the Bay," 2:345–46.
65 Mansfield, "At the Bay," 2:346.
66 Vivekananda, *Raja Yoga*, 84.

67 Millar Dunning, "The Subconscious Influence of Nature," *The New Age* 24, no. 19 (March 13, 1919): 311.
68 Katherine Mansfield, "Prelude," in *Collected Fiction*, Kimber and O'Sullivan, 2:87.
69 Katherine Mansfield, "Prelude," 2:87. "There were times when he was frightening—really frightening. When she just had not screamed at the top of her voice: 'You are killing me'" (87).
70 Katherine Mansfield, "Prelude," 2:88.
71 Dunning, "Subconscious Influence," 311.
72 Dunning, "Subconscious Influence," 311.
73 Vivekananda, *Raja Yoga*, 53.
74 Mansfield to Dorothy Brett, September 12, 1921, 4:278.
75 Dunning, "Sanatana Dharma," 381.
76 Mansfield to Murry, December 6, 1922, 5:330.
77 Mansfield to Ida Baker, December 12, 1922, 5:334.
78 Edith Hamilton, *Mythology* (1940; repr., New York: Little, Brown & Company, 1963), 33.
79 Jones, *Story Teller,* 36.
80 Dunning, "Sanatana Dharma," 381–82.
81 Mansfield to Murry, October 4, 1922, 5:285.

8

Turning the Tables: Katherine Mansfield and W. L. George

Ann Herndon Marshall

Katherine Mansfield's early sketch "Sunday Lunch" (1912) lampoons the Georgian scene, exposing the uncivilized "hunting, killing, eating ground of the George-the-Fifth-and-Mary English artists." The narrator locates this savage cult which "kicks hardest (strictly under the table) in Chelsea, in St. John's Wood, in certain squares, and (God help them) in gardens."[1] While W. L. George did have his "at homes" in St. John's Wood, there is no host equivalent to George in "Sunday Lunch," only an English hostess who asks the non-English narrator to welcome other exotic outsiders like the Hungarian "Kaila Scarrotski":

> He's just read your "Pallors of Passion" and he swears you've Slav blood… Remember I didn't ask you to my lunch to wait until the food was served and then eat it and go. Beat your tom-tom, dear.[2]

But any hospitality recedes when "a victim is seized by the cannibals": "A middle-class mind [… whose] bones are picked." The "obvious slaughter of the absentees" introduces subtle pricks across the table.[3] In "Sunday Lunch," Mansfield shows the cutthroat competition and a salon hostess struggling to manage the scene. But while she reveals a clear disdain for such gatherings from the perspective of an outsider told to beat her "tom-tom," Mansfield's view of Georgian artists and their patrons grew more nuanced as she became more involved in London's artist culture.

In Mansfield's writing, two larger-than-life figures, Lady Ottoline Morrell and W. L. George, are counterparts, both "repaid" in Mansfield's fiction but in very different fashions. When Mansfield first went to Garsington in 1917, she brought along an unfavorable notion of the salon lady revealed in her early sketch, but as her friendship developed with Ottoline Morrell, her sympathies changed. For George, her resentment steadily grew. Much has been written on Mansfield's relationship with Morrell, but George's presence in the London salon has been reduced to a few mentions. In this article I contend that George has equal influence on Mansfield's view of literary society and its pitfalls.

We know from Katherine Mansfield's letters and John Middleton Murry's autobiography that the philandering host of "Bliss" (1918), Harry Young, was "touched with W. L. G.," the novelist and London host to writers. C. A. Hankin notes: "It was at the St. John's Wood home of Walter (Willy) Lionel George [...] that Mansfield and Murry first met. Six years later Katherine repaid George by using his house as the setting for 'Bliss' and himself as the model for the emotionally empty Harry Young."[4] However, neither Hankin nor other critics have examined closely Mansfield's "repayment" to George nor the extent to which her unflattering portrait draws on George's provocative personality. George was a contradictory figure, a womanizing defender of woman's freedom.[5] Though a husband three times and a father twice, George questioned the survival of the patriarchal family and disparaged families as compulsory groups. He also challenged rarefied notions of the writer's vocation with a pragmatic commercialism that went against the grain of literary authors.[6] Mansfield's resentment of him built over time as she witnessed George's calculated self-promotion.

The friendship and the send-up of the Georges

To the extent that Harry Young's irreverent quips in "Bliss" are amusing, we can assume Mansfield recognized George's power to charm. Others found him charming. Both Alec Waugh and Douglas Jerrold recall him as a remarkable host. Waugh writes that George "always had his eye upon his guests; he was quick to observe when a conversation had begun to flag. [...] I learnt from George one very valuable social lesson, not to be a guest at your own party."[7] Jerrold also praises George's skill: "George indeed had a spark of genius, particularly as a host. [... He] had, like all of his race, the gifts of an *impresario*."[8] Jerrold further describes a tea with Murry and Mansfield in 1914 when George came up for discussion: "we talked first about H. G. Wells and then about W. L. George, whose impertinences had obviously come as a relief to her after so much flattery."[9]

George's Parisian upbringing and his arrival in England the same year as Mansfield perhaps reinforced their acquaintance. George shared Mansfield's interest in music halls and even her curiosity about the lives of prostitutes.

Mansfield's interest in prostitutes would have been piqued by a memorable chapter from George's best-selling and notorious novel *A Bed of Roses* (1911); the chapter takes place in the St. John's Wood home of the successful prostitute Victoria Fulton. Influenced by a socialist who lent her his books, Victoria invites three prostitutes for lunch hoping to interest them in organizing a kind of union. "Accustomed to their small flats off Shaftesbury Avenue," they are overwhelmed by the elegant house.[10] This scene could have inspired Mansfield's odd suggestion to Beatrice Campbell that they pretend to be prostitutes who have never seen a home as grand as Ottoline Morrell's London house.[11] That Mansfield named her character "Pearl Fulton" in "Bliss" is another suggestive connection with George's *A Bed of Roses* and its heroine Victoria Fulton.

Thinking back on first meeting Mansfield at the Georges' St. John's Wood home in 1911, Murry interprets Mansfield's contradiction of George's description of her as both "formidable" and "cynical" as a calculated challenge to George's habit of assigning labels to his coterie. Consequently, Murry was surprised by her demure "dove grey" frock and her "quiet poise" as she defied George's labeling of her and advocated not "starkness" but "simplicity" in writing: "Instead of playing up to [her 'bitter and witty'] part, she somehow subtly turned the tables on W. L. George, so that he appeared rather like a kindly, well-groomed, but not very quick-witted dog."[12] Murry was obviously taken with the young Mansfield's ability to "turn the tables" on the older, more established writer. In his letters to Mansfield, he often recalled fondly that first encounter. In financial straits in 1914, he fixed on the story of meeting Mansfield to cheer himself: "I had to tell the Campbells all the story of how we met and how we lived together—two years ago—to keep from feeling miserable."[13] As late as 1920, he elevates the memory of meeting Mansfield at the Georges': "light and beautiful (you always have been the incarnation of these things to me since first I met you in your gauze scarf at the Georges')."[14]

Mansfield, however, mythologizes that evening in a different way. Amused as she may have been by George's racy reputation and piquant conversation, Mansfield did not want to be one of George's protégées; she did not want a "literary uncle," the title Waugh uses to describe George's relation to "a number of young women."[15] Three months after her introduction to Murry at the Georges', Mansfield published "A Marriage of Passion" (1912), a satire of a flamboyant host, Vivian De Voted, who strives to overawe his guests.[16] Antony Alpers calls the story a "gibe at bourgeois marriage," but it is better described as a gibe at bohemian gatherings like the one where Mansfield had met Murry.[17] George's stress on how modern marriage must retain passion, a tenet highlighted in his feminist speeches and tracts, helps explain the story's title. In "Feminist Intentions" (1913), George vehemently defends the role of passion for men like himself:

> If the death of love had to be the price of woman's emancipation, I for one would support the institution of the *zenana* and the repression of women by brute force; but, I do not think we need to be anxious.[18]

The De Voteds do not hide their passion, embodied in their pink-lighted bedroom with its "big pink velvet bed."[19] Vivian with "black velvet jacket buttoned over his Bohemian bosom" prepares his wife before the party, "you might ask me to sing 'Loosen Your Girdles, Ye Rosebuds.'" When the time comes, she prompts him. He observes his wife shiver and draws attention to it, whispering, "Draught?" She passionately responds to his concern, "You know I always shiver when you sing; it's—it's emotion."[20]

Keen to show off the markings of a modern, successful marriage, Vivian De Voted specializes, like George, in promoting the New Woman, having recently lectured on "The Infant at Nature's Fount, or Shall the Modern Mother Suckle?"[21] He further displays parental expertise, parading baby Cedric on his shoulder, taking pride in his gender-bending nursery care. However, "A Marriage of Passion" raises the dubious marriage for inspection. After Vivian returns Cedric to the nursery, Mrs. De Voted playfully grabs Vivian's lapels to accuse him of marital boredom. With mock melodrama she suggests it is silly for a thoroughly modern couple to feel any threat from boredom, but the overcompensation of her manic performance conveys a hollow center to their "passionate" marriage.[22]

George's popular feminism

George's well-known womanizing and promotion as New Woman's advocate helped to inspire Mansfield's critical treatment of modern husbands in at least two of her stories, "A Marriage of Passion" and "Bliss." She witnessed George's life with his first wife Helen, mother of their two sons.[23] While it is hard to imagine Mansfield devoting time to reading George's prophetic feminist tracts like *Woman and To-Morrow* (1913) and *The Intelligence of Woman* (1916), his short editorials and advertisements were hard to avoid. His articles appeared throughout the war, as did advertisements for his books. Little as he is known today, he was a celebrity in his time, and his radical opinions as a feminist and reformer were widely sought. Like many of his ads, the ad for *The Stiff Lip* (1922) touts his remarkable access to women's thoughts: "There is perhaps no novelist of the younger school who understands women as well as Mr. George." This unsigned blurb speaks of his "witty dialogue" and "terse straightforward narrative," concluding with a mildly prurient touch: "He can set a woman at her dressing table and tell you her life while she lifts her powder-puff to her nose."[24] George and his publishers cultivated the idea that he was uniquely tied to women by featuring fan mail from enthusiastic readers. Sheila Kaye-Smith mentions an article that George engineered. He posed "sheepishly" holding up silk stockings, purportedly a gift from a female admirer so impressed by George's understanding of women that she assumed he must be one and in need of stockings.[25]

Mansfield had socialized with George before she met Murry, and if Vivian De Voted in "A Marriage of Passion" is any indication, George made social occasions platforms for his social views. In his writing and in his lifestyle, he celebrated the end of the oppressive Victorian family with the emergence of a new sort of woman, liberated by the Marriage Act, the social acceptance of divorce, and the cooperation of befuddled patriarchs. George's study of the changing family appears in the jovial, celebrative chapter of *The Intelligence of Woman*, "Downfall of the Home": today's patriarch is "rather uncomfortable when in the evening his wife appears dressed in a Russian ballet frock or even a little less."[26] Seasoned with characteristic impertinence, *The Intelligence of Woman* forecasts the end to the "mutual tyranny" of the patriarchal family: the old family sickened because it was a compulsory gathering based on "too much propinquity."[27] George prophesied a future when the patriarch hands over his power, every woman realizes a healthy sexuality, and the human race benefits. Mansfield's stories run counter to his utopian vision and challenge this easy, popular image of the New Woman promulgated by George and other middlebrow writers.[28]

George's image comes as something of a surprise given his initial career. He began as a serious social critic in *Engines of Social Progress* (1907) and *Labour and Housing at Port Sunlight* (1909), a study of the Lever Brothers' factory village. But the commercial success and notoriety of *A Bed of Roses* changed the course of his writing life. Retaining the themes of a sociological study, the novel included details of a respectable woman's fall into prostitution. British libraries banned it, sales skyrocketed, and the novel soon appeared "with a lurid jacket [...] in a shilling edition in Villiers Street beside damaroids and contraceptives."[29] The commercial success of *A Bed of Roses* carried over in impressive sales of his later woman-centered novel, *A Second Blooming* (1914), which focused on the hard-fought triumph, this time of an adulterous wife.[30] His publishers were keen to have him continue the success in writing about women who challenge Victorian mores. Sheila Kaye-Smith sees George as a victim of his own scheme, "his idea that every author should wear a label, in order to impress his work more clearly on the public's mind."[31] He had often recommended labels to young writers as a method of finding a niche and enhancing their prospects. Alec Waugh, his second publisher, makes a case for George's interest in sex as more than the pursuit of a publishing niche: "He wrote articles about sex, he lectured on sex; though he did not boast of his conquests, he did not conceal that the pursuit of women was his chief preoccupation."[32] A man and his image are always hard to disentangle. In the case of George, it is hard to tell where liberalism left off and libertinism began.

Mansfield's resentment of George

As a successful writer in 1911, George was generous to Murry and Mansfield. He insisted upon their meeting, "a necessary *confrontation*."[33] He did not just introduce Mansfield and Murry; he was on the managing committee and signed the letter proposing a Limited Liability Company for "the well known publication, RHYTHM, which is the organ of the advanced artists of this country and, to a certain extent of the Continent."[34] That cosmopolitan claim has the ring of George's expert promotion. The letter asks those who want shares to communicate with W. L. George at his address. George's involvement with *Rhythm* included the initial recommendation of Mansfield's "A fairy story" to Murry and his own poem "The Negress," which appears in the third issue of *Rhythm*.[35] Although Mansfield satirizes the "Sunday Lunch" hostess and her Orientalizing her guest as a "tom-tom player," she and Murry as editors were evidently not opposed to George's poem with its shades of the Hottentot Venus: "Her breasts are black as ebony:/She sways, as she walks, on her hips."[36] George was, after all, an enthusiastic backer of their magazine. His sage advice was advantageous to their marketing.[37] He was an astute manager of his own contracts at a time when a good deal of money could be made from fiction in England.[38] Murry writes to Mansfield twice of plans to have lunch with George between 1912 and 1914, the year Murry declared bankruptcy and needed good advice.[39] And Mansfield approves George as part of Murry's circle: "glad that Campbell is looking after you well—glad too that you went to see W.L.G."[40]

However, a striking change in her attitude comes between 1914 and 1915. Writing to Murry from a Paris café in May 1915, Mansfield is exasperated with "Willy":

> I found a photograph of Willy today—he looked like Edward VII in spirits of wine—an awful fat-head—of course he has got *some*thing but he's terribly small beer, I'm afraid—And a snob and heartless. So I feel.[41]

With "So I feel," she makes a show of leaving room for Murry's disagreement should he retain respect for, or need of George, and she immediately launches into another disappointment, Frank Harris, featured in the *Continental Times*, "writing Pro-Germanics." Murry would have understood this segue to "Pro-Germanics." The cosmopolitan George had been educated in Germany, and according to Jerrold, "defined himself as a Frenchman *sans patrie*."[42] Murry and Mansfield may have read the "illuminating aside to one of his reviews," which Jerrold cites, "he wrote apropos of a denunciation by Saki of German militarism, 'at bottom I should not at all mind being annexed by Germany. I can see nothing against it, as I do not walk on the grass.'"[43] Mansfield's exasperated letter may also have been provoked by George's photo featured in *The Times* (London) ad for the "Grand Easter Number" of the *Daily Mirror's Sunday Pictorial* (April 4, 1915) which would contain his article on the War's impact, "Will We Be More Serious?"[44] It is possible that Mansfield had caught some of the publicity surrounding George's pacifism: It was reported he did not wish to fight because of the risk of a disfigurement that might spoil his appeal to women.[45] George's audacity having once amused had lost its luster as the war progressed. On the heels of Rupert Brooke's early death, a loss that haunted Mansfield's dreams—and most certainly after the death of her brother, Leslie, later the same year—such a trivial response to the war would indeed offend.

No longer charmed by what Jerrold describes as George's "impertinence," Mansfield increasingly saw him as a *bête noire*, his writing an open joke: "They are selling huge asparagus here—so big that it looks like the first sentence of a Willy novel," writes Mansfield to Murry.[46] Mansfield mocks George's derivative and bombastic style and his exaggerated social awareness; she continues to be preoccupied with George's verbosity and falsity. The animus toward George's style reinforces her value of literary economy. It comes as no surprise, then, that the questionable modern attitude of Harry Young in "Bliss" is "touched with W.L.G.," who was, according to Jerrold, "in a curious detached way, the most selfish man I ever met."[47]

W.L.G. and "manly bluffness"

If George had been just a progressive who oversimplified social issues, Mansfield might not have fixed on him as her target. But his promotion and success as a feminist made him an irresistible target. He published widely on women's issues in English and American magazines and even traveled across America on a popular lecture tour, defending feminists in a way that would appeal to both sexes, presenting himself as a manly lover of women: "the death of love" must not be "the price of woman's emancipation."[48] By making a career as a sought-after advocate for feminism, he raised questions about his sincerity. Was he more interested in helping women or in keeping himself in the headlines? In his private life, the pursuit of women was George's "sport."[49] Add to this sporting attitude George's audacious manner and Harry, the exploitative charmer in "Bliss," is born.

George the materialist and the iconoclast inspired Harry's anti-aestheticizing speech in "Bliss." George opposed "highfalutin" notions about the arts that might hamstring a writer's publishing success; he encouraged those he advised to approach writing as a business employing hard-headed tactics when they negotiated with publishers. Jerrold credits George with bringing about a new age in publishing: "[His autobiographical novel] *The Making of an Englishman* [...] was more than a piece of characteristic cosmopolitan impertinence. George was the precursor, the prophet of an age when Englishmen were to be made, not born; when writing was to become a branch of commerce, and commercial success the goal of social ambition."[50]

In "Bliss," Mansfield does not name Harry's profession: he may be a literary agent, journalist, producer, or another sort of successful man acting as patron. But it is clear he does not regard the artist guests with the same awe that Bertha does. Thus, the couple's conflict, the earthy materialist versus the *artist manqué*, first appears in the story as an age-old battle of the sexes. Wheeler credits Murry's understanding of Bertha as an *artist manqué*, taking seriously the philosophical conflict in "Bliss," especially Bertha's conviction that the "life of a human being is, or at least can be a work of art."[51] This high-mindedness conflicts with Harry's aggressive frankness, contributing a humorous tension that even Bertha finds amusing. Along with his erotic appreciation of food, "manly bluffness" is Harry's most salient characteristic. I draw on George for this phrase. In his novel *Caliban* (1920), the journalist hero, Bulmer, assumes a bluff style to get the public's attention. He is the new breed of journalist ever willing to use insult to keep himself in the public's gaze: "[He] flaunted an aggressive Liberalism and a manly bluffness which caused noses to sniff and eyebrows to rise among the brethren of Fleet Street."[52]

George links Bulmer's "bluffness" to his success in a competitive world: "For he was beginning to say brief, dramatic things. He was not quite thirty-two. He was incredibly successful."[53] As Bulmer focuses on manipulating the masses, like George, he rejects antiquated aesthetic concerns in favor of worldly ones. In the same vein, Harry's brief, dramatic utterances show his studied rejection of excessive refinement when he diagnoses Pearl with "a touch, perhaps, of anaemia of the brain," or when he counters Bertha's making too much of Pearl's holding her head "a little on one side" by suggesting it is a symptom of "most likely a good stomach."[54] Harry's habit of saying "brief, dramatic things" amuses the imaginative Bertha:

> He made a point of catching at Bertha's heels with replies of that kind ... "liver frozen, my dear girl" or "pure flatulence" or "kidney disease," ... and so on. For some strange reason Bertha liked this and almost admired it in him very much.[55]

However, Bertha Young does not take seriously Harry's deflating diagnosis of Pearl; nor is she stopped by his materialism from her own aestheticizing. She constructs her own image of Pearl with natural symbols as generative alternatives to a conventional language: the "tall slender pear tree" links her to Pearl; she also registers the imminent threat of the grey cat "dragging its belly" shadowed by the black cat on the lawn. One cat stalking the other fills her with unnamable dread and foreshadows the painful revelation of Harry's erotic interest in a woman he has reduced to brain, liver, and kidney.

When Bertha defends Pearl's tardiness as her fashionable mobility, Harry challenges her glamorized vision: Bertha relishes that Pearl "lives in taxis"; "She must run to fat if she does," says Harry.[56] Significantly, Harry's bluffness seems to arouse Bertha's desire for him. His crass comments may be his style of flirting, which she takes as manly frankness. We, however, get only a glimpse of the psychology of the philanderer. Perhaps he relishes Bertha's responsiveness to his bluffness as a marital benefit of the affair with Pearl. It is just after his brusque offer of the jumbled box of cigarettes to Miss Fulton that Bertha experiences her strongest attraction to him. In the "warm bed" tonight with Harry she plans to explain Pearl Fulton to her husband. Whatever Harry's intentions, Bertha's unconscious pandering, as she plans to "explain" her discovery, makes the revelation of Harry's infidelity a devastating self-betrayal. Mansfield does not mention the vulnerability of the hostess Mrs. George in her letter to Murry about "Bliss," but it is likely that Bertha is touched with her as well.

Mansfield's response to George's "fashionable" novels

As early as Murry's first meeting with her, Mansfield was at odds with George about his mistaken labeling of her outlook as "cynical." Her forceful argument for simplicity revives as she reviews George's overstuffed novels. Murry understands her distaste for reading George and tries to cheer up Mansfield as she tackles the task. In 1919, he spots an advertisement he hopes will show he understands her distaste:

> I saw in a 'bus today an advertisement for O.K. sauce which might come in useful to you when describing a novel of the W.L.G. kind. "O.K. Sauce consists of 'fruity' elements mixed with a choice of oriental spices, and a natural acidity derived from pure malt. The use of this sauce compensates for the absence of fresh fruit & vegetables from the daily diet."[57]

In her reply she acknowledges the joke: "W.L.G. should have … [the O.K. sauce] on a paper wrapper or done into Latin for a motto perpetual for the House of George."[58] She had to take heart from the opening sentence of Virginia Woolf's review of George's *A Novelist on Novels* (1918): "Mr. George is one of those writers for whom we could wish, in all kindness of heart some slight accident of the fingers of the right hand, some twinge or ache warning him, that it is time to stop, some check making brevity more desirable than expansion."[59]

Although Mansfield would not have acknowledged George himself as witty, his irrepressibility is the frequent cause of wit in Mansfield and Murry. In her illness while living in France, Mansfield was detached from her former circle, but she continued to hear and read of George. She writes about George to Raymond Drey after he mentions servants at a large party:

> You are very grand *but* not as grand as Willy. His party must have been a very powerful affair, Drey. Talk about numbered cloakroom tickets. Willy will have to have them for his wives, next time. He will be a terribly busy man in Heaven. I am sure the restitution of conjugal rights is a spécialité de la maison, there.[60]

Gossiping about George's three marriages, Mansfield adopts a conspiratorial tone, in French no less. She is "Campbelling," Gordon Campbell's style of good-humored gossip, sharing her joke about "Willy." The sprightly comparison of Drey to George suggests nostalgia for an earlier day when she had constant inspiration to gossip, and not seldom about the marriages of W. L. George.

Mansfield is able to put gossip aside when reviewing George. She is mostly serious and generally fair in her criticism. Her review of *Blind Alley* (1919), George's socialist and pacifist treatment of the war industry, damns it with faint praise. The dominance of ideology over character often makes *Blind Alley* a plodding instrument of the author's political views. However, Mansfield begins with its falsity of style. The title of her review, "The Exoticist," introduces a comparison of George's novel to the exotic contents of a London emporium. The reader of the extended analogy may expect an endorsement until Mansfield marshals her examples. George's retired banker, his family, and their subplots are absurd. She introduces the patriarch's apology:

> Picture a father, a retired banker, and now a country gentleman, an eminently practical man, hushing a quarrel with a rebellious daughter in this fashion:
>
> > he felt remorseful. So he sent by a messenger boy an enormous bunch of Parma violets and a note: "Sylvia, your father has the pride of age, and the temper of youth. He asks pardon of his beautiful daughter and hopes that, when next she comes to cheer his waning years, she will bring forgiveness in her eyes of amber."[61]

Mansfield knows bankers. As the rebellious daughter of one, she finds George's character laughable in his fawning solicitude. Mansfield concludes slyly, "Perhaps from these extracts the reader may gather that whatever else Mr. George's long strong book may be, it is not dull." "Not dull," she suggests, because it is ludicrous. "Long and strong" because it lavishes attention on preposterous, unwanted detail: "The completeness, however, is but symptomatic of Mr. George's method [...] with not a detail missing." She ends by drawing attention to the precious frame narration from the point of view of Kallikrates, the Persian cat, who "composes his squat head into the sumptuous silk of his ruff and begins to purr.... If we may say so without disrespect, we can almost hear the author joining in."[62] Mansfield conflates the cat's cozy purring with the self-satisfaction of the author.

Mansfield was unsparing in her cool denunciation of George's excesses. She engages with *Blind Alley,* reporting on its preposterous flights, even enjoying its failed devices. The later *Caliban,* on the other hand, leaves her cold. In contrast to the playful criticism of *Blind Alley,* her review of *Caliban* is direct and impatient. "A Dull Monster" she entitles her review of George's "latest novel," which is "very late indeed." She argues George's work retains all the ills of the Edwardian generation whom she dubs the "Fire Brigade." She reduces their tiresome audacity to a fetish for attacking all things Victorian: "'*Toujours de l'audace*'—we actually said it then."⁶³ Even as she resists clichés about the war's sobering influence, she identifies it as a watershed. She depicts a generation marked by war and loathes to repeat the posturing of Edwardian provocateurs like George:

> It is impossible for us to recapture the emotional state in which it was presented to us then. To say the war has changed our attitude to life is not a very useful thing to say, neither is it wholly true. But what it has done is to fix forever in our minds the distinction between what is fashion and what is permanent.⁶⁴

It is rare that Mansfield speaks for her generation, but her identification of *Caliban* as embodying a prewar sensibility supports her case for a necessary shift in values. The overreaching egoism of George's "Dull Monster" fails to entertain because it embodies empty prewar fashions. The novel is like the inferior "D.G.T. [*Daily Gazette* Tea]" Bulmer promotes to fans of his newspaper.⁶⁵ It is a poor rehashing of H. G. Wells's *Tono-Bungay*. Mansfield blurs the line between Bulmer's failures and those of the author by focusing on a tortured simile which Bulmer uses to try to please Janet: "He buys men, women, houses, Power, but slim, cool Janet, with her graceful untidy hair and her look [he describes] as 'warm snow' he cannot buy."⁶⁶ Mansfield questions the novel's project to lampoon shallowness. Bulmer is a sad version of George's carefully constructed image, a lover who strives to understand women.

In 1921, it is Murry who reviews George's *The Confession of Ursula Trent* along with Stephen McKenna's *The Secret Victory*, but Mansfield writes to Elizabeth von Arnim about preparing to review both herself. She describes George and McKenna as typical of current vulgarity and emotional falsity:

> I have also been reading [...] Stephen McKenna and W. L. George & Co [...] They are a vulgar, dreary lot. Why all this pretense? When we have not said a quarter of what there is to say. Why can't writers be warm, living, simple, merry or sad as it pleases them. All this falsity is so *boring*.⁶⁷

Mansfield's rebuke of both authors echoes her elevation of simplicity when turning the tables on George back in 1911. In the case of *Ursula Trent*, she cheers on others who acknowledge the weakness of George's novel. In a letter to Robert Lynd, she compliments his wife Sylvia for her negative review in the *Daily News*: "How *excellentissimo* Sylvia was on W. L. George's novel!"⁶⁸ Having prepared to review George and McKenna herself in November, it is likely she collaborated with Murry on his review of both in *The Nation and the Athenaeum* in December. That review never dignifies *Ursula Trent* as a feminist novel. Apart from its "'smartness' and 'sex,'" the new formula reflected in the novel involves very few requirements, "the most important thing to remember is that a miscarriage enables you conveniently to allow your heroine all the adventures necessary to her process of liberation, and gives you—what is still more necessary—the tense expectation of the unwanted child, while permitting you to get her into the arms of the noble-minded hero without any distressing encumbrances."[69] By over-valorizing a woman's sexual drive, writers like George and McKenna slight the physical and emotional realities of sexual experimentation. There is one last stab reminiscent of Mansfield's review of George's *Blind Alley*: "Mr. George pays unusual attention to the details of his heroine's dress; to an intelligent reader his book is the equivalent of a gift of a dozen free patterns."[70]

Antony Alpers writes of Mansfield's eventual exhaustion with Ottoline Morrell, or at least with the intensity of that friendship, which is well documented in biographies from Alpers's *The Life of Katherine Mansfield* (1980) to Jones's *Katherine Mansfield: The Story-Teller* (2010). In contrast, there seems to be no end to the usefulness of W. L. George as a defining antagonist.[71] To illustrate the staying power of Mansfield's antagonism to "W. L. G.," there is a very late entry in her notebook from January 2, 1922:

> I dreamed I was at the Strand Palace, W.L.G. having married Marie Dahlerup—big blonde—in quantities of white satin.... There was a great deal more snow this morning; it was very soft, "like wool."[72]

Mansfield has a habit of recording dreams, but the subject of this late one is especially cherished in a perverse way. The dream imagines a fourth marriage for George, this time to an old friend of Mansfield's school days. It could be read as the projection of a worst fear, that she will be, by association, forever tied to "W. L. G.," or as a revelation of the strength of his usefulness to her. Though Pearl Fulton is not a "big blonde," like Marie Dahlerup in the dream, the bridal white satin recalls Pearl's silver allure. The transition to snow recalls the clumsy "warm snow" comparison Mansfield mocks in her review of *Caliban*. As a writer, Mansfield has the last word: in contrast to George's monstrous falsity, she writes the unadorned truth of the Psalmist, "like wool."[73]

George is the unlikely muse that continues to inspire. What Murry described as a singular "turning the tables" on her erstwhile host initiates a prolonged unmasking of George's falsity. George is the anti-Gurdjieff. He initially pursued Mansfield to be one of his coterie, but he came to represent for her the false prophecy of an entire generation of authors whose audacious rejection of Victorian values offered no bulwark in the face of war. Mansfield lampooned

London's artistic society as cannibalism in her early "Sunday Lunch," but she unmasks a more insidious savagery in her later portraits of liberated, anti-Victorian households inhabited by George's spiritual offspring. She works over George's dubious feminism in Mr. De Voted's advocacy of the New Woman, a performance that makes doubtful a so-called marriage of passion. Harry Young's mordant wit and sexual predation amount to a deadening misogyny. George's precious literary method is not spared in her reviews. He is an incurably audacious Edwardian. She cannot forgive W. L. George and his brethren for never learning what she tried to teach them, the lesson of simplicity. George purports to show women as they are, but in falsifying their circumstances and emotions, he trivializes them. His method of piling on "smart" detail in lieu of truthful emotion leads to his failure both as a writer and as a prophet for a new age.

Notes

1. Katherine Mansfield, "Sunday Lunch," *Rhythm* 2, no. 9 (October 1912): 223. *The Modernist Journals Project*, http://www.modjourn.org/render.php?id=1159896829341976&view=mjp_object (accessed December 17, 2016).
2. Mansfield, "Sunday Lunch," 224.
3. Mansfield, "Sunday Lunch," 224–25.
4. C. A. Hankin, ed., *The Letters of John Middleton Murry to Katherine Mansfield* (New York: Franklin Watts, 1983), 18n. Murry later regrets Mansfield's use of George's house "as the background for 'Bliss'—on false pretenses." See *The Autobiography of John Middleton Murry: Between Two Worlds* (New York: Julian Messner, Inc., 1936), 185.
5. Alec Waugh comments on George's womanizing in "W. L. George," in *My Brother Evelyn, and Other Portraits* (New York: Farrar, Straus, and Giroux, 1968), 106.
6. Waugh, "W. L. George," 106.
7. Waugh, "W. L. George," 108.
8. Douglas Jerrold, *Georgian Adventure* (London: Collins Pall Mall, 1937), 90–91. By "race" Jerrold seems to mean George's French upbringing and not his Jewishness.
9. Jerrold, *Georgian Adventure*, 104.
10. W. L. George, *A Bed of Roses* (London: Frank Palmer, 1911), 309–35.
11. Beatrice Campbell, *Today We Will Gossip* (London: Constable, 1964), 80.
12. Murry, *Autobiography*, 186–87.
13. John Middleton Murry to Katherine Mansfield, February 10, 1914, in Hankin, *Letters of JMM*, 31. Unless otherwise noted, all subsequent letters from Murry are from this source.
14. Murry to Mansfield, February 16, 1920, 282.

15 Waugh, "W. L. George," 107. Sheila Kaye-Smith lists George's other protégés in *All the Books of My Life* (New York: Harper and Brothers, 1956), 98.
16 Katherine Mansfield, "A Marriage of Passion," in *The Collected Works of Katherine Mansfield, The Collected Fiction 1916–1922*, 2 vols., ed. Gerri Kimber and Vincent O'Sullivan (Edinburgh: Edinburgh University Press, 2012), 1:261–66. The story first appeared in *The New Age* (March 1912).
17 Antony Alpers, *The Life of Katherine Mansfield* (New York: Viking Press, 1980), 135–36.
18 W. L. George, "Feminist Intentions," in *The Intelligence of Woman* (Boston: Little, Brown, and Co, 1916), 88. The essay originally appeared in *The Atlantic Monthly*, December 1913.
19 Mansfield, "A Marriage of Passion," 1:265.
20 Mansfield, "A Marriage of Passion," 1:261, 1:265.
21 Mansfield, "A Marriage of Passion," 1:262.
22 Frank Harris first saw the very modern Georges at a party in Chelsea around 1910: "Suddenly I was asked by someone to notice that Mrs. George was smoking a pipe or it may have been a cigar. In any case, attention was drawn to the couple rather by force than by charm." *Contemporary Portraits, 3rd Series* (New York: The Author, 1920), 143.
23 Waugh highlights the popularity of George's second wife "Russet" whose presence on the scene corresponds with the 1918 composition of "Bliss" ("W. L. George 110); there is no record of Mansfield meeting her, only the first Mrs. George who, like Bertha, served red plum soup (Murry, *Autobiography*, 186).
24 *The Times* (London) (September 29, 1922): 15, *Times Digital Archive*.
25 Kaye-Smith, *All the Books*, 97.
26 George, *The Intelligence of Woman*, 166.
27 George, *The Intelligence of Woman*, 165.
28 Todd Martin links Mansfield's questioning of the New Woman to her desire for a real home with the stability of marriage and children: "just as Mansfield became disillusioned by the artistic elite, […] she likewise exposed the potential vapidity of the 'modern' woman who, for all her promise, tramples the rights of other women." See "'Why haven't I got a "real" home?': Katherine Mansfield's Divided Self," *Journal of New Zealand Literature* 31 (2013): 75.
29 Waugh, "W. L. George," 105–6. "Damaroids" were pills to enhance male sexual performance.
30 See Kenneth Womack, "W. L. George," in *Dictionary of Literary Biography: Late-Victorian and Edwardian British Novelists*, 2nd Series, ed. George M. Johnson (Detroit, Washington, DC, London: Gale Research, 1999), 110–16, 111.
31 Kaye-Smith, *All the Books*, 97.
32 Waugh, "W. L. George," 106.
33 Murry, *Autobiography*, 185.

34 Katherine Mansfield to Compton MacKenzie, November 1912, in *The Collected Letters of Katherine Mansfield*, 5 vols., ed. Vincent O'Sullivan and Margaret Scott (Oxford: Clarendon Press, 1984–2008), 1:115. All subsequent letters from Mansfield are from this source.

35 W. L. George, "The Negress," *Rhythm* 1, no. 3 (Winter 1911): 5. http://www.modjourn.org/render.php?id=1159894157369395&view=mjp_object (accessed December 17, 2016). Angela Smith notes the "weary Orientalist familiarity" of "The Negress." See *Katherine Mansfield: A Literary Life* (London: Palgrave Macmillan, 2001), 81.

36 George, "The Negress," 5.

37 Jerrold, *Georgian Adventure*, 89.

38 Rosa Maria Bracco, *Betwixt and Between: Middlebrow Fiction and English Society in the Twenties and Thirties* (Melbourne: History Department, University of Melbourne, 1990), 9. Bracco records that titles rose from about 6000 in 1901 to over 12,000 by 1913.

39 Murry to Mansfield, March 26, 1912, 18, February 8, 1914, 30.

40 Mansfield to Murry, February 9, 1914, 1:135.

41 Mansfield to Murry, May 8, 1915, 1:178.

42 Jerrold, *Georgian Adventure*, 90.

43 Jerrold, *Georgian Adventure*, 90.

44 His title, along with a promotional photo of George, appears in an ad for the *Sunday Pictorial* in *The Times* (April 3, 1915): 3, *Times Digital Archive*.

45 Waugh, "W. L. George," 106.

46 Mansfield to Murry, May 14, 1915, 1:188.

47 Jerrold, *Georgian Adventure*, 90.

48 W. L. George, "Feminist Intentions," 88.

49 Waugh, "W. L. George," 106.

50 Jerrold, *Georgian Adventure*, 89.

51 Kathleen Wheeler, *Modernist Women Writers and Narrative Art* (New York: Farrar, Strausss, Giroux, 1994), 124.

52 W. L. George, *Caliban* (New York and London: Harper & Brothers, 1920), 161.

53 George, *Caliban*, 161.

54 Katherine Mansfield, "Bliss," in *The Collected Fiction*, Kimber and O'Sullivan, 2:144.

55 Mansfield, "Bliss," 2:145.

56 Mansfield, "Bliss," 2:147.

57 Murry to Mansfield, October 16, 1919, quoted in *Collected Letters*, 3:39n1.

58 Mansfield to Murry, October 21, 1919, 3:38.

59 Virginia Woolf, "The Claim of the Living," *Times Literary Supplement* (London) (June 13, 1918): 275.

60 Mansfield to Raymond Drey, December 27, 1921, 4:358.

61 Katherine Mansfield, "The Exoticist," in *The Collected Works of Katherine Mansfield, Poetry and Critical Writings*, vol. 3, ed. Gerri Kimber and Angela Smith (Edinburgh: Edinburgh University Press, 2014), 3:471–72.
62 Mansfield, "The Exoticist," 3:473.
63 Katherine Mansfield, "A Dull Monster," in *Collected Works*, ed. Kimber and Smith, 3:662.
64 Mansfield, "A Dull Monster," 3:663.
65 George, *Caliban*, 208.
66 Mansfield, "A Dull Monster," 3:663.
67 Mansfield to Countess Russell, November 19, 1921, 4:322.
68 Mansfield to Robert Lynd, November 23, 1921, 4:324.
69 John Middleton Murry, "The Fashionable Novel," *The Nation and the Athenaeum* (December 17, 1921): 474.
70 Murry, "The Fashionable Novel," 474.
71 In *The Life of Katherine Mansfield,* Alpers does not treat George's ongoing importance to Mansfield, though he does consider his discovery of Mansfield; he characterizes George in a reductive phrase as "a syphilitic Anglo-French Jew" (134). To clarify, George was half-Jewish but did not practice the faith. See William D. Rubinstein, Michael Jolles, Hilary L. Rubinstein, ed., *Palgrave History of Anglo-Jewish History* (New York: Palgrave, 2011), 317. The purported "syphilis" may have been a rumor based on his rakish image. George died from Parkinson's disease in 1926, under the care of his devoted third wife Kathleen (Waugh, "W. L. George," 114).
72 Margaret Scott, ed., *The Katherine Mansfield Notebooks*, vol. 2 (Minneapolis: University of Minnesota Press, 2002), 312.
73 Mansfield probably recalls "[God] giveth snow like wool" (Psalms 147:16).

Part Two

Katherine Mansfield and Literary Bloomsbury

9

Katherine Mansfield: A Fauvist, Colonial Outsider Encounters Bloomsbury

Mary Ann Gillies

But I don't feel anything but intensely a longing to serve my subject as well as I can—But the unspeakable thrill of this art business. What is there to compare! And what more can one desire. Its not a case of keeping the home fire burning for me. Its a case of keeping the home fire down to a respectable blaze and little enough.[1]

"'[T]he paradox of art making nature is nothing but a serious and sober truth," wrote Roger Fry in an early essay "The Philosophy of Impressionism" (1894). This paradox, he continues, is founded on the notion that things "only exist when they are perceived, and they are never consciously perceived by the ordinary eye until attention has been called to them by the trained observer— for of the infinite in number of sensations falling on the retina only those that training or habit has prepared us for, stir up any response in consciousness."[2] Fry was to modify his position on the Impressionists as well as on the concepts of sensation, consciousness, and perception over the course of his career, yet his remarks capture an important thread in the intellectual conversations of late nineteenth- and early twentieth-century Britain. Indeed, Fry's comments speak to a paradigm shift in not only painting, but also in the arts more generally. Virginia Woolf's famous articulation of this shift in "Mr Bennett and Mrs Brown"—"on or about December 1910, human character changed"[3]—is arguably better known than Fry's comments, but both gesture to the same realization: how humans understood their world was changing. That change emerges not only in the art and literature that has become known as modernist, but also in science and philosophy where new theories and approaches to existing concerns and problems transformed our knowledge of the world—both the inner realms of consciousness and the outer landscape in which we live.

This chapter is part of a larger project in which I explore the ways that modernists Katherine Mansfield and Virginia Woolf, as well as the Canadian artist/writer Emily Carr, responded to this perceptual shift by enacting new ways of perceiving of and representing consciousness in their art. Here, I want to focus much more narrowly, looking at Mansfield through the lens of late twentieth-century theories of perception, and making a brief comparison of her aesthetics with those of Bloomsbury's foremost art critic, Roger Fry, whose own ideas were formed within the framework of early twentieth-century notions of perception. What I contend is that it is Mansfield's characteristic mode of perception, rooted in her New Zealand childhood, that draws her to Fauvism, that sets her at odds with Fry and other Bloomsburies, and that makes her work resonate with our contemporary audience, which finds itself embroiled in yet another epistemic shift in perception.

Theories of perception

While we might want to debate various aspects of Woolf's famous claim about human nature changing in 1910,[4] it is clear that the perceptual shift that it referenced has continued to be an object of discussion and investigation in diverse fields well into the twenty-first century.[5] To look specifically at theories of perception, philosophers Alva Noë and Evan Thompson tell us, in their "Introduction" to *Vision and Design*, that current orthodox views of perception, which are built on work from earlier in the twentieth century, maintain that perception "is a process whereby the brain, or a functionally dedicated subsystem of the brain, builds up representations of relevant features of the environment on the basis of information encoded by the sensory receptors."[6] They continue: "In other words, the beliefs and expectations of the perceiver are thought to have no influence on the character of the subpersonal computations that constitute perception." And they claim that "most adherents of the orthodox view also believe that for every conscious perceptual state of the subject, a particular set of neurons exists whose activities are sufficient, as a matter of scientific law, for the occurrence of that state."[7] Put more plainly, mainstream views of perception argue that it is an internal mental process involving the brain's sophisticated neural networks, and these networks may be correlated to specific perceptual activities.

Alternative views of perception have contested orthodox ones—whatever they might have been—throughout history, but from the middle of the twentieth century onwards the debate has intensified in part due to advances in science, particularly brain imaging technology. Embodied and enactive perceptions are prominent concepts among these heterodox theories, and they are what I use here, though I want to emphasize that both remain highly contested and I provide condensed and selective accounts of them.

The research of neuroscientists Humberto R. Maturana and Francisco J. Varela provides a good starting point. Their work set the foundation for an embodied theory of perception. They claim that "it is a mistake to think of the nervous system as an input-output system that encodes an internal representation of the outside world. [...] Rather than representing an independent, external world, the nervous system generates or brings forth, on the basis of its own self-organized activity, the perceptuo-motor domain of the animal."[8] Thus, each animal's perception derives from its interactions with its environment—perception is no longer situated solely inside the brain; it is an interactive construct between brain and external world. In a fascinating article on color vision, for example, Thompson, Palacios, and Varela claim that "Color can be understood only in relation to the visual perception of a given individual or species (contrary to objectivism); but such visual experience can be understood only in the context of its ecological embodiment (contrary to subjectivism)."[9] For instance, forager honey bees and human beings are both trichromats—that is, they possess three independent channels for conveying color information, derived from the three different cone types that are found on the surface of the eye's retina. However, "bee color vision is shifted toward the ultraviolet" spectrum, and the theory is that "this distinctive form of trichromacy coevolved with the colors of flowers, which often have contrasting patterns in ultraviolet light."[10] Over time, bees' vision developed certain functionality in order to detect these subtle differences in ultraviolet light; this adaptation allowed them to discern in a range of flowers the specific flowers from which to collect nectar. Though bees may have the same basic perceiving "equipment" as humans, if you will, bees and humans perceive the world very differently because they live in it very differently. In this perceptual framework, neither species creates identical, or even similar, internal, mental models of the external world.

Alva Noë's sensorimotor approach extends theories of embodied perception and in doing so becomes a theory of enactive perception. By sensorimotor he means what Andy Clark calls "relations between movement or change and sensory stimulation."[11] Noë argues that "the enactive approach seeks to explain the quality of perceptual consciousness not as a neural function caused by and realized in the brain […] but rather in terms of patterns and structures of skillful activity. In the enactive approach, brain, body, and world work together to make consciousness happen."[12] The brain is thus no longer the main driver of consciousness; it is one component among others in the process. Again, an example is helpful here. "When a painter works from life," Noë writes,

> he or she makes continuous and ongoing reference to the world. The painter looks to the world, then back to the canvas, then back to the world, then back to the canvas. Eye, hand, canvas, paint, world are brought into play in the process of constructing the picture. Seeing, like painting, involves the temporally extended process of reaching out and probing the scene.[13]

In other words, painting, like seeing, is "an activity of learning about the world by learning how things look." It is an example of how "experience is realized in the active life of the skillful animal."[14] We are who we are not solely because of our genetics or social influences, but also because of where we live and how we live in that environment; in turn, our actions on our environment shape it as well.

So, what do trichromats and honeybees have to do with Katherine Mansfield and the Bloomsburies? Well, using the embodied and enactive models of perception I have just outlined, I want to make three linked points that explain, in part, the fundamental difference between Mansfield's and Fry's approaches to art and the gulf this difference created between Mansfield and Bloomsbury. I start with Roger Fry whose theories were very influential not just in Bloomsbury's aesthetics, but also in the Anglo-American art world of the early twentieth century. His views are those against which I situate Mansfield's. I then move on to Mansfield, looking first at how her early childhood physical environment shaped her perceptual foundations; then at how these perceptions were situated within a nonindigenous environment—the social and built environment of colonial New Zealand; and finally at Mansfield and Fauvism. In the paper's concluding section, I draw out explicitly the differences between Mansfield and Fry.

Roger Fry: Bloomsbury's art theorist

Roger Fry was arguably one of the most important art critics of his generation, though art would have seemed a highly unlikely career given his family background.[15] The Frys were a well-established and prosperous Quaker family that provided Roger with, as Virginia Woolf notes in her biography of Fry, a "highly comfortable life"[16] centered on a "family circle" whose interests were principally "legal and scientific."[17] Frances Spalding comments that his early years were spent at No. 6, The Grove, Highgate, a "solid red-brick house" with "ample but restrained proportions [that] set a standard of elegance [Fry] was never to forget."[18] "Aside from the house, with its retrained wealth and lofty position,"[19] Spalding says that his home life was "austere and full of high principles: there was very little gaiety, affection or fun."[20] His parents imbued him with a moral and intellectual framework which both served him well throughout his life and against which he chafed more and more as he became his own man. His father passed along to his young son a love of science, and especially a keen interest in botany that was to remain with Fry throughout his life. As Spalding notes, "science and intellect ruled in the Fry household, [while] art received only passing attention."[21] Fry was also provided with an excellent education, first at home and then in public schools where his love of science was further cemented. His studies at Cambridge, where he read natural sciences, permitted Fry to move beyond his family circle and eventually led him to the study of art—both as a painter and as a critic. Indeed, despite measured and persistent opposition from his parents whose financial and emotional support he continued to rely on for many years, from 1887 onward Fry committed himself to art, travelled widely in Europe, worked in his own studio space in London, and launched a career as a lecturer and art critic.

By the turn of the century, Fry had developed a reputation as a "coming man," with his work appearing in leading journals such as *The Burlington Magazine* (which he helped to found), the *Athenaeum*, *The Nation*, and *The Fortnightly Review*. While perhaps remembered today more for his championing of Post-Impressionist art through his staging of two exhibitions at the Grafton Galleries in 1910 and 1912, his theories of art were as influential in literary modernism's evolving aesthetics, particularly among the Bloomsbury circle of which he was a member. In keeping with the perceptual framework I have established, I want to suggest that the foundation of Fry's aesthetics can be seen in his childhood, with its "emphasis on simplicity and dignity and [its] distrust of entertainment and ostentation [that] encouraged an austere cast of mind."[22] It is no surprise, then, that a sensibility thus shaped in childhood would develop an art theory which privileges "purposeful order and variety in an object"[23] alongside an "intense disinterested contemplation that belongs to the imaginative life, and which is impossible to the actual life of necessity and action."[24]

Fry is perhaps best known for articulating a formalist view of art. This approach was signaled in his 1901 essay on "Giotto" and confirmed in the 1920 publication *Vision and Design*, a selection from the many articles he published in periodicals over nearly twenty years. Fry sets out this vision in "Retrospect," the closing essay in the collection: "I think we are all agreed that we mean by significant form something other than agreeable arrangements of form, harmonious patterns, and the like. We feel that a work of art which possesses it is the outcome of an endeavor to express an idea rather than to create a pleasing object."[25] At "the core of [Fry's]" formalist aesthetics, art critic Michael Fried suggests, is

> the conviction that all persons capable of experiencing esthetic emotion in front of paintings [...] are responding when they do so to relations of pure form—roughly of ideated volumes in relation both to one another and to the surface and shape of the canvas—rather than to whatever dramatic expressiveness the work in question may be held to possess.[26]

A work of art for Fry was separate from the sentimental, personal, mundane experiences of everyday life; it was impersonal in that particular way that other modernists such as T. S. Eliot used that term. In Fry's theory, what emotions one might feel standing in front of a Cézanne painting, say, would be aesthetic, engendered by an appreciation of the interplay of the formal qualities—line, color, shape, volume, space—on the canvas. As Adrianne Rubin remarks, "The narrative aspects of a work of art are of secondary importance, [Fry] believed, for in most cases they are culturally or temporally contextual, and therefore limited or transitory in their appeal. Form, on the other hand, is universal, for it is not reliant upon any external context for appreciation, according to him."[27]

Even more important, and particularly so for the line of thought I am developing in this chapter, was Fry's emphasis on the role and function of perception in art. As Rubin suggests, "In order for Fry's theories to be properly understood, it is necessary to recognize that what is common to them, from his early essays of the 1890s to his *Last Lectures* of the 1930s, is the emphasis he places upon perception."[28] Fry's understanding of perception—and the way he deployed that understanding in his art criticism—evolved over time, though its core features were established early in his career. We see Fry addressing this issue in "An Essay in Aesthetics" (1909) where he distinguishes between perceptions arising from actual life and those from imaginative life. He argues that "with regard to the greater clearness of perception" the

> needs of our actual life are so imperative, that the sense of vision becomes highly specialised in their service. With an admirable economy we learn to see only so

much as is needful for our purposes; but this is in fact very little, just enough to recognize and identify each object or person; that done, they go into an entry in our mental catalogue and are no more really seen. In actual life the normal person really only reads the labels as it were on the objects around him and troubles no further. Almost all things which are useful in any way put on more or less this cap of invisibility. It is only when an object exists in our lives for no other purpose than to be seen that we really look at it.[29]

Two years later, in "Post Impression" (1911), Fry goes beyond this distinction between the perception of actual life and imaginative life, making his aim "to discover the visual language of the imagination. To discover, that is, what arrangements of form and colour are calculated to stir the imagination most deeply through the stimulus given to the sense of sight."[30] Fry develops this line of argument later in the essay: "There is no immediately obvious reason why the artist should represent actual things at all. [...] We may get, in fact, from a mere pattern, if it be really noble in design and vital in execution, intense aesthetic pleasure."[31]

Fry's emphasis on the interplay between sensory input and affective response suggests an understanding of perception that is similar to the orthodox views I quoted above from Noë and Thompson. Even more telling are Fry's own words, which I quoted at the outset of this paper: that we form our perceptions from "the infinite in number of sensations falling on the retina." It is evident that although Fry emphasizes the difference between the perceptions of the trained observer and those of the habitual observer and develops his aesthetic around those differences, he nonetheless relies on a model of perception in which the brain constructs images from sensory input and these images then evoke an affective response. The response differs depending on the perceiver's aesthetic training, but the process is similar across perceivers. Such a model permits Fry to maintain one of his core positions: that art is universal, transcending time and place. For him, the best art of any period or location is recognizable to viewers in other places and time because they respond to its formal qualities and not to its specific context.[32]

Katherine Mansfield: A Fauvist, colonial outsider

As was the case with Fry, the basic facts of Katherine Mansfield's biography are familiar. Born in 1888, she was the third daughter of Annie and Harold Beauchamp, who were living at 11 Tinakori Road, Wellington, when she was born. They subsequently moved their growing family to Karori—then a small village in the countryside and now a Wellington suburb. Mansfield's early years have been written about extensively, much of it focusing on the loneliness and alienation she experienced as a child in a family where she felt out of place.[33] Most critics would agree, however, that one of the saving graces in Mansfield's childhood was her ample opportunity to play in and explore the bush, paddocks, and gardens near her various homes, to swim in the ocean and play in the sand at her family's seaside cottage, and to engage in the many other activities that the children arranged to amuse themselves—her sisters remember Mansfield making "peep" shows from colored glass to entertain them, for instance. The relative freedom that nature provided to her was counterbalanced by the more conventional pursuits of a girl of her era and class: school—first the small public school in Karori and later private schools in Wellington—music lessons, tea parties, tennis parties, and dances—activities that Mansfield always claimed to dislike. Her father's increasing wealth and influence allowed him to provide his daughter with educational and cultural opportunities in Wellington and "at home" in London that not only opened her eyes to life beyond the provincial capital, but also made it impossible for Mansfield to live her life there. As is well known, she turned away from the path set for her by her family and, despite his initial opposition to the path she had chosen, her father provided her with crucial financial support that made it possible for her to pursue her life's purpose. At nineteen she left Wellington for London and for a career as a writer.[34]

Though anxious to escape from Wellington to London, her early years in New Zealand were to form the basis for the best of her mature fiction. I am not referring just to the biographical content of stories such as "Prelude" (1917), "At the Bay" (1921), or "The Doll's House" (1921), for example, or to the fact that so much of her fiction is anchored in a New Zealand landscape, topics which have been well covered by various critics. Rather, as I have already suggested was the case for Fry, I want to claim that the basis of Mansfield's art, as I would argue it is for all great artists, is her unique perception of the world in which she lived—how she sees, smells, or feels her surroundings and how she represents these experiences in her stories—and that this perception is fundamentally rooted in her childhood experience of New Zealand. There are two points to make here.

If perception is, indeed, the product of "brain, body and world" working together during active exploration, as Noë has argued, then what we experience in the various environments in which we find ourselves and how we make sense of what we experience constitute our conceptual framework—how we understand the world in which we live. From the earliest moments of our life, our sensory interactions with our surroundings play a central role in shaping our consciousness. Current theories of neuroplasticity emphasize the brain's capacity to rewire itself even in old age, but most of these theories recognize the importance of early childhood experiences in setting a basic foundation which remains with us throughout life. A toddler living in, and interacting daily with, an environment which is arid, containing little vegetation, bathed in harsh light, and subject to extreme temperatures, for example, will develop a very different perceptual matrix or baseline than would a toddler whose environment was humid, lush with vegetation, subject to soft, diffuse light, and moderate temperatures. And they would do so even if the human influences on them—social structures and built environments, for example—were similar. Mansfield's perceptual base is conditioned by the fact that it is determined, at least in part, by her sensorimotor interactions with her early physical environment in Karori and Wellington: the wind that is characteristic of the city on the bay, the clarity of light that was a feature noted by settlers and visitors well into the twentieth century, the temperate climate, the lush and unique vegetation, to name a few elements.

We see clear signs of this foundation in an early story such as "In the Botanical Gardens" (1907) with its counterpointing of "the broad central walk, with the orthodox banality of carpet bedding on either side" and the "bush [...] silent and splendid."[35] But it is as evident in later works such as "The Wind Blows" (1920), with its references to the ubiquitous Wellington winds: "shaking the house, rattling the windows, banging a piece of iron on the roof and making her bed tremble."[36] More subtly, yet perhaps more evocatively, the physical landscape that shaped Mansfield's sensibility occupies prominent positions in some of her best stories. In "At the Bay," for example, the opening section, with its "big bush-covered hills," "paddocks," "silvery, fluffy toi-toi," and "sea [that] had been beaten up softly in the darkness,"[37] does more than set the scene for the story to come. It is a powerful evocation of life that is timeless and universal yet grounded in the particularity of Mansfield's childhood excursions to the seaside near her Wellington home.

My second point is that it is also clear that her perceptions were placed within a conceptual framework that was not indigenous to New Zealand—here I mean both her built environment and the social structures which were modeled on British norms. Looking again at "At the Bay," we see how the evocative natural world in the opening scene is swept aside by the modern man-made world with the emergence of Stanley Burnell from "the back door of one of the bungalows."

His energetic dash across "the paddock [...] through the tussock grass [...] up the sandy hillock [... and] over the cold, wet pebbles, on to the hard sand" and into the sea results in a short-lived triumph: "First man in as usual!"[38] His triumph overshadows the landscape in which it occurs. Stanley is later more firmly linked to colonial Wellington in which a "blue serge suit, a stiff collar and spotted tie"[39] are the required uniform even at the height of summer, and in which the inhabitants ride in coaches to town where they work in offices that Jonathan Trout likens to a prison where "the cage door opens and clangs to upon the victim."[40] And this is a key source of conflict for Mansfield: how she sees/perceives the world through which she moves with relative freedom as a young child is different than how she is told and taught to see it. As I will argue in my larger project, I believe this conflict is the impulse which drives her toward art—music, literature, painting—and particularly toward theorists of art in the broad sense: There is a long list familiar to us all, which includes Wilde, Nietzsche, Symons, and Pater in her teens, for example. Art, for Mansfield, becomes a way to reconcile—or not—the conflict between what she experiences/perceives and how she is told to interpret it. And this is where Fauvism comes in.

I am indebted to Angela Smith's perceptive treatment of Mansfield and Fauvism, and particularly her accounts of Mansfield's association with J. D. Fergusson and *Rhythm*. She makes a strong case for her assertion that the "exclusion both [Mansfield] and Fergusson experienced because they did not speak the language of Oxbridge and Bloomsbury led them to a colourist, Fauvist language, where line and structure could liberate them into a new means of expression."[41] However, in keeping with the perceptual theories I have been discussing, I approach Mansfield and Fauvism from a somewhat different angle. I believe that when Mansfield met Fergusson in Paris in 1912, she was, as she had with such intensity in Wellington on her return from London, still searching for an aesthetic theory that would reconcile her manner of perceiving the world with how she was told the world should be seen. She was, in effect, looking for some external explanation or perhaps validation of what she already was attempting to express in her early stories.

Henri Matisse's remarks on art may add further weight to this point. Though written in 1939, his comments on drawing give us a glimpse of the qualities of Fauvist art that would have attracted Mansfield:

> My line drawing is the purest and most direct translation of my emotion. The simplification of the medium allows that. However, these drawings are more complete than they may appear to some people who confuse them with a kind of

sketch. They generate light; seen on a dull day or in indirect light they contain, in addition to the flavor and sensitivity of the line, light and value differences that quite clearly correspond to color. These colors are also evident to many in full light. […] Once my emotive line has modeled the light of my white paper without destroying its precious whiteness, I can neither add nor take anything away. The page is written, no correction is possible.[42]

If we replaced the word "drawing" with "short story," we might be able to read this as a description of Mansfield's work, and in the process we might see why Fauvism was so compelling to her. Think, for a moment, of the opening scene of "The Woman at the Store" (1912), with its depiction of dynamic movement so typical of Fauvist works: "The wind blew cross to the ground—it rooted among the tussock grass—slithered along the road" and "There was nothing to be seen but wave after wave of tussock grass."[43] In keeping with the Fauvist aesthetic, the dominant white and gray colors of the natural landscape—"the white pumice dust," "the sky was slate colour," "manuka bushes covered with thick spider webs" of white flowers—are punctuated with the exotic "purple orchids" and the bold colors of the riders' clothing: "a blue galatera shirt," a "white handkerchief spotted with red," and "a pair of blue duck trousers."[44] Strong colors, harsh light, and definite lines shape the opening scenes of this story, just as they feature in a Matisse or a Fergusson painting. No doubt, meeting Fergusson and their subsequent friendship provided her with much needed companionship and support as she continued to develop her aesthetic theory. But rather than Fauvism "liberat[ing] [Mansfield] into a new means of expression," I believe the situation was actually the reverse—Mansfield found Fauvism so liberating because it was a familiar lexicon: it was how she already saw the world and aimed to represent it in her own art.

Mansfield continued to develop her own aesthetics, and it was in her postwar reviewing for the *Athenaeum*—as Jenny McDonnell and others have noted[45]—that she finally formalized her unique vision. Reading through the more than 100 reviews, one gets a sense of a mature artist, ever more sure in her sense of what fiction ought to be and what it clearly ought not to be. I cannot do justice to them here, but I do want to quote from a few reviews that not only give us a sample of Mansfield's views, but also do so in a manner that illustrates what I have been discussing.

In her review of a new edition of George Moore's *Esther Waters*, the key role that emotion plays in art is on show: "There must be an initial emotion felt by the writer, and all that he sees is saturated in that emotional quality. It alone can give incidence and sequence, character and background, close and intimate unity."⁴⁶ In her review of Allan Monkhouse's new novel, she insists on the importance of experimentation: "However deep the knowledge the writer has of his characters, however finely he may convey that knowledge to us, it is only when he passes beyond it, when he begins to break new ground, to discover for himself, to experiment, that we are enthralled."⁴⁷ In her comments on Dutch author Louis Couperus's novels, she addresses the question of the author's vision:

> The troubling question which would seem to lie so heavily upon the pen of many a modern writer: "How much can I afford to take for granted? How much dare I trust to the imagination of the reader?" is answered here. We are too often inclined to think it may be solved by technical accomplishment, but that is not enough; the reason why Mr. Couperus can afford to dismiss the question, to wave it aside and to take everything for granted, is because of the strength of his imaginative vision. By that we mean it is impossible in considering these books not to be conscious of the deep breath the author has taken; he has had, as it were, a vision of the Van Lowe family, and he has seen them as souls—small souls—at the mercy of circumstance, life, fate.⁴⁸

From these and other reviews, we see Mansfield articulating the essential qualities that mark her best fiction—depth of emotion, formal experimentation, breadth of imaginative vision, insight into the human soul, among other qualities. She has, in effect, finally developed an aesthetic theory that matches her artistic vision.

Opposing approaches to art and aesthetics

Even these overly brief treatments of Fry and Mansfield show us the gulf that exists between their aesthetics. One way to characterize the two is to suggest that Mansfield works from a position of lived experience moving toward theory, whereas Fry works in a reverse pattern, seeking an art to correspond with his theories. And this is not just the difference between a practicing artist and a practicing critic; both were practicing artists and critics. The opposite approaches of the two speak to fundamentally different visions of art and those different visions are, at least in part, the result of the fundamentally different perceptual frameworks from which the two started. Mansfield's perceptual baseline, as I have illustrated, is the sensibility of a female, colonial outsider—as so many critics have noted—while Fry's is that of a privileged, English male insider. The gulf between Bloomsbury and Mansfield that can be attributed to her gender, class, or nationality have all been well documented. But what has not been sufficiently or adequately addressed are the differences caused by their fundamental perceptual frameworks that I have focused on in this chapter. Mansfield saw, innately, if you will, the boldness of color, the importance of line and form, the interplay of light and shade, and the dynamism of nature that comes to be associated with modern art, but her vision was firmly situated within the everyday world with all its emotions and personal complications, and her stories showcase that vision. Fry's aesthetic—shaped as it was from his own unique perceptual baseline—emphasizes the interplay of forms, colors, lines, and dynamism, as well, but his vision is very different than Mansfield's given his privileging of the imaginative life over the everyday world and his insistence on aesthetic detachment.

Fry's place as Bloomsbury's foremost art theorist accentuated the gulf between Mansfield and Bloomsbury. He spoke and wrote with authority about art; even when his views were at odds with others in the Bloomsbury circle—including Virginia Woolf's—they were debated seriously and with respect. Mansfield was not accorded similar respect, though Woolf, as we know, learned much from her. There is little wonder, then, given Fry's influence among the Bloomsbury group, that Mansfield felt excluded from that circle. Yet I would argue that Mansfield's approach resonates more fully with subsequent generations of writers in large measure because her perceptual framework was fashioned outside the "imperial capital" that was home to Fry and Bloomsbury. Her way of seeing and being in the world—and how she represents them in her fiction—drew attention to the act of perception, and it also helped her to devise a markedly new form of fiction and an aesthetics that were different from both the British "norm" of the day and Bloomsbury's. The success of Mansfield's fiction created space for others to speak from their own "non-normative" perspectives, and in the process she transformed the art of short fiction. She may have felt like a "little colonial outsider," but it is that very position that allowed her to create a lasting legacy.

Notes

1 Katherine Mansfield to Dorothy Brett, October 11, 1917, in *The Collected Letters of Katherine Mansfield*, vol. 1, ed. Vincent O'Sullivan and Margaret Scott (Oxford: Clarendon Press, 1984), 332.
2 Roger Fry, "Post Impression," in *A Roger Fry Reader*, ed. Christopher Reed (Chicago: University of Chicago Press, 1996), 15.

3   Virginia Woolf, "Mr Bennett and Mrs Brown," in *Collected Essays of Virginia Woolf*, vol. 1, ed. Leonard Woolf (London: Hogarth Press, 1966), 320.
4   Woolf's remarks have become something of a touchstone for scholars interested in tracing connections between her writing and Fry's first Post-Impressionist Exhibition, but some critics have also shown how Woolf's comments relate to the broader intellectual concerns of the era. See, for example, Anne Banfield's *The Phantom Table* (Cambridge: Cambridge University Press, 2000) and Patricia Waugh's "Science and the Aesthetics of English Modernism," *New Formations* 49 (Spring 2003): 32–47.
5   The scope of this chapter makes it impossible to delve into the extensive research and scholarship of this era on perception and allied concepts such as sensation and consciousness. Of importance to this paper, Adrianne Rubin makes evident that Roger Fry was well versed in this scholarship and used it in developing his own aesthetic. There is no evidence that Katherine Mansfield was as well versed in these theories. See Rubin's *Roger Fry's "Difficult and Uncertain Science": The Interpretation of Aesthetic Perception*, Cultural Interactions: Studies in the Relationship between the Arts 28 (Oxford: Peter Lang AG, 2013).
6   Alva Noë and Evan Thompson, introduction to *Vision and Mind*, ed. Alva Noë and Evan Thompson (Cambridge, MA: MIT Press, 2002), 2.
7   Noë and Thompson, "Introduction," 2–3.
8   Noë and Thompson, "Introduction," 5.
9   Evan Thompson, Adrian Palacios, and Francisco J. Varela, "Ways of Coloring: Comparative Color Vision as a Case Study for Cognitive Science," in *Vision and Design*, ed. Noë and Thompson, 370.
10 Thompson, Palacios, and Varela, "Ways of Coloring," 370, 392.
11 Andy Clark and Naomi Eilan, "Sensorimotor Skills and Perception," *Aristotelian Society Supplementary Volume* 80, no.1 (2006): 44.
12 Alva Noë, *Action in Perception* (Cambridge, MA: MIT Press, 2004), 227.
13 Noë, *Action in Perception*, 223.
14 Noë, *Action in Perception*, 227.
15 As Adrianne Rubin notes in *Roger Fry's "Difficult and Uncertain Science,"* Fry's reputation as a significant art critic has waxed and waned over the last century. She argues that while his "theories informed those of other formalist critics, specifically Kenneth Clark, Herbert Read and Clement Greenberg" (197), others, including his contemporary Howard Hannay and later twentieth-century critics such as Andrew Hemmingway and Charles Harrison, attacked Fry on several fronts.
16 Virginia Woolf, *Roger Fry: A Biography* (London: The Hogarth Press, 1969), 25.
17 Woolf, *Roger Fry*, 65.
18 Frances Spalding, *Roger Fry: Art and Life* (London: Granada, 1980), 3.

19 Spalding, *Roger Fry*, 3.
20 Spalding, *Roger Fry*, 9.
21 Spalding, *Roger Fry*, 11.
22 Spalding, *Roger Fry*, 3.
23 Roger Fry, "An Essay in Aesthetics," in *Vision and Design* (London: Chatto & Windus, 1920), 20.
24 Fry, "An Essay in Aesthetics," 24.
25 Roger Fry, "Retrospect," in *Vision and Design*, 199.
26 Michael Fried, "Roger Fry's Formalism," *The Tanner Lectures on Human Values* (Ann Arbor, MI: University of Michigan, November 2–3, 2001): 6. http://tannerlectures.utah.edu/lecture-library.php (accessed December 17, 2016).
27 Rubin, *Roger Fry's "Difficult and Uncertain Science,"* 44–45.
28 Rubin, *Roger Fry's "Difficult and Uncertain Science,"* 2.
29 Fry, "An Essay in Aesthetics," 16.
30 Fry, "Post Impression" in *A Roger Fry Reader*, ed. Reed, 100.
31 Fry, "Post Impressionism," 105.
32 Fry's privileging of the imaginative world over the actual one does not lead him to the exclusion of the natural in art. As Rubin suggests, for Fry, "the artist interprets rather than copies nature; in so doing, he creates a world equal and parallel to the natural world" (*Roger Fry's "Difficult and Uncertain Science,"* 51).
33 The major biographies deal with Mansfield's childhood in varying ways. See Antony Alpers, *The Life of Katherine Mansfield* (New York: Viking Press, 1980); Jeffrey Meyers, *Katherine Mansfield: A Darker Place* (Hamish Hamilton, 1978); Gillian Boddy, *Katherine Mansfield: The Woman and the Writer* (Ringwood, Victoria: Penguin Books, 1988); Claire Tomalin, *Katherine Mansfield: A Secret Life* (London: Viking, 1987); and Kathleen Jones, *Katherine Mansfield: The Storyteller* (Edinburgh: Edinburgh University Press, 2010).
34 Space constraints make my treatment of her childhood necessarily brief. It was not idyllic, as her biographers have made evident, but it did have a profound impact on her writing career.
35 Katherine Mansfield, "In the Botanical Gardens," in *The Collected Works of Katherine Mansfield, The Collected Fiction*, 2 vols., ed. Gerri Kimber and Vincent O'Sullivan (Edinburgh: Edinburgh University Press, 2012), 1:84, 85.
36 Katherine Mansfield, "The Wind Blows," in *Collected Fiction*, ed. Kimber and O'Sullivan, 2:74.
37 Katherine Mansfield, "At the Bay," in *Collected Fiction*, ed. Kimber and O'Sullivan, 2:342.
38 Mansfield, "At the Bay," 2:344.
39 Mansfield, "At the Bay," 2:346.
40 Mansfield, "At the Bay," 2:365.

41 Angela Smith, *Katherine Mansfield: A Literary Life* (London: Palgrave Macmillan, 2000), 22
42 Henri Matisse, "Notes of a Painter on His Drawing, 1939" in *Matisse on Art*. rev. ed., ed. Jack Flam (Berkley: University of California Press, 1995), 130–31.
43 Katherine Mansfield, "The Woman at the Store," in *Collected Fiction*, ed. Kimber and O'Sullivan, 1:268.
44 Mansfield, "The Woman at the Store," 1:268.
45 While a number of critics have commented on Mansfield's *Athenaeum* reviews over the years, Jenny McDonnell makes perhaps the best case to date for the important role they play in Mansfield's maturation as a professional writer. See her *Katherine Mansfield and the Modernist Marketplace* (New York: Palgrave Macmillan, 2010).
46 Katherine Mansfield, "Esther Waters Revisited," *Athenaeum* no. 4710 (August 6, 1920): 176.
47 Katherine Mansfield, "Control and Enthusiasm," *Athenaeum* no. 4674 (November 28, 1919): 1259.
48 Katherine Mansfield, "The Book of the Small Souls," *Athenaeum* no. 4703 (June 18, 1920): 798.

10

Modernist Emotions: The Critical Writings of Katherine Mansfield and Virginia Woolf

Chris Mourant

In April 1919, the first issue of the *Athenaeum* was published under the editorship of Katherine Mansfield's husband, John Middleton Murry. Entrusted by Arthur Rowntree with the task of transforming this established Victorian weekly into a modern literary review, Murry had quickly set about gathering together a group of contributors culled from the circles of Bloomsbury and Garsington. These included Leonard and Virginia Woolf, T. S. Eliot, Lytton Strachey, Bertrand Russell, Roger Fry, Clive Bell, Aldous Huxley, and E. M. Forster. Mansfield was also integral to the success of the periodical, contributing at least one book review to the *Athenaeum* every week before resigning in December 1920. Until recently, this vast body of work has remained almost entirely overlooked by scholars. Prior to the welcome interventions of Sydney Janet Kaplan and Jenny McDonnell, Mansfield's reviews have been interpreted predominantly as motivated by either feelings of duty toward her husband or resentment toward Virginia Woolf, with hundreds of contributions and two years of literary work often reduced to a single notorious review of Woolf's novel *Night and Day*. As this chapter examines, however, Mansfield's critical writings for the *Athenaeum* provide a more detailed and extensive material record of her sustained engagement with Woolf's ideas than this accepted interpretation suggests. Deploying a shared vocabulary of empathetic "emotion" and deep "feeling," the critical writings produced by Mansfield and Woolf at this time highlight the degree to which their professional relationship was based upon what Woolf herself termed a "common certain understanding."[1]

The week following the publication of the first issue of the *Athenaeum* under Murry's editorship, Woolf's seminal essay "Modern Novels" was printed in the *Times Literary Supplement*. Later substantially revised under the title

"Modern Fiction" for inclusion in *The Common Reader* (1923), this essay outlines distinctions that have come to define how we understand literary modernism. Contrasting "modern fiction" with the "old," Woolf begins by stating that her quarrel is not with the "classics" (Fielding, Thackeray, Austen), but with the "materialists" (Wells, Bennett, Galsworthy).[2] Each of these Edwardian novelists, she writes, has been too concerned with "the solidity of his fabric" and "more often misses than secures the thing we seek": "Whether we call it life or spirit, truth or reality, this, the essential thing, has moved off, or on, and refuses to be contained any longer in such ill-fitting vestments."[3] "Modern Novels" is Woolf's manifesto for a new kind of fiction; it is her rallying cry for a new literary form that would be adequate to the task of representing the "essential thing." In this essay, Woolf famously states that the task of the modern writer is to record the myriad "impressions" that fall upon the surface of the mind like "an incessant shower of innumerable atoms, composing in their sum what we might venture to call life itself."[4] A writer who goes some way to achieving this, Woolf argues, is James Joyce. In contrast to the "materialists" of the Edwardian period, Joyce is the preeminent example of a modern writer who is "spiritual" because he is "concerned at all costs to reveal the flickerings of that innermost flame which flashes its myriad message through the brain."[5] However, Joyce's writing is so "centred in a self" that it never "reaches out or embraces or comprehends what is outside and beyond."[6] This is an important distinction. For Woolf, modern fiction must look to mediate between the external world and the inner self; it must look to find a middle ground between lifeless realism and disconnected solipsism, communicating personal experience at a level that is universally comprehensible; only then can fiction capture the "essential thing."

Woolf ends "Modern Novels" by noting that the writers to date who have successfully mediated between the external and internal realms are the Russian writers of the nineteenth century, and particularly Anton Chekhov. The essential quality of Russian literature, Woolf suggests, is something between "matter" and "spirit": it is its "heart."[7] These works, filtering through to a British readership for the first time in translation, convey "sympathy for the sufferings of others, love towards them."[8] Unlike Joyce, Woolf argues, the Russian writers reach "outside and beyond" the self and thus achieve a degree of universality in their work; she observes, for instance, that the "Russian mind" is "comprehensive and compassionate."[9] These word choices in Woolf's essay, of "heart," "sympathy," "love," and "compassion," underscore an implicit emphasis on emotion, feeling, sentiment, and sensibility as that which can mediate between the internal and external, the personal and universal. Moreover, Woolf further highlights her resistance to the "solidity" of plot-driven Edwardian fiction by praising the "inconclusiveness" of Russian literature, observing that such works give "the sense that there is no answer, that if honestly examined life presents question after question which must be left to sound on and on."[10] The work of Chekhov, in particular, "leaves us with the suggestion that the strange chords he has struck sound on and on" and that "there is perhaps no answer to the questions which [he] raises."[11]

On reading "Modern Novels" in April 1919, Mansfield immediately wrote to Woolf to relate her enthusiasm for the essay. What's more, Mansfield surely had this essay in mind when she wrote to Woolf again the following month, describing the translation of a letter by Chekhov that she had made with S. S. Koteliansky that was about to be printed in the *Athenaeum*. Echoing Woolf's emphasis on the unresolved "question" of Russian literature, Mansfield writes thus: "Tchekhov has a very interesting letter published in next week's A…what the writer does is not so much to *solve* the question but to *put* the question. There must be the question put. That seems to me a very nice dividing line between the true & the false writer—Come & talk it over with me."[12] Throughout their letters and diaries, Mansfield and Woolf continually refer to the importance of their "talk" with each other. After one of their first meetings together, for example, Mansfield wrote this to Woolf: "It was good to have time to talk to you. We have got the same job, Virginia & it is really very curious & thrilling that we should both, quite apart from each other, be after so very nearly the same thing."[13] Throughout the autumn and winter of 1918, Mansfield and Woolf met weekly. While these visits became irregular in 1919 and 1920, interrupted by Mansfield's worsening health, Woolf records in her diary in June 1920 that they had "2 hours priceless talk—priceless in the sense that to no one else can I talk in the same disembodied way about writing" and considers this "exalted talk" and "intercourse" as "more fundamental than many better established ones": "I can talk straight out to her."[14] Talking to Mansfield, Woolf experiences "the queerest sense of echo coming back to me from her mind the second after I've spoken."[15] Likewise, in December 1920, Mansfield wrote to Woolf: "I think of you often—very often. I long to talk to you […] You are the only woman with whom I long to talk *work*. There will never be another."[16] And after Mansfield's death in 1923, it is this "exalted talk" that Woolf misses: "there are things about writing I think of & want to tell Katherine."[17]

Through the critical writings that they produced at this time, I argue in this chapter, Mansfield and Woolf established a dialogue in print, each echoing the terms of debate and conceptual ideas advanced in the literary reviews written by the other. This dialogue and "talk" exemplify the "conversational model for modernism" that Suzanne Churchill and Adam McKible suggest early twentieth-century periodicals looked to enact.[18] Indeed, Woolf often used conversation as a formal device for her essays, as in "A Talk about Memoirs" (1920), "Mr Conrad: A Conversation" (1923), and "Bryon & Mr Briggs" (drafted in 1922), in which characters from her own novels talk about literature. In Woolf's "How It Strikes a Contemporary" (1923), the idea of the talking voice and "random chatter" dominates.[19] And in "On Being Ill" (1926), Woolf envisions heaven as a place of conversation and gossip between writers and readers. As Hermione Lee has observed, these thematic strands of open conversation and "random chatter" highlight Woolf's wider aims for her essays and reviews. Woolf disclaimed the kind of literary "authority" that she associated with the (usually male) forms of literary criticism that set out to dictate and delineate: as Lee writes, Woolf's essays are instead conversational in tone and open-ended in form, resisting "definitiveness, closure and opinionated certainties," and are thus "closely connected to her recommendations for a democratic literary community."[20] In other words, Woolf's essays deliberately opened up a space for dialogue, and Mansfield responded to this. After Woolf wrote a review of Dorothy Richardson's novel *The Tunnel*, for instance, she records in her diary visiting Mansfield: "At once she flung down her pen & plunged, as if we'd been parted for 10 minutes, into the question of Dorothy Richardson; & so on with the greatest freedom & animation on both sides."[21] Two weeks later, Mansfield's own review of *The Tunnel* appeared in the *Athenaeum*, echoing Woolf's emphasis on the novel's superficial "surface" impressions by arguing that it was lacking in those "large pauses in which we creep away into our caves of contemplation" and each thing that happens in the mind is "judged" and given "its appointed place in the whole scheme."[22] In the absence of specific instances such as these, whereby a diary entry or letter helps us to trace particular correlations between an actual conversation and the reviews, we can measure the impact of Mansfield's "talk" with Woolf through the remarkably similar language choices made by each writer in their critical works.

Throughout her contributions to the *Athenaeum*, for instance, Mansfield continually employs "emotion" as a critical standard for evaluating literature, arguing that "[w]ithout emotion writing is dead" and that "emotion is essential to a work of art; it is that which makes a work of art a unity."[23] In her review of Joseph Conrad's *The Rescue*, for example, she states that the "feeling that we are not so much reading a story of adventure as living in and through it" arises "from the quality of the emotion in which the book is steeped."[24] Likewise, Woolf identifies books with the "shock of emotion" that they produce.[25] In a notebook entry made under the heading "Misc. Reading," for example, Woolf writes, "One grades one's feelings."[26] This emphasis on "emotion" and "feeling" can be seen in relation to the idea of "significant form" advanced by Clive Bell. While the Bloomsbury group had no specific manifesto, as Andrew McNeillie observes, Bell's *Art* (1914) has been claimed by many as having served "as a platform for the group cause."[27] In this book, Bell states that "[t]he starting-point for all systems of aesthetics must be the personal experience of a peculiar emotion" and then asks, "What quality is shared by all objects that provoke our aesthetic emotions?"[28] In answer to this question, he outlines the notion of "significant form," arguing that it is "lines and colours combined in a particular way, certain forms and relations of forms, [that] stir our aesthetic emotions."[29] In their critical writings, Mansfield and Woolf can be seen to respond to this idea of "aesthetic emotion." For Woolf, however, it is emotion that creates form, rather than form that elicits emotion. In an article written in 1922, for instance, she responds to Percy Lubbock's argument in *The Craft of Fiction* by stating that the "book itself" is not "form which you see, but emotion which you feel": "we feel with singular satisfaction, and since all our feelings are in keeping, they form a whole which remains in our minds as the book itself."[30] This clearly parallels Mansfield's assertion that it is emotion "which makes a work of art a unity." This privileging of "emotion" distinguishes Mansfield and Woolf's critical writings from the entirely formalist approach adopted by Bell. Whereas Bell states that it is "significant form" that stirs "aesthetic emotions," Mansfield and Woolf argue that it is "emotion" that creates form, making the book a "unity" or "whole."

With both Mansfield and Woolf writing for the *Athenaeum*, their shared emphasis on "emotion" can also be contextualized against other contributions to this periodical. In his own articles for the *Athenaeum*, for example, Murry consistently argues that "reading is, essentially, a process of enlarging our experience by the direct absorption of emotion"; that literature "is rooted in emotion, and that it grows by the mastery of emotion, and that its significance finally depends upon the quality and comprehensiveness of the emotion."[31] In his essay "Hamlet and His Problems," which was first published in the *Athenaeum* in September 1919, moreover, T. S. Eliot famously argues that the "only way of expressing emotion in the form of art is by finding an 'objective correlative' […] a set of objects, a situation, a chain of events which shall be the formula of that *particular* emotion."[32] Murry later illustrated this concept in his book *The Problem of Style* (1922) by distinguishing between the author who pursues the "active ideal of art" and "the matter-of-fact vision of the professional accumulator of details": "For in the latter case, the detail, having been the cause of no emotion in the writer, can awaken none in the reader."[33] Mansfield responds to this distinction in her own critical writings, arguing that when an author's method is simply to amass observations, "we feel that no one observation is nearer the truth than another."[34] This clearly echoes Woolf's argument in "Modern Novels," that "truth" can no longer be contained in the "ill-fitting vestments" of an outdated form of literary realism focused almost exclusively on recording the material details of the external world.

Indeed, the idea of "emotion" shaped the response to the so-called "materialists" in Mansfield and Woolf's critical writings. When they reviewed a reissue of George Moore's novel *Esther Waters*, for example, both emphasized "emotion" in contrast to the "object." Mansfield argues that Moore's novel presents "a world of objects accurately recorded" but "it has no emotion" and, therefore, "who cares?" Emphasizing the same idea of "unity" when discussing "emotion," Mansfield writes: "To contemplate the object, to let it make its own impression—which is Mr. Moore's way in 'Esther Waters'—is not enough. There must be an initial emotion felt by the writer, and all that he sees is saturated in that emotional quality. It alone can give incidence and sequence, character and background, a close and intimate unity."[35] This assessment is directly echoed in Woolf's review:

> Vivid, truthful, so lightly and yet so firmly constructed as it is, what then prevents us from talking of immortality and greatness? In one word, the quality of the emotion. [...] The conception springs from no deep original source, and the execution has that sort of evenness which we see in the work of a highly sensitive student copying on to his canvas the picture of some great master.[36]

When Mansfield and Woolf reviewed Joseph Hergesheimer's *Java Head*, moreover, they both reiterated the argument of "Modern Novels," devoting considerable space to detailing the novel's plot, for example, and thereby foregrounding that aspect of contemporary writing that they were both trying to counter in their own fiction. When critiquing Hergesheimer for his extensive descriptions of clothing, Woolf also echoes "Modern Novels" by celebrating the "heart": "It is very difficult to write beautifully about the heart. When Mr Hergesheimer has to describe not what people wear but what they feel, he shows his lack of ease or of interest."[37] In her own review, likewise, Mansfield calls attention to Hergesheimer's focus on the materiality of clothing, arguing that it "is not enough to be comforted with colours, to finger bright shawls [...]

our curiosity is roused as to what lies beneath these strange rich surfaces. Mr. Hergesheimer leaves us wondering and unsatisfied."[38] For both Mansfield and Woolf, therefore, the object must be related to that which is below the surface; it must become the formula for a particular "emotion" that springs from a "deep original source."

In the critical writings produced by Mansfield and Woolf at this time, a constellation of interrelated words and concepts forms around this idea of deep "emotion." In one review, for example, Mansfield states: "*revelation* comes from that *emotional reaction* which the artist felt and was impelled to communicate" (my emphasis).[39] To be taken seriously, authors must make this "serious attempt at revelation."[40] For example, a novel such as R. O. Prowse's *A Gift of the Dusk*, which narrates the life of a consumptive exiled to a retreat in the Swiss mountains, affects Mansfield because it "is not only a record of suffering" but is "a revelation."[41] When reviewing fictions about the First World War, in particular, it is the revelation of a personal, "spiritual truth" that is the essential thing for Mansfield, "a revelation of [the author's] inner self which would perhaps never have been revealed in times less terrible and strange."[42] In their correspondence, Mansfield and Murry highlight the importance of this idea of "revelation" in the postwar context. Murry writes, for instance: "The War *is* Life; not a strange aberration of Life, but a revelation of it. It is a test we must apply; it must be allowed for in any truth that is to touch us."[43] For Mansfield, the modern writer must attempt to find a new form through which to communicate the "revelation" of new emotions following the war. Writing to Murry, for example, she states: "'I feel in the *profoundest* sense that nothing can ever be the same that as artists we are traitors if we feel otherwise: we have to take it [the war] into account and find new expressions new moulds for our new thoughts & feelings."[44] Advancing the idea of a "new word" throughout her reviews, this concept of "revelation," by which an emotional reaction or inner truth is communicated by the writer, was placed at the center of Mansfield's prescriptions for modern fiction.[45]

In an article published in the *Athenaeum* in November 1919, Murry borrows the title of one of Thomas Hardy's poetry collections, *Moments of Vision*, to clarify what is meant by this contemporary idea of "revelation":

> The word "revelation" is fertile in false suggestion; the creative act of power which we seek to elucidate is an act of plenary apprehension, by which one manifestation, one form of life, one experience is seen in its rigorous relation to all other and to all possible manifestations, forms, and experiences. [...] In a "moment of vision" the poet recognises in a single separate incident of life,

life's essential quality. The uniqueness of the whole, the infinite multiplicity and variety of its elements, are manifested and apprehended in a part.[46]

In this article, Murry both echoes Woolf's emphasis in "Modern Novels" on the "essential thing" and anticipates her later idea of "moments of being," which Hermione Lee has observed was developed out of an essay on Hardy that Woolf published in 1928, in which she also borrowed the title *Moments of Vision* to describe the "sudden quickening of power" in a novel when "a single scene breaks off from the rest."[47] In the essay "A Sketch of the Past," written in 1939, Woolf distinguishes "moments of being" from the "cotton wool of daily life": each of these moments, she writes, is like a violent "shock" of recognition that "is or will become a *revelation* of some order; it is a token of some real thing behind appearances" (my emphasis).[48] For both Murry and Woolf, then, the idea of "revelation" was connected with perception or "vision" and the notion of a privileged "moment."

When Mansfield uses a specific vocabulary in her reviews, therefore, we can see how these word choices register a set of interrelated concepts also advanced by her immediate contemporaries. Reiterating the idea of a "sudden quickening," for instance, Mansfield tells us that we must ask of each book: "Has it quickened our perception, or increased our mysterious response to Life? Do we feel that we have partaken of the author's *vision*—that something has been *revealed* that we are the richer for having seen?" (my emphasis)[49] Similarly, she praises Conrad's "peculiar responsive sensitiveness to the significance of everything, down to the slightest detail that has a place in his *vision*": "in this heightened, quickened state of awareness we are made conscious of his passionate insistence upon the importance of extracting from the *moment* every drop of life that it contains" (my emphasis).[50] In letters and notebook entries, likewise, Mansfield elaborates on this notion of a revelatory "moment of vision." In a letter to Ottoline Morrell composed in July 1918, for instance, she anticipates Woolf's idea of the "moment of being," later conceptualized as "a token of some real thing behind appearances," when she writes:

> My secret belief—the innermost "credo" by which I live is that *although* Life is loathsomely ugly and people are terribly often vile and cruel and base, nevertheless there is something at the back of it all—which if only I were great enough to understand would make *everything* everything indescribably beautiful. One just has glimpses, divine warnings—signs—[51]

Likewise, in a notebook entry pointedly given the title "The Glimpse" when it was published posthumously by Murry, Mansfield develops this idea of a revelatory "moment":

The waves, as I drove home this afternoon, and the high foam, how it was suspended in the air before it fell … What is it that happens in that moment of suspension? It is timeless. In that moment (what *do* I mean?) the whole life of the soul is contained. One is flung up—out of life—one is "held", and then,—down, bright, broken, glittering on to the rocks, tossed back, part of the ebb and flow.[52]

This idea of experiencing a privileged "moment" or glimpsing a "timeless" truth shapes the language of Mansfield's reviews. Assessing Vita Sackville-West's novel *Heritage*, for example, she argues that "the form of the novel" is lost without "central points of significance": "the gradual unfolding in growing, gaining light" must "be followed by one blazing moment"; without this "blazing moment," Mansfield asks, "how are we to appreciate the importance of one 'spiritual event' rather than another?"[53] And what impresses Mansfield about Woolf's short story "Kew Gardens" is precisely the "blazing moment" of illumination and revelation that is presented to the reader: "for a moment the secret life is half-revealed […] we believe these things are all [the author's] concern until suddenly with a gesture she shows us the flower-bed, growing, expanding in the heat and light, filling a whole world."[54] As such, it is possible to trace in Mansfield's writings a genealogy of ideas through which Woolf would later go on to develop the celebrated concept of the "moment of being."

Importantly, the passage from Murry's article on Hardy quoted above highlights how this shared vocabulary of the "moment," "vision," and "revelation" was also employed to signal the belief that literature should connect the subject and the object, the self and the other, the part and the whole, the particular and the universal; that each "creative act" should look to be a manifestation of all life. In August 1920, Woolf records in her diary that Mansfield told her that "one ought to merge into things."[55] We see this articulated further in Mansfield's famous letter to Dorothy Brett about the "moment" of merging between the subject and the object: "There follows the moment when you are *more* duck, *more* apple or *more* Natasha than any of these objects could ever possibly be, and so you *create* them anew."[56] In their reviews, both Mansfield and Woolf emphasize this idea of merging the self and the other in order to move beyond the particular. As in Woolf's "Modern Novels," both writers argue that literature should be "comprehensive and compassionate," reaching out and embracing "what is outside and beyond." As such, Mansfield and Woolf consistently advocated the idea that "modern fiction" should seek to blur the lines between the inner ego and outer world. In 1920, for example, Mansfield writes: "The word that haunts me is egocentric."[57] Looking to move beyond the ego in her own fiction, Mansfield sought to rise "above all pain, and all infirmity—rising above everything."[58] As such, she defined her "philosophy" at this time as "the defeat of the personal": "People today are simply cursed by what I call the *personal* ... What is happening to ME. Look at ME. This is what has been done to ME. Its [*sic*] just as though you tried to run and all the while an enormous black serpent fastened on to you."[59] As Lee notes, Woolf also "wanted her criticism to express deep feeling, but not to be personal."[60] Right from the beginning of her essay-writing career in 1905, Woolf set herself against what she termed "the unclothed egoism" of many of the essayists of her time.[61] The critical writings by Mansfield and Woolf highlight a sustained attempt to negotiate a position between personal "emotion" and the world beyond. Throughout their essays and literary reviews, both writers seek to find a language and vocabulary by which to celebrate "emotion" and "feeling" yet resist "unclothed egoism," appraising those books that successfully relate personal experience at a level that is comprehensive and universal. As Woolf observes in a notebook entry, for example: "The better books universalise/disinfect personality. Simply they are dealing with important feelings."[62]

This resistance to the "egocentric" shaped how Mansfield and Woolf responded to the so-called "stream of consciousness" technique and the contemporary vogue for fiction influenced by psychoanalysis. In her first review for the *Athenaeum*, for instance, Mansfield criticizes Dorothy Richardson for "registering every single thing that happens in the clear, shadowless country of her mind": "There is Miss Richardson, holding out her mind, as it were, and there is Life hurling objects into it as fast as she can throw."[63] In a later review of Richardson's novel *Interim*, titled "Dragonflies," Mansfield argues that the habit of "registering every single thing" in the novel blocks the possibility of any one object or event being imbued with the "importance" that she elsewhere associates with the "blazing moment": "everything being of equal importance to her, it is impossible that everything should not be of equal unimportance."[64] In her review of *The Tunnel*, likewise, Woolf argues that reality exists "beneath the surface": like Mansfield's image of a dragonfly "[d]arting through life, quivering, hovering," and skimming the water,[65] Woolf argues that Richardson is too content to focus on surface impressions and that she fails to penetrate any deeper: "sensations, impressions, ideas and emotions glance off her, unrelated and unquestioned, without shedding quite as much light as we had hoped into the hidden depths."[66] Instead, Woolf argues, the writer "should make us feel ourselves seated at the centre of another mind" and "we should perceive in the helter-skelter of flying fragments some unity, significance, or design."[67] Again, therefore, Mansfield and Woolf both promote the idea that the inner ego should be connected to the outer world, and that particular "emotions" and "sensations" of the inner life should be communicated at a level that is immediately comprehensible to others; only then can the work of art become a "unity" of importance or significance.

Richardson's novels were first described as presenting a "stream of consciousness" by May Sinclair in 1918, who borrowed the term from the philosopher and psychologist William James. Famously, this was a term that Richardson herself didn't favor, but the work of the so-called "stream of consciousness" novelists revealed a pressing problem for the modern author and critic: how to relate the insights of psychology and psychoanalysis to fiction. In "Modern Novels," for instance, Woolf states: "The tendency of the moderns and part of their perplexity is no doubt that they find their interest more and more in [the] dark region of psychology."[68] Likewise, in an article titled "Is There a New Generation?" published in the *Athenaeum*, Murry observed: "The 'modern' is too fond of thinking that he has shown up life. What he shows up is not life at all. He is typified by the novelist who pathetically believes that psycho-analysis has added a cubit to his stature, whereas he staggers like a pygmy under the burden."[69] Mansfield critiqued Sinclair for staggering under this burden, writing: "she has allowed her love of writing to suffer the eclipse of psycho-analysis."[70] Elsewhere, Mansfield expresses exasperation at the recurring "character in modern English fiction […] who from childhood up has suffered from what our psycho-analytical skimmings have taught us to call the sex-complex."[71] Again, therefore, the focus of Mansfield's critique is on the failed attempt to access hidden depths, with English fiction never getting beyond superficial "skimmings." Similarly, when Woolf reviewed J. D. Beresford's *The Imperfect Mother* in the *Times Literary Supplement*, in a review titled "Freudian Fictions," she critiqued the novel for being "strictly in accordance with the new psychology," observing that "all the characters have become cases" and, in becoming so, "they have ceased to be individuals":

> We must protest that we do not wish to debar Mr Beresford from making use of any key that seems to him to fit the human mind. Our complaint is rather that in *An Imperfect Mother* the new key is a patent key that opens every door. It simplifies rather than complicates, detracts rather than enriches. The door swings open briskly enough, but the apartment to which we are admitted is a bare little room with no outlook whatever.[72]

When she reviewed this novel in the *Athenaeum*, Mansfield employed a very similar spatial metaphor to Woolf in order to highlight its deficiencies. Beresford and R. H. Bretherton, turning "from the vague outlines and spaces of the open country, have chosen to build their new novels in what might be called the Garden

City of literature," a "desirable site" lately "discovered by the psychoanalysts" in which "the houses are still scattered and few, but there is no doubt as to its dawning popularity with the novelists."[73] However, Mansfield argues, Beresford "brings nothing from the vasty deep" and reveals only the "essential emptiness" of the psychoanalytical novel: "The house is not furnished at all; nobody lives there."[74]

Mansfield and Woolf's criticism of those novelists following the "new psychology" reflects their wider argument that modern literature must not attempt to answer a question, but simply pose it: characters must not be made into "cases" and human experience must not be explained away; intellect and reason must always be combined with "emotion" and "imagination." Where Mansfield criticizes Frank Swinnerton for leaving "expression" out of his novel *September*, for example, Woolf also describes his "lucid rather than […] beautiful mind, intellectual in its scope, rather than imaginative."[75] Moreover, positioning the "intellect" and "vision" in a dialectical relation in an article published in December 1919, Woolf writes: "The greatest poets, having both the visionary imagination and the intellectual imagination, deal with both sides of life; in the lesser poets either the one kind of imagination or the other predominates."[76] Likewise, Mansfield writes in one of her reviews:

> [W]hat is the use, to your artist at any rate, of thought that is not the outcome of feeling? You must feel before you can think; you must think before you can express your-self. It is not enough to feel and write; or to think and write. True expression is the outcome of them both, yet a third thing, and separate.[77]

In other words, both Mansfield and Woolf argued that literature must seek to mediate between "vision" and "feeling" (intuition) and "intellect" and "thought" (reason), producing a third, separate thing out of this dialectic: only then might the author approximate, in the words of Woolf's "Modern Novels," "what we might venture to call life itself." In a review of a novel by Louis Couperus, for example, Mansfield asks:

> What is it then that differentiates these living characters from the book-bound creatures of even our brilliant modern English writers? Is it not that the former are seen ever, and always in relation to life—not to a part of life, not to a set of society, but to the bounding horizon, life, and the latter are seen in relation to an intellectual idea of life? In this second case life is made to fit them; something is abstracted—something quite unessential—that they wouldn't in the least know what to do with … and they are set in motion. But life cannot be made to "fit" anybody.[78]

For Mansfield and Woolf, the writer staggering under the burden of psychoanalysis presumes to explain that which cannot be explained, fitting people to a theory of life that diminishes rather than enhances lived experience. This idea was in part derived from Chekhov. In letters translated by Mansfield for publication in the *Athenaeum*, for example, Chekhov writes that it is "not the business of a psychological writer to understand that which he does not understand" or to "pretend that he understands that which nobody understands"; instead, the writer must simply be "an impartial witness": "For writers, particularly for writers who are artists, it is high time to confess [...] that you can't understand anything in this world."[79] As such, rather than try to answer the question, the artist can only pose it; and rather than attempt to explain life, the artist must learn to accept it. In her review praising Couperus, for instance, Mansfield concludes: "It is only by accepting life as M. Couperus accepts it that the novelist is free—through his characters—to question it profoundly."[80]

Throughout her letters and diaries at this time, Mansfield argued that one must learn to accept life and "learn to submit": "Its [sic] only by risking losing yourself—giving yourself up to Life—that you can ever find out the answer."[81] This submission meant merging the self with the other, as Mansfield made clear on several occasions: "when I am writing of 'another' I want to lose myself in the soul of the other that I am not"; the artist "must accept Life, he must submit, give himself so utterly to Life that no personal quâ personal self remains"; one "must learn, one must practise, to *forget* oneself."[82] Through this "act of surrender" the artist will be able "to lose oneself more utterly, to love more deeply, to feel oneself part of life,—not separate" and will thereby "pass from personal love to greater love."[83] As such, the submission of the "personal" self would lead to a more universal comprehension and compassion: "This is the moment which, after all, we live for,—the moment of direct feeling when we are most ourselves and least personal."[84]

Like Woolf in "Modern Novels," therefore, Mansfield postulates "love" and "direct feeling" as that which can mediate between the self and the other, the subject and the object, the part and the whole. Like Woolf, too, Mansfield derived this idea from her reading of Chekhov, a writer praised across the *Athenaeum* at this time. In his articles for the periodical, for instance, Murry argues that Chekhov is not an "intellectualist" who seeks to explain human experience or answer life's great problems; instead, he is a writer "driven to art by the excess of his humanity" and his work maintains "sensibility at its most sensitive, and experience at its most comprehensive."[85] This emphasis on comprehensiveness and universality is key: for Murry, the "great writer" is one who can refine "emotional experience" into "a system of emotional conviction" and thereby apprehend "the quality of life as a whole" and "make the particular a symbol of the universal."[86] Mansfield and Woolf promoted very similar ideas when reviewing Chekhov's work. Appraising Constance Garnett's translation of Chekhov's *The Bishop and Other Stories*, for example, Woolf writes of his story "The Steppe": "Without metaphor, the feelings of his characters are related to something more important and far more remote than personal success or happiness."[87] Corresponding with Koteliansky about "The Steppe," likewise, Mansfield writes: "One feels about this story not that it *becomes* immortal—it always was."[88] In this way, both writers place emphasis on how Chekhov's story moves beyond the particular, relating personal "feelings" at a level that is universal or timeless; as made clear in "Modern Novels," Chekhov's work conveys a comprehensive vision of "love" and "sympathy" that exceeds personal interest and egoism. In her review of a production of "The Cherry Orchard" published in July 1920, furthermore, Woolf writes: "I do not know how better to describe the sensation at the end of *The Cherry Orchard*, than by saying that it sends one into the street feeling like a piano played upon at last, not in the middle only but all over the keyboard and with the lid left open so that the sound goes on."[89] And in her own review of this production for the *Athenaeum*, Mansfield describes how all "that comes under the author's spell is bathed, is steeped and saturated in an emotional atmosphere."[90] For both Mansfield and Woolf, then, the work of Chekhov exemplified the qualities of emotion, sensation, compassion, and universality on which "modern fiction" should be based.

Attacked by both modernist writers themselves and subsequently dismissed in our critical accounts of the period, notions such as "sensibility" and "sympathy," or "emotion" and "empathy" have historically served to structure and stabilize a set of gendered and class-inflected binaries, between male/female, individual/community, reason/emotion, serious/popular, and minority/mass. As such, a despised and feminized mass culture of the mediocre and "sentimental" has often helped to bolster claims for modernist (male) exceptionality. On occasions, Woolf herself clearly subscribed to these distinctions, voicing suspicions of excessive personal "emotion" and self-indulgent "sentimentality." On reading Mansfield's "Bliss," for example, she dismissed the story as "so hard, & so shallow, & so sentimental."[91] Similarly, writing to Jacques Raverat in 1923, Woolf explained that she didn't like Mansfield's writing because as soon as she tried to "put thoughts, or feelings, or subtleties of any kind into her characters," she became either "hard" or "sentimental."[92] While these comments were perhaps motivated by professional jealousy on Woolf's part, Mansfield's contemporaries often accused her of producing "sentimental" writing. When Beatrice Hastings reviewed Mansfield's first short story collection for the *New Age* in 1911, for example, she accused the younger writer of exhibiting a "lachrymose sentimentality" that obscured an otherwise "amusing and refreshing" gift for observational satire.[93] This denigration of Mansfield's "sentimentality" served to place her beyond the pale of an emerging modernist culture of aesthetic impersonality and "classicism" then being developed within the pages of the *New Age* by the likes of T. E. Hulme and Ezra Pound. Arguably, Mansfield's posthumous reputation has also suffered under this charge of being too "sentimental." The gendered condemnation of "sentimentality" and "emotion" has inevitably served as a rod with which to beat the literary endeavors of women writers in particular. As Suzanne Clark has shown, however, the "sentimental" also provided a site of transgression, enabling women writers to conceptualize their own modernist "revolution of the word."[94] More recently, Meghan Marie Hammond has argued that modernism can be understood not only as a turn toward abstraction and a concomitant break with "empathy" but also as a reinvestment in the idea of "fellow feeling."[95] Hammond points to a number of modernist writers of the late nineteenth and early twentieth centuries, including Mansfield and Woolf, who promoted "sympathetic imagination" or "empathy" as integral to the modernist project, advancing the idea of "feeling with" or "feeling oneself into" the other. While Hammond points to the ways in which Mansfield and Woolf depict these empathetic acts with a certain ambivalence, noting the "psychological violence" often involved in the merging between the self and the other in Woolf's political writings and late novels, in particular, the notion that modernist writing should aim to overcome the barriers between different subjective entities through "compassion" or "emotion" runs directly counter to a version of modernism based upon the distancing techniques of abstraction and radical interiority.[96] In the current scholarly context of revisionary work that is exploding and complicating previously entrenched oppositions in our understanding of modernism, then, attentiveness to the ways in which individuals were committed to the idea of "emotion" as the basis for a new form of writing helps to reveal another strand or internal contradiction within modernist thought.

In the essays and reviews written in the years immediately following 1919, both Mansfield and Woolf emphasized deep "emotion" and "feeling" as essential to the coming "new word" of "modern fiction." Reading these critical writings, a common vocabulary emerges around the concept of "emotion" that suggests the extent to which Woolf's writings "talk" to Mansfield's, and vice versa. In particular, both writers employ "emotion" as a critical standard against which to evaluate works by the so-called "materialists" and those contemporary novelists influenced by the "new psychology." Moreover, it is the concept of "fellow feeling" that shapes Mansfield and Woolf's shared idea that modern fiction should aim to reach "outside and beyond" by mediating between the self and the other. On occasions, Mansfield's writings even preempt some of Woolf's later, more celebrated ideas, such as the concept of a revelatory "moment of being." Indeed, after Mansfield's death in 1923, her writings continued to speak to Woolf. When she read the posthumously published journals, for instance, Woolf was provoked by Mansfield's observation that writing should come from "deep feeling" into asking of herself: "Am I writing *The Hours* [*Mrs Dalloway*] from deep emotion? [...] Have I the power of conveying the true reality? Or do I write essays about myself?"[97] As Lee observes, "[t]his passage, so often quoted, where [Woolf] asks herself the crucial questions of her writing life, [came] directly out of her argument with Katherine."[98] As this chapter has examined, each woman's work provoked the other into questioning how the modern writer might produce fiction from the "deep original source" of emotion while avoiding the trap of personal sentimentality, thus conveying the "essential thing" or "true reality." Throughout their contemporaneous critical writings, then, Mansfield and Woolf can be seen to enact a dialogue in print, formulating remarkably similar ideas that help us to place "emotion" at the heart of literary modernism.

Notes

1 Anne Olivier Bell, ed. *The Diary of Virginia Woolf*, 5 vols. (London: Hogarth Press, 1978–1984), 2:45.
2 Virginia Woolf, "Modern Novels," in *The Essays of Virginia Woolf*, 6 vols., ed. Andrew McNeillie and Stuart Clarke (London: Hogarth Press, 1987–2000), 3:30–32.
3 Woolf, "Modern Novels," 32–33.
4 Woolf, "Modern Novels," 32–33.
5 Woolf, "Modern Novels," 34.
6 Woolf, "Modern Novels," 34.
7 Woolf, "Modern Novels," 35.
8 Woolf, "Modern Novels," 35.
9 Woolf, "Modern Novels," 36.

10 Woolf, "Modern Novels," 36.
11 Woolf, "Modern Novels," 35.
12 Katherine Mansfield to Virginia Woolf, c. May 27, 1919, in *The Collected Letters of Katherine Mansfield*, 5 vols., ed. Vincent O'Sullivan and Margaret Scott (Oxford: Clarendon Press, 1984–2008), 2:320. All subsequent letters from Mansfield are from this source.
13 Mansfield to Woolf, c. August 23, 1917, 1:327.
14 Bell, *Diary of Virginia Woolf*, 2:45–46.
15 Bell, *Diary of Virginia Woolf*, 2:61.
16 Mansfield to Woolf, December 27, 1920, 4:154.
17 Bell, *Diary of Virginia Woolf*, 2:227.
18 Suzanne W. Churchill and Adam McKible, introduction to *Little Magazines and Modernism: New Approaches*, ed. Churchill and McKible (Aldershot: Ashgate, 2007), 12–13.
19 Virginia Woolf, "How It Strikes a Contemporary," in McNeillie, *Essays of Virginia Woolf*, 3:354.
20 Hermione Lee, "Virginia Woolf's Essays," in *The Cambridge Companion to Virginia Woolf*, 2nd ed., ed. Susan Sellers (Cambridge: Cambridge University Press, 2010), 93.
21 Bell, *Diary of Virginia Woolf*, 1:257.
22 Virginia Woolf, "The Tunnel," in McNeillie, *Essays of Virginia Woolf*, 3:11; Katherine Mansfield, "Three Women Novelists," in *The Collected Works of Katherine Mansfield, Poetry and Critical Writings*, vol. 3, ed. Gerri Kimber and Angela Smith (Edinburgh: Edinburgh University Press, 2014), 446.
23 Katherine Mansfield, "Esther Waters Revisited," in Kimber and Smith, *Collected Works*, 643–44.
24 Katherine Mansfield, "Mr. Conrad's New Novel," in Kimber and Smith, *Collected Works*, 623.
25 Virginia Woolf, "Mr Byron & Mr Briggs," in McNeillie, *Essays of Virginia Woolf*, 3:487.
26 Virginia Woolf, Notebook, B2q (Silver, XLIX), Monk's House Papers, University of Sussex, quoted in Hermione Lee, *Virginia Woolf*, 2nd ed. (London: Vintage, 1997), 410.
27 Andrew McNeillie, "Bloomsbury," in Sellers, *Cambridge Companion to Virginia Woolf*, 3.
28 Clive Bell, *Art* (London: Chatto & Windus, 1914), 6; 8.
29 Bell, *Art*, 8.
30 Virginia Woolf, "On Re-reading Novels," in McNeillie, *Essays of Virginia Woolf*, 3:340.
31 J. M. M. [John Middleton Murry], "On Reading," *Athenaeum* no. 4712 (August 20, 1920), 235; "The Condition of English Poetry," *Athenaeum* no. 4675 (December 5, 1919), 1284–85.

32 T. S. E. [T. S. Eliot], "Hamlet and his Problems," *Athenaeum* no. 4665 (September 26, 1919), 941.
33 John Middleton Murry, *The Problem of Style* (London: Oxford University Press, 1922), 100.
34 Katherine Mansfield, "Observation Only," in Kimber and Smith, *Collected Works*, 673.
35 Mansfield, "Esther Waters Revisited," 643–44.
36 Virginia Woolf, "A Born Writer," in McNeillie, *Essays of Virginia Woolf,* 3:251.
37 Virginia Woolf, "Java Head," in McNeillie, *Essays of Virginia Woolf*, 3:49.
38 Katherine Mansfield, "Glancing Light," in Kimber and Smith, *Collected Works*, 477.
39 Mansfield, "Esther Waters Revisited," 643–44.
40 Katherine Mansfield, "Letters," in Kimber and Smith, *Collected Works*, 660.
41 Katherine Mansfield, "The Silence Is Broken," in Kimber and Smith, *Collected Works*, 683.
42 Katherine Mansfield, "A Citizen of the Sea," and "Portrait of a Little Lady," in Kimber and Smith, *Collected Works*, 452; 453.
43 John Middleton Murry to Katherine Mansfield, November 14, 1919, in *The Letters of John Middleton Murry to Katherine Mansfield*, ed. C. A. Hankin (London: Constable, 1983), 211.
44 Mansfield to John Middleton Murry, November 10, 1919, 3:82.
45 Katherine Mansfield, "Wanted, a New Word," in Kimber and Smith, *Collected Works*, 620.
46 J. M. M. [John Middleton Murry], "The Poetry of Mr. Hardy," *Athenaeum* no. 4671 (November 7, 1919), 1148.
47 Hermione Lee, introduction to *Moments of Being: Autobiographical Writings*, ed. Jeanne Schulkind (London: Pimlico, 2002), vii.
48 Virginia Woolf, "A Sketch of the Past," in Schulkind, *Moments of Being*, 85.
49 Katherine Mansfield, "A Model Story," in Kimber and Smith, *Collected Works*, 610.
50 Mansfield, "Mr. Conrad's New Novel," 623.
51 Mansfield to Ottoline Morrell, July 16, 1918, 2:254.
52 John Middleton Murry, ed., *Journal of Katherine Mansfield: Definitive Edition* (London: Constable, 1954), 202–3.
53 Katherine Mansfield, "A Novel without a Crisis," in Kimber and Smith, *Collected Works*, 467.
54 Katherine Mansfield, "A Short Story," in Kimber and Smith, *Collected Works*, 474–75.
55 Bell, *Diary of Virginia Woolf*, 2:61–62.
56 Mansfield to Dorothy Brett, October 11, 2017, 1:330.
57 Murry, *Journal of Katherine Mansfield*, 212.
58 Murry, *Journal of Katherine Mansfield*, 212.

59 Murry, *Journal of Katherine Mansfield*, 195; Mansfield to Richard Murry, c. January 25, 1920, 3:196.
60 Lee, "Virginia Woolf's Essays," 104.
61 Virginia Woolf, "The Decay of Essay-Writing," in McNeillie, *Essays of Virginia Woolf*, 1:27.
62 Woolf, Notebook, quoted in Lee, *Virginia Woolf*, 410.
63 Mansfield, "Three Women Novelists," 446.
64 Katherine Mansfield, "Dragonflies," in Kimber and Smith, *Collected Works*, 558.
65 Mansfield, "Dragonflies," 558.
66 Woolf, "The Tunnel," 10–11.
67 Woolf, "The Tunnel," 11.
68 Woolf, "Modern Novels," 35.
69 [John Middleton Murry], "Is There a New Generation?" *Athenaeum* no. 4703 (June 18, 1920), 789.
70 Katherine Mansfield, "Ask No Questions," in Kimber and Smith, *Collected Works*, 676.
71 Katherine Mansfield, "The 'Sex Complex,'" in Kimber and Smith, *Collected Works*, 501.
72 Virginia Woolf, "Freudian Fiction," in McNeillie, *Essays of Virginia Woolf*, 3:196–97.
73 Katherine Mansfield, "Two Modern Novels," in Kimber and Smith, *Collected Works*, 584.
74 Mansfield, "Two Modern Novels," 586.
75 Virginia Woolf, "September," in McNeillie, *Essays of Virginia Woolf*, 3:104.
76 Virginia Woolf, "The Intellectual Imagination," in McNeillie, *Essays of Virginia Woolf*, 3:134.
77 Katherine Mansfield, "Looking On," in Kimber and Smith, *Collected Works*, 609.
78 Katherine Mansfield, "A Foreign Novel," in Kimber and Smith, *Collected Works*, 546.
79 Anton Chekhov, "Letters of Anton Tchehov II" and "Letters of Anton Tchehov III," trans. by Katherine Mansfield and S. S. Koteliansky, in Kimber and Smith, *Collected Works*, 209–11.
80 Mansfield, "A Foreign Novel," 547.
81 Mansfield to Sylvia Lynd, c. February 12, 1921, 4:180; Mansfield to Richard Murry, c. January 25, 1920, 3:196.
82 Mansfield to Sydney Schiff, mid-February 1921, 4:180–81; Murry, *Journal of Katherine Mansfield*, 269.
83 Mansfield to Murry, November 10, 1920, 4:105; Murry, *Journal of Katherine Mansfield*, 228–29.
84 Murry, *Journal of Katherine Mansfield*, 205.
85 John Middleton Murry, "More Notes on Tchehov," *Athenaeum* no. 4732 (January 7, 1921), 12.

86 Murry, *Problem of Style*, 92–93.
87 Virginia Woolf, "The Russian Background," in McNeillie, *Essays of Virginia Woolf*, 3:85.
88 Mansfield to S. S. Koteliansky, August 21, 1919, 2:353.
89 Virginia Woolf, "The Cherry Orchard," in McNeillie, *Essays of Virginia Woolf*, 3:248.
90 Katherine Mansfield, "The Cherry Orchard," in Kimber and Smith, *Collected Works*, 632.
91 Virginia Woolf to Janet Case, March 20, 1922, in *The Letters of Virginia Woolf*, ed. Nigel Nicolson and Joanne Trautmann, 6 vols. (Hogarth Press, 1975–80), 2:514, quoted in Lee, *Virginia Woolf*, 393.
92 Virginia Woolf to Jacques Raverat, July 30, 1923, in Nicolson and Trautman, *Letters of Virginia Woolf*, 3:59, quoted in Lee, *Virginia Woolf*, 399.
93 [Beatrice Hastings], "In a German Pension," *New Age* 10, no. 8 (December 21, 1911): 188.
94 Suzanne Clark, *Sentimental Modernism: Women Writers and the Revolution of the Word* (Bloomington: Indiana University Press, 1991).
95 Meghan Marie Hammond, *Empathy and the Psychology of Literary Modernism* (Edinburgh: Edinburgh University Press, 2014).
96 Hammond, *Empathy and the Psychology of Literary Modernism*, 153.
97 Bell, *Diary of Virginia Woolf*, 2:248.
98 Lee, *Virginia Woolf*, 399.

11

Space of Debate, Debating Space: A Look at Irreverent Bloomsbury through the Lens of Mansfield's Stories

Ruchi Mundeja

There were tangerines and apples stained with strawberry pink. Some yellow pears, smooth as silk, some white grapes [...] and a big cluster of purple ones. These last she had bought to tone in with the new dining room carpet [...] When she had finished with them [...] she stood away from the table to get the effect—and it really was most curious. For the dark table seemed to melt into the dusky light and the glass dish and blue bowl to float in the air. This of course in her present mood was so incredibly beautiful.[1]

Her eyes had been going in and out among the curves and shadows of the fruit, among the rich purples of the lowland grapes [...] putting a yellow against a purple, a curved shape against a round shape [...] every time she did it, she felt more and more serene [...] She looked at Rose [...] How odd that one's child should do that![2]

Two moments couched in the domestic economy of the bourgeois home— moments where art seeks to reinvigorate the domestic, an art that is a hybrid mélange, a polyphonous riot, much like the buoyant experimentalism of the Bloomsbury interior. I have chosen to begin with these two vignettes as an indication of how the unorthodoxy of the "Blooms Berries" found its creative acme in lifestyle modernism and in Katherine Mansfield's reading/rendering of the same. As recent work by scholars such as Christopher Reed on Bloomsbury interiors has established, the aesthetic of the "Blooms Berries" pitched itself at the crossroads of the "domestic" and the "anti-domestic."[3] This chapter, through a sustained reading of the minutiae in some of Mansfield's stories, focuses on how, read against the backdrop of Empire, the overhauling of the traditional domestic partook liberally of the Empire's polyvocality. Monographs such as those by Reed and Mica Nava frame my reading of Bloomsbury's eclectic tastes. For instance, Mica Nava's work on consumer patterns in the Western metropolises becoming increasingly inflected by the impact of empire carries references to how the pale pastels of women's attire as well as domestic interiors were edged out by the more "barbaric" hues of jade, scarlet, and orange.[4] Nava's observation, intriguingly, finds a direct echo in a letter Vanessa Bell wrote to her sister in which she speaks of how the white walls of their dwelling were regally transformed by "Indian shawls of brilliant colors" that, draped strategically all over, "look rather fine and barbaric."[5] My subsequent discussion hinges around how Mansfield, with a minute eye, worked the (imperial) consumerism that undergirded Bloomsbury's cultivation of anti-insularity into her stories. The stories that I propose to look at become test cases for how Mansfield consumes the Bloomsburian spatial ethos, and how her own spatial positionality, as a woman *and* as a "colonial," is the interpretative filter.

To look a little more closely at the two passages: While the pear tree dominates critical discussion on "Bliss," the whiff of fruit enters the story through another side door—the blue dish overladen with fruit arranged to perfection by Bertha as soon as she reenters the house. As the feeling of bliss overwhelms Bertha, this radiant centerpiece of the dining table becomes one of its creative signifiers. In Woolf's *To the Lighthouse* the bowl of fruit, colorful and innovative, arranged with gay abandon by the Ramsay daughter, Rose, is admired by Mrs. Ramsay for the *experimentalism* of the arrangement. Woolf treads delicately between recognizing the autonomous creative genius of the girl and also registering how this aligns itself with Mrs. Ramsay's creative domesticity, that which lifts the Ramsay household above the level of "clucking domesticities."[6] Hence Mrs. Ramsay's "serenity"—she sees her daughter's artistry as a bequest; its "oddness," coalescing into a marvel of aestheticism, is seen as a continuation of her own legacy—that gift she possesses of merging and unifying is juxtaposed throughout the scene against the sterile, univocal, linearity of the masculine world. What both vignettes offer are polychromatic canvases. Read from within the frame of gender, the two scenarios are a creative riposte to the idea of (masculine) regimentation. And if one were to employ the prism of empire, they can be read as suggestive of how the landscape of the imperial metropolis, impacted by the hybridized flux of empire, was rendered, in the words of Urmila Seshagiri, "marvelously supple."[7] The two passages speak of an embrace of fluidity and malleability, key concepts in Bloomsbury's iconoclastic understanding of both empire and gender. This leads forward to my later discussion of how, for the women in the stories I have chosen, the unhomely becomes a way to escape/critique the homely. In both cases, by a virtuoso display of a hybrid mix-up of elements, a staid domestic arrangement is turned into a statement by the women characters. But while in Woolf it is of a piece with her theoretical standpoint vis-à-vis gender, in Mansfield, Bertha's "bliss" is in the ultimate analysis, a more tentative groping for self-expression. Authors like Mansfield, with their own off-center positioning, bring in a sense of the more conflicted, even compromised (given the fact that Mansfield keeps Bertha's class privileges firmly in view), nature of rebellion.

These two passages, then, are a suggestive entry point into the different positionalities of the two writers, one at the vanguard of Bloomsbury experimentalism, and the other occupying a more fraught inside-outside space. Woolf's cerebral engagement with otherness throughout her fiction can be read against Mansfield's more direct experience of finding herself "othered" (as her journals and letters reflect) in the subculture of coteries. This would also help readdress the debate on the "contours of privilege" in women's writing and to recognize that though gender is certainly a focal point in the works of women writers of the early decades of the twentieth century, it is equally important to read them along the multiple axes of class, nationality, background, and race.[8]

The Bloomsbury experiment was seminally related to an overhauling of domestic space. Bloomsbury's nerve center of the privatized conversational arena can be read as the locus of a transgressive challenge to, vis-à-vis its cerebral and sexual heterodoxy, the "moralizing solemnity" of the domestic.[9] Both Woolf and Mansfield register its liberatory potential for women in particular. But while "Bliss" does show Bertha as partaking of the bohemianism of her set in arranging the dish, it is contextualized as aligned to her current state of rapture. These moments of women's self-expression in Mansfield are not knitted into an ideological whole as they are in Woolf. Mansfield does not effect the transition from the experiential to the ideological in quite the way that Woolf does. Mansfield leaves us with unresolved issues, curtailed epiphanies, all of which bespeak qualified, truncated, half-articulated moments of revolt, such as Bertha's, as I argue later. Mrs. Ramsay's reading of her daughter's creative flourish is contiguous with Woolf's conceptual economy where heroines like Clarissa Dalloway, whose terrain is the domestic arena, interrupt its patriarchal solemnity by their gift for assemblages. Mansfield's women often enact covert acts of nonacceptance unfolding shadowily in the interstices of conformism and protest, not quite as definitive as Woolf's more programmatic and exhortative feminism.

That this difference can to some extent be linked to the dynamics of center/periphery, high/low, European/"colonial," privilege/delinquency, and emplacement/marginality strands in modernist studies is perhaps best glossed by one of Mansfield's own statements: "How I envy Virginia; no wonder she can write. There is always in her writing a calm freedom of expression as though she were at peace—her roof over her, her own possessions round her."[10] While Mansfield's statement is open to contestation, it does importantly raise the question of authorial and locational positionality. Mansfield identifies Woolf as emplaced, in implicit juxtaposition to her own displaced, itinerant existence. Not only did Mansfield cross continents and countries but, as Gillian Boddy points out, John Middleton Murry's estimate was that they lived in no fewer than thirteen houses in two years.[11] Thus, though Bloomsbury is the common frame for these writers, the parallels are not seamless, and Mansfield's hyphenated status makes her more a skeptical consumer of the Bloomsbury milieu than its acolyte. As the "little colonial," Mansfield stood at a distance from this self-perpetuating mythos of modernist heresy, of which Bloomsbury was such a vociferous component. Though there is much in Mansfield's writing that is steeped in modernist aesthetics, there is also a component that looks askance at what Molly Hite terms their "canon forming polemics."[12] It is these resistant nerve centers that this chapter explores.

The spaces of modernism are rife with "rooms" that inseminate the literary firmament with a surcharged vitality. Domestic space was so much the crucible of oppositionality and avant-gardism, whether one thinks of Garsington Manor, Ford Madox Ford's and Violet Hunt's "South Lodge" Villa in Kensington, or of course Bloomsbury itself. Inside accounts of Bloomsbury, in consonance with the high-adrenalin narrative of modernist iconoclasm, configure it as a platform for nonconformist stances. How does this measure against formulations on bourgeois domestic space? Commenting on the prohibitive repressiveness written into the "normative" domestic economy of the bourgeois home in *The Production of Space*, Henri Lefebvre observes how the "bourgeois space implies a filtering of the erotic, a repression of *libidines*."[13] He argues that in the increasing spatial subdivisions of the bourgeois home, bodily functions are thrust out of sight. Victoria Rosner, commenting on how the Victorian bourgeois home worked along the principle of a sanctimonious compartmentalization, says, "A 'good' house, a proper house, is one in which rooms maintain social and spatial discretion."[14] It is in the radicalization and sexualization of that same bourgeois interior that Bloomsbury's adversarialism is located. That "climactic" moment when Strachey uttered the word "semen" in the drawing room has been enshrined in the accounts of the Stephen sisters as in most subsequent modernist histories as the moment when the domestic was penetrated by the sexual. As Peter Brooker points out, this set the agenda for "the remorseless sniping at sham and hypocrisy," and for Vanessa Bell, it indicated what "complete freedom of expression and mind" meant.[15]

How then was this compelling narrative of heterodoxy read and consumed by a writer participating in these formations and yet often in a precariously poised relationship with them? Though arguably Mansfield is seen as casting her lot with the "Blooms Berries," her piquant location modulates her reception of Bloomsbury's gestures of self-construction. One might frame the argument in terms of the distinction Lefebvre draws (though in a different context) between space of consumption, that is, how Bloomsbury's radicalism of design and performance drew on imperial goods and idioms, and consumption of space,[16] which would pertain to how Mansfield watchfully perceived and read this hotbed of irreverence.

Inveighing against Victorian prudery, sexual talk pervaded the Bloomsbury interior, but that its registers of heterodoxy were compromised by class, race, and nationality is also clear. For instance, there was Strachey holding forth on how "one's amours are very like the British Empire—all over the shop, in every sort of unexpected ridiculous corner. One plants one's penis on so many peculiar spots!"[17] Whether this be read as an ironic glance at the expansionary zeal of the empire or in terms of Strachey's own sexual nonconformity, the imagery of phallic *jouissance* he evokes reads rather unfortunately for a postcolonial reader, since it bespeaks a sensibility insouciantly at home in the imperial imaginary. The Bloomsburians quite self-consciously staged their scandalous tableaux as a peeling away of the layers of accreted conventionalisms to reveal the provocative substratum beneath, contiguous with the project of modernism. Women, such as the Stephen sisters, were decidedly active participants in these exhumatory experiments of Bloomsbury. Thus, this would on one level have been attractive to a free-spirited woman such as Mansfield. My reading registers that, but equally pressingly pays heed to traces of the ironically resistant in her stories dealing with the "Blooms Berries." Mansfield's positioning as a woman writer from the colonial periphery shapes her qualified depiction of the irreverence of the "Blooms Berries" even as she grasps its emancipatory potentialities for women. Interestingly, in the stories that this chapter examines, it is the women who are most conspicuously associated with the cosmopolitanized imperial landscape. This would imply that, as a reader, one needs to tread carefully, to be attuned to how the satirizing of imperial consumerism in Mansfield's stories is held in careful balance against the opportunities for expansiveness the overhauling of the domestic offered to women chafing against the confinement of the "homely."

The stories I have chosen for analysis, "Bliss," "A Cup of Tea," and "Marriage à la Mode," engage with the modernist provenance of Bloomsbury in an interesting way since they mime its movement from outside to inside, a microspace jousting with the macrodynamics of empire, war, gender, and so on. Writers like Mansfield who wrote on the peripheries of the developing canon of modernism provide an insight into what I term the inverted narcissism of modernist writing: that is, how each movement outward, its gestures of "centrifugal patronage" (to borrow a phrase from Timothy Bewes), was ultimately directed inward, geared toward either the angst of self-examination or the quest for self-revitalization.[18] In *Culture and Imperialism* Edward Said speaks of how, from the point of view of the West, other cultures have been either pathologized or embraced as therapeutic.[19] In keeping with modernism's anti-institutional spirit, while the bourgeoisie was wary of the unhomely, the modernists cast it as the necessary therapy for an increasingly mechanized civilization and also played on its primitive uninhibitedness as the much needed shock to the puritanical bourgeoisie, such as in "Bliss" when Mrs. Norman Knight revels in how her unconventional dress scandalized all the people on the train. Thus, the way in which the domestic space can be approached in these stories looks back at an essential feature of Bloomsbury—its aesthetic embrace of the other, as the cross-traffic of imperialism told on the consumer spectacle. The trope of *flânerie* brings into modernist literature an apprehension of increasing metropolitan polyphony. Bloomsbury sought to rework the domestic interior to reflect this cosmopolitanized flavor, but with scant concern for the geographical or material coordinates of these gleanings. In a wily parallel enactment, Mansfield brings the variegated panorama of the shopping arcades into the bourgeois home in these narratives.

In "Bliss," the story opens to reveal Bertha's present rhapsodic mood of bliss, where the bohemianism of her set is adopted in an individualized manner by her. That Bertha's experimental flings are bolstered by the consumerist paradise easily accessible to someone of her class is a fact not glossed over by the writer. For instance, the reference to the fruit as displayed in a blue dish with a strange sheen, given her husband's later reference to how the very sourcing of the objects in their home evokes a dynamic colonial circuitry, brings into the story the specter of imperial consumerism. In fact, in a characteristically blustering manner, Harry preens in front of Pearl Fulton as he shakes a silver box full of cigarettes at her: "Egyptian? Turkish? Virginian? They're all mixed up."[20] The terminology (the allusion to "mix-up") is directly evocative of a culturally miscegenated imperial landscape. The subsequent characterization of Harry as a man whose swagger is based on his possessions brings to mind Carole Sweeney's observation that "An aesthetic appreciation of non-Western culture as artefactual domestic commodity does not produce an equivalent political tolerance."[21] That the exploitative antecedents of these imperial collectibles that increasingly graced upper-middle-class bourgeois homes would scarcely concern someone as self-absorbed as Harry is self-evident. This would also be in line with this comment from Lefebvre: "Produced or worked objects pass from the space of labor to the enveloping social space only once the traces of labor have been effaced from them."[22]

It is in how Mansfield portrays this toying with otherness vis-à-vis Bertha that her own inside-outside stance manifests itself. In the plush interiors of Bertha's bourgeois salon, this foregrounding of otherness furthers Bertha's nascent stirrings to transgress the boundaries of the heterosexist marital bind. Bertha's consumerist forays are treated more tolerantly by Mansfield; the annoying, fawning eclecticism of the Norman Knights, on the other hand, is panned with a delightfully ironic flourish. Mansfield reserves her wickedest satire for the poseur-guests at Bertha's party. Koppen speaks of the sartorial derring-do of the Bloomsburians as a crucial facet in their self-invention.[23] As the Norman Knights enter, the narrator lingers over the attire sported by Mrs. Norman Knight, a bright orange coat with a procession of monkeys embroidered on its hem. The coat comes off to reveal a dress of vivid yellow, made out of scraped banana skins. If one recalls Vanessa Bell's account of Duncan Grant's inspired visualization of her studio at Gordon Square as a giant tropical forest,[24] or if we turn for a minute to Eric Hobsbawm's reminder of how tropical fruits like bananas flooded the imperial city,[25] one sees how the riotous excess built into her look visually elucidates Janet Lyon's reference to an imperializing cosmopolitanism.[26] The lady follows up the visual challenge with this remark: "Why! Why! Why is the middle class so stodgy—so utterly without a sense of humor! […] For my darling monkeys so upset the train that it rose to a man and simply ate me with its eyes. Didn't laugh—wasn't amused—that I should have loved. No, just stared—and bored me through and through."[27] Writing against the backdrop of empire, Mansfield would want us to take note of the imperial-racial registers of both the design elements and the phobic hostility with which it is received. Recent work on colonialism has revealed that with imperial progeny and the empire's material spillover dotting the imperial corridors, the colonial gaze was transplanted into the metropolis. While the passengers on the train enact its hysterics, Mrs. Norman Knight parades her willingness to plunge into the diaphanous folds of the imperial fabric. Modernism's fascination with cultural difference is legendary, but what these moments make us ask is: Did that necessarily entail a dialogue between cultures?

What Mansfield brings into the story with the entry of the arty clique is "the unremitting newness of modernity," which is portrayed in all its cannibalistic zeal, borrowing from other, (ironically) older cultures and art forms.[28] In her almost filmic description, Mansfield draws on her own experiences of being witness to Bloomsbury hijinks. Alison Light reminds us, for instance, that "The Stephen siblings were not Bohemians glorying in […] eating scratch meals" and that their bohemianism existed in uneasy conjunction with a thorough "dependence" on servants.[29] With her own brushes with poverty and deprivation, Mansfield in her of/not of position could catch these ironies better.

Mansfield's conflictual and divided relationship with Bloomsbury is figured in "Bliss" in terms of the split between Bertha and the rest of the arty set. Bertha's toying with Bloomsburian notions is seen as gendered and personalized, as opposed to the facetious and parodic Bohemianism of the others. Mansfield's edgy positioning vis-à-vis the Bloomsburian insiders rendered her recalcitrant to its expansive gestures—the earthbound nature of her vision resisted their etherealized flights and stubbornly brought the unsublime corporeal into the frame. Again, in "Bliss" this is presented more from the inside in Bertha's revolt against civilization's wanting to keep the body shut in a case like a "rare, rare fiddle," her desire to open out her body to taste the "brimming cup of bliss."[30] But the irony turns sharper in that wonderful vignette where Eddie Warren quotes what he considers an incredibly beautiful line—"Why must it always be tomato soup?"—as the story moves toward the analogically predictable denouement of adultery. Mansfield achieves a double effect here—even as the Bohemian wannabe's poetic credentials are held up to scorn, the discovery of infidelity is itself shorn of a glamorized portrayal, so "dreadfully eternal" like tomato soup.[31] Mansfield treads carefully between portraying Bertha's heartbreak but also an acute awareness of the deceptions that pull at the marital structure. My argument is in line with Aimee Gasston's strong emphasis not on the transcendent quality of her work, but its material obduracy, which Gasston sees as an "anti-aristocratic formulation of modernism."[32] Could Woolf's aversion to the story be traced back to Mansfield's stubborn refusal to sublimate quotidian domestic infelicities at the end, leaving us only with that intensely visceral image of the nakedly carnal, "hideous grin" that Bertha sees on Harry's face as he bends toward Pearl?[33]

While the domestic space in "Bliss" foregrounds the conspicuously exoticist through attire and objects, the next story I look at, "A Cup of Tea," centers its title on an item that is more complexly poised vis-à-vis the quotidian and the exotic. As I go on to discuss, this story plays with the implications of the homely/unhomely through the symbolization of tea. Urmila Seshagiri argues that the recurrent symbols of tea and china in modernist fiction render impossible any belief in "the unified, undifferentiated white English subject," and that even as these commodities were through the centuries transformed into "signifiers of Englishness," one needs to bear in mind that they were originally appropriated from the East.[34] Eric Hobsbawm points out how by the end of the nineteenth century Britons increasingly filled their teapots from India and Ceylon.[35] This engagement with the exotic is thus contained in the title of "A Cup of Tea" and how it is pressed into service to enliven the domestic space. Erika Rappaport does an extensive analysis of "Empire Tea." She shows how a colonial product like tea became the site for an accreting imperial conversation, reaching a crescendo in the 1930s. She describes the 1931 massive Drink Empire Tea campaign that "intended to teach British tea buyers and drinkers to prefer teas from India, Ceylon and British East Africa to those from the Netherlands East Indies."[36] She also points out how women in particular were recruited into the Empire Buying ideology. There was the Primrose League that looked at shopping as knitting together "Home, Nation and Empire," and the League of Empire Housewives that adopted as their motto the making of "Every Kitchen an Empire Kitchen."[37] She argues emphatically that no commodity was as inextricably associated with empire as was tea. Thus, the Buy Empire campaign, though impelled by commercial considerations, also harnessed the talismanic appeal of the Empire. There is also a reference in Rappaport's article to how there was a difference between the informed, discerning upper-middle-class buyer of imperial goods and the lower-rung citizens who "were generally receptive to the idea of empire shopping [but] on the whole ignorant about tea production and imperial geography."[38]

"A Cup of Tea" centers around a cup of the brew shared between two women divided by the gulf of class. Rosemary Fell belongs to the plush set, and the girl she befriends and brings home is portrayed as a wastrel. The story opens with a peek into Rosemary's life, and the consumerist paradise that defines her is the focus of the description. The cosmopolitan strivings of Rosemary are contained in references to how, while most people would shop in Bond Street, Rosemary's refined pursuits take her to Paris, where in her "rather exotic way" she finds herself in her element.[39] Friedberg notes how "By the middle of the nineteenth century, as if in a historical relay of looks, the shop window succeeded the mirror as a site of identity construction."[40] The shop windows that beckon and the stores Rosemary visits go into her self-presentation as "extremely modern."[41] In bringing the "quaint" into her home, whether it be in the form of bohemian artists or antiques, she partakes of the experimental proclivities of the modernist salons. That Mansfield relates Rosemary's sourcings to women's resistance to marital anonymity is clear from the desultory emptiness that overcomes her as she walks away without purchasing an unusual box, with the battered young woman appearing miraculously as a substitute for it. What is interesting is that just at that juncture, Rosemary thinks of having an "extra-special tea" to assuage her sense of unfulfillment.[42] Tea here becomes a measure of her knowledgeable consumerism since this could be read as evidence of her awareness of special blends and brands and another manifestation of the co-optive embrace of the "other" to give a density to her own life.

The other implication, that the ubiquitous presence of these products made them almost English in their wide usage, is also present in the story. This comes in through the girl who, in line with the argument of Rappaport, is the passive, uninformed consumer for whom tea is only a familiar English custom. She refuses brandy and only pines for the warmth that a cup of tea can give her. Rosemary ensures that she has her fill of it: "Every time her cup was empty she filled it with tea, cream and sugar. People always said that sugar was so nourishing."[43] In the introduction to *Empire of Tea*, the authors identify tea and sugar as foremost among the nonnative material commodities that had a radically transformative effect on patterns of British consumption.[44] One wonders whether Mansfield was deliberately playing upon the knowledge of empire since the story quite startlingly "orients" itself to such a reading. Joanna de Groot speaks of how complexly interwoven the "circuits of capital, exchange and consumption" were in imperial times.[45] This would account perhaps for a blurring of the origins of tea. Arguing also that tea chains such as the ABC were "aimed at those of modest means," de Groot cites Forrest's point that on the metropolitan map the "natural habitat of the teashops was … the less exclusive shopping streets"; this landscape would account for the girl's metropolitan at-homeness with tea, her unawareness of its imperial origins.[46]

The nourishing effects of tea and sugar conjoined conflate in the young woman's case into a homely narrative. But the postcolonial reader cannot but make the connection with the colonial horrors that silently reside in colonial products like sugar in particular. To that extent, a readjustment of perspective can reveal how close the émigré writers from the colonial peripheries sometimes come to the later insights of postcolonial theorists. Stuart Hall's self-scrutiny of immigrants to England like himself reads thus:

> People like me who came to England in the 1950s have been there for centuries: symbolically, we have been there for centuries. I was coming home. I am the sugar at the bottom of the English cup of tea […] There are thousands of others beside me that are, you know, the cup of tea itself. Because they don't grow it in Lancashire, you know. Not a single tea plantation exists within the United Kingdom. This is the symbolization of English identity—I mean, what does anybody in the world know about an English person except that they can't get through the day without a cup of tea?[47]

The tea and the sugar that are viewed in the story as rejuvenating and nourishing are as exotic as the other objects that Rosemary craves, though their ubiquity in English life, as Hall suggests, belies this. Interestingly, when Rosemary visits the little treasure-house of antiques and collectibles, one of the objects she sees on display is a teakettle. Mansfield's story evokes through the symbol of tea the intermeshing, indeed blurring, trajectories of the homely and the unhomely.

Having partaken of the cornucopia of empire, the girl displays the languor of the satiated imperial consumer and transforms into a "new being."[48] It is now time for another kind of consumerism to come into play—Rosemary's aestheticization of the young woman as the "model" of alterity: "Rosemary lit a fresh cigarette; it was time to begin."[49] The girl becomes another collectible in Rosemary's appropriative and eclectic consumerism. The ritual of tea that is the site of assembly thus marks various levels of consumerist incursions into distant, alien, "unhomely" realms. Through her interaction with the young woman, Rosemary ventures into the unfamiliar realm of the underclass. Rosemary's acute self-consciousness is evidence of how Mansfield is ironizing the anti-insular gestures that animated high modernism. This is Rosemary's social experiment, her induction into the domestic sphere of the alien. When her husband plays on her wifely possessiveness to get rid of the intruder, Rosemary cultivates an exoticism to rival that of the stranger. Mansfield explores both the possibilities and limits of domestic experiments. Her fine-grained irony allows for an understanding of Rosemary's consumer forays as both appropriative and self-defining. The self-absorption of Rosemary's sourcings is recorded with unerring honesty by Mansfield, yet employing the filter of gender, she writes from the inside of Rosemary's connoisseurship as the *raison d'être* of her marital existence. In line with the self-performativity of modernist culture, Mansfield's married protagonists bring the performative into the home to combat, even disrupt, the staid normativity of their bourgeois existence.

Mica Nava has written extensively on how the department store culture of the first few decades of the twentieth century drew upon the pervasive iconography of the oriental. Nava points out that the stores staged their own tableaux to parallel the imperial exhibitions: "Spectacular oriental extravaganzas which included live tableaux of Turkish harems, Cairo markets, or Hindu temples with live performers, dance, music, and of course oriental products" were frequently organized.[50] She discusses how Selfridges created a business empire out of this symphonic interplay between consumerism and the exotic.[51] In *Bohemia in London*, Peter Brooker's engaging study of the "lifestyle modernism," that is, the fashions, fads, lifestyles of the artistic set in the modernist period, he cites John Drummond to point out that following the premiere of *Scheherazade*, blue, orange, turquoise, and velvet found favor with the dressmakers of Paris.[52] That Bloomsbury was a part of this sartorial and cultural frenzy to embrace the new is corroborated by Brooker's account. Relying on Vanessa Bell's reminiscences, he mentions how at the Post-Impressionist ball, the Bloomsbury denizens draped themselves in cloth worn by natives in Africa sourced from Burnett's and completed the impression by browning their legs and arms and by sporting flowers and beads.[53]

Employing a similar frame of consumerism, "Marriage à la Mode" traces the fluctuating marital fortunes of Isabel and William through consumer patterns, with Isabel's turn to novelty contrasted against William's loyalty to the familiar. Mansfield cleverly uses a consumerist idiom to map out the faltering trajectory of their married life. This is a particularly difficult tale to bracket since while Mansfield's examination of marital existence inclines toward an understanding of women's entrapment, the critique of the Bohemian necessarily entails recognizing Isabel's complicity in its trendy shallowness. However, the two strands are also interwoven where Isabel's taking to its theatrics is a reaction against William's refusal to grant her individuality—like when he wishes to control who she consorts with, his greatest regret being her introduction to Moira Morrison. Whether his instincts about her "crowd" are correct or not is another matter, but what is incontrovertibly present in their relationship is his complete inability to see the element of stasis that plagues Isabel. For instance, when Isabel points out how they needed to move out of their too tiny, "poky little" house, he sees her point at one level, yet cannot let go of the nostalgia as the pride of that house in London remains his most precious memory of the idyll he feels those years were.[54] It is space that is at the crux of the debate: For William it is a space that disallows room for Isabel's expansion. For him, the understanding that it could be cramped for her can be measured vis-à-vis spatial dimensions, yet he is reluctant to face up to its other resonances: "He hadn't the remotest notion […] that she was desperately lonely, pining for new people and new music."[55]

It is this impulse that guides what might be seen as Isabel's callous toying with the marital space in "Marriage à la Mode." Interestingly, the story opens with William's thoughts on his marriage and children, a clear indication of how he is far more invested in the domestic structure than Isabel. There are, of course, the satirical flashes, such as Isabel's newly acquired taste in foreign toys that will improve her children's "sense of form."[56] William's ruminations on how Isabel is in his mind allied to a world of childhood freshness betray his own refusal to grow up, his childish desire to freeze-frame his marriage as a never-ending idyll, which leads to his lack of awareness of Isabel's loneliness. More generally, too, William's seeing life through the lens of prearranged categories is clear from the pronouncements he makes at the spectacle he sees through the train window: a girl running alongside the train is cast as an instance of (feminine?) "hysteria," and a workman at the end of the platform is viewed as an example of "filthy" low life.[57] Conversely, Mansfield does not let Isabel's Bohemian gang off the hook. The story details how their artistic flamboyance feeds off William. Mansfield wickedly delineates a parallel between the gastronomic excesses and artistic dilettantism of Isabel's artistic finds such as when the nougat is described as "a perfect little ballet" by Bobby Kane.[58]

Woolf's essay, "Bloomsbury," reflects how she envisaged their move to the new location—it is the domestic that becomes the bearer of transgressive rupture with the past: "We were full of experiments and reforms. We were going to do without table napkins, we were to have [large supplies of] Bromo instead; we were going to paint; to write; to have coffee after dinner instead of tea at nine o'clock. Everything was going to be new; everything was going to be different. Everything was on trial."[59] So we come back again to how the laboratory for the Bloomsbury experiment was the home and that the throwing over of old consumer commodities and patterns were the sites of transgression.

"Marriage à la Mode" opens with William anguishing over how he has again bought fruits for his children. Thus, Mansfield engages with the lifestyle modernism of the Bloomsbury set, and hence her chosen site, too, is the domestic. William's buying sprees seem repetitive and nonadventurous when juxtaposed against the avant-garde pretensions of Isabel's friends. William's reminiscences circle around how the domestic was earlier cozily shorn of these novelties: he recalls how initially homely domestic objects doubled up as the children's toys—many a mock battle fought with shovels, tongs, and so on. A little down the years, they were playing with familiar choices like toy animals, and he fondly remembers finding lopped-off limbs of the toy animals strewn around the house. Mansfield again gives the reader very little room for glib pronouncements in the way she juxtaposes William's conservative consumerism and the related implication of unimaginativeness to the annoyingly self-serving consumerist éclat of Isabel's friends. Isabel's experimental jauntiness is at times rendered from the outside, but Mansfield also creates space for an alternate interpretation. Mansfield holds the balance between William's nostalgic need for sameness—"And he was still that little boy"—and Isabel's yearning for change, though the "rebels" she chooses as her cronies are presented in the most unflattering manner.[60] Isabel might strike one as vapid and uninvolved, but that is the deliberate space Mansfield provides her women characters for preservation of autonomy, the possibility of uninhabitation, if one may coin that word. By not investing completely in the domestic structure, by enacting a withdrawal, her women retain a private voice of critique and commentary.

"Marriage à la Mode" makes for a telling as also perplexing study in Mansfield's conflicted take on the "Blooms Berries," how she both ironizes them yet at the same time holds on to their liberatory agenda, specifically vis-à-vis women. This story, too, like "A Cup of Tea" and "Bliss," plays off an increasingly cosmopolitanized landscape against William's attempt to hold on to a more knowable, identifiably English one. Early on in the story, William feels nonplussed by how his buying sprees for his children are now complicated by the influx of foreign goods on display: "In the old days, of course, he would have taken a taxi off to a decent toyshop and chosen them something in five minutes. But nowadays they had Russian toys, French toys, Serbian toys—toys from God knows where."[61] The vocabulary here points to the insular in his consciousness—his resistance to newness/change. Pitted against that are the anti-insular flourishes of Isabel's friends—their overeager embrace of the foreign, all in their pursuit to "make it new." As the unhomely enters the homely in this story, it is analyzed in terms of its self-serving fashionableness, yet at the same time it becomes an important leveraging point to expose the paranoias of the "old." With her experience of both colony and periphery, artists like Mansfield were especially primed to read into the hysteria of self-protection exhibited by the imperial metropolis, as also its obverse, the triumphal note of self-reinvigoration through an embrace of the alien that ruled in artistic circles. The ambivalence of the tale gathers into that one line at the end, as Isabel, after sharing an intensely private missive from her husband with her "set," withdraws in a moment of distress into her room: "Down she sat on the side of the bed. 'How vile, odious, abominable, vulgar,' muttered Isabel."[62] Who is the reference to? Is it to Isabel herself? Is it meant to be a castigation of her friends? Or could it be a reference to William's (as suggested by the word "vulgar") unfashionable sentimentalism? I believe that the fact that it could be any or all of these is where the complexity of Mansfield's response to Bloomsbury resides.

In this chapter, I have tried to examine the fine line that Mansfield treads as both a participant in and a caustic reader/recorder of the conversational, performative, and ideational exuberance of the "Blooms Berries." Given her locational ambivalence, Mansfield reads astutely the coterie nature of the group, such as in her recording of how the "other" is rendered a consumable commodity in the search for novelty, as in Rosemary's "exoticizing" of poverty in "A Cup of Tea." At one point the Norman Knights are referred to as a very "sound" couple.[63] Is this Mansfield's antipodean backlash against how the compelling narrative of modernist heresy was made possible by entrenchment in a sound, secure, privileged structure? If immersion in the flourishes of its gestures of iconoclasm is modernism's hubris, then outré figures like Rhys and Mansfield expose these fissures by writing a sly counternarrative to it. One can appreciate how prescient these critiques were in terms of the long critical afterlife they have had, such as in Gretchen Holbrook Gerzina's mention of Sir Christopher Ondaatje's remarks on the telling silence of most Bloomsbury denizens on Leonard Woolf's anti-imperial *The Village in the Jungle*. Gerzina mentions this by way of problematizing Bloomsbury's aesthetic engagement with the other.[64] Mansfield's stated ambition to "write with acid" finds fullest expression in her skeptical consumption of the Bloomsburian narrative.[65] Again one wonders if Woolf's dislike of "Bliss" was founded on Mansfield's writing with venom, a mode of writing Woolf inveighed against in *A Room of One's Own*, a proviso significantly stemming from Woolf's discomfiture with Charlotte Bronte's recording of the inchoate, infantile rage of Bertha Mason, the colonial other. By letting the rancor and acid seep into her writing, Mansfield implicitly problematizes the exclusionisms of the Bloomsbury set.

Notes

1. Katherine Mansfield, "Bliss," in *The Collected Works of Katherine Mansfield, The Collected Fiction 1916–1922*, vol. 2, ed. Gerri Kimber and Vincent O'Sullivan (Edinburgh: Edinburgh University Press, 2012), 142–43.
2. Virginia Woolf, *To the Lighthouse* (1927; London: Penguin Books, 1992), 118.
3. Christopher Reed, *Bloomsbury Rooms: Modernism, Subculture and Domesticity* (New Haven: Yale University Press, 2004), 3. Reed's extended argument revolves around how the radicalized politico-aesthetic agenda of the Bloomsbury group found its materialization in "the modernist dwelling, which becomes a kind of anti-home."
4. See Mica Nava, *Visceral Cosmopolitanism: Gender, Culture and the Normalization of Difference* (Berg: Oxford University Press, 2007), 32.
5. Reed, *Bloomsbury Rooms*, 23.
6. Woolf, *To the Lighthouse*, 27.
7. Urmila Seshagiri, *Race and the Modernist Imagination* (New York: Cornell University Press, 2010), 7.
8. Rosemary Marangoly George, "Feminists Theorize Colonial/Postcolonial," in *Cambridge Companion to Feminist Literary Theory*, ed. Ellen Rooney (Cambridge: Cambridge University Press, 2006), 220.
9. Henri Lefebvre, *The Production of Space*, trans. Donald Nicholson-Smith (Oxford: Blackwell Publishing, 1974), 315.
10. Katherine Mansfield to John Middleton Murry, November 30, 1919, quoted in Gillian Boddy, *Katherine Mansfield: The Woman and the Writer* (Victoria: Penguin Book, 1988), 71. Jean Rhys, another "savage" from the colonies, similarly commented on the cliquey, clubby feel of metropolitan art coteries: "Everything is clubs in London, isn't it? Clubs, clubs…" Jean Rhys, *Good Morning, Midnight* (1939; London: Penguin Books, 2000), 131.
11. Boddy, *Woman and the Writer*, 41.
12. Molly Hite, "The Public Woman and the Modernist Turn: Virginia Woolf's *The Voyage Out* and Elizabeth Robins's *My Little Sister*," *Modernism/Modernity* 17, no. 3 (2010): 523. Hite uses this phrase while discussing how Woolf, in her nonfictional writings such as her "great modernist polemic" "Mr Bennett and Mrs Brown," left out in the cold her women precursors from the Edwardian period, thus relegating them to relative obscurity.
13. Lefebvre, *Production of Space*, 315.
14. Victoria Rosner, *Modernism and the Architecture of Private Life* (New York: Cambridge University Press, 2004), 65.
15. Vanessa Bell, *Sketches in Pen and Ink: A Bloomsbury Notebook*, ed. Lia Giachero (London: Hogarth Press, 1997), 106, quoted in Peter Brooker, *Bohemia in*

London: The Social Scene of Early Modernism (New York: Palgrave Macmillan, 2007), 161.
16 Lefebvre, Production of Space, 352.
17 Lytton Strachey, Manuscript, vol. 3, King's College, Cambridge University, quoted in Gretchen Holbrook Gerzina, "Bloomsbury and Empire," in The Cambridge Companion to the Bloomsbury Group, ed. Victoria Rosner (Cambridge: Cambridge University Press, 2014), 115.
18 Timothy Bewes, The Event of Postcolonial Shame (Princeton, NJ: Princeton University Press, 2011), 78.
19 Edward W. Said, Culture and Imperialism (New York: Vintage Books, 1994), 303.
20 Mansfield, "Bliss," 150.
21 Carole Sweeney, From Fetish to Subject: Race, Modernism and Primitivism 1919–1935 (Westport: Praeger Publishers, 2004), 106.
22 Lefebvre, Production of Space, 212.
23 R. S. Koppen, Virginia Woolf, Fashion and Literary Modernity (Edinburgh: Edinburgh University Press, 2009), 22–23.
24 Morag Shiach, "Domestic Bloomsbury," in Rosner, Cambridge Companion to the Bloomsbury Group, 64.
25 Eric Hobsbawm, The Age of Empire, 1875–1914 (London: Abacus, 1987), 64.
26 Janet Lyon, "Cosmopolitanism and Modernism," in The Oxford Book of Global Modernisms, ed. Mark Wollaeger and Matt Eatough (Oxford: Oxford University Press, 2012), 394. Lyon cites Pheng Cheah's concept of an imperializing, assimilative cosmopolitanism, to argue that cosmopolitan "plundering" had a "strong geographical inflection" with the routes of empire opening up "intercultural" zones.
27 Mansfield, "Bliss," 146.
28 Jane Garrity, "Modernist Women's Writing: Beyond the Threshold of Obsolescence," Literature Compass 10, no. 1 (2013): 19. doi:10.1111/lic3.12043.
29 Alison Light, Mrs. Woolf and the Servants (London: Penguin, 2007), 53; xvii.
30 Mansfield, "Bliss," 142, 148.
31 Mansfield, "Bliss," 152.
32 Aimee Gasston, "Consuming Art: Katherine Mansfield's Literary Snack," Journal of New Zealand Literature 31, no. 2 (2013): 178.
33 Mansfield, "Bliss," 151.
34 Urmila Seshagiri, "Orienting Virginia Woolf: Race, Aesthetics and Politics in To the Lighthouse," Modern Fiction Studies 50, no. 1 (Spring 2004): 69.
35 Hobsbawm, Age of Empire, 64.
36 Erika Rappaport, "Drink Empire Tea: Gender, Conservative Politics and Imperial Consumerism in Inter-War Britain," in Consuming Behaviours: Identity, Politics and Pleasure in Twentieth-Century Britain, ed. Erika Rappaport, Mark J. Crowley, and Sandra Trudgen Dawson (London: Bloomsbury Academic, 2015), 140.
37 Rappaport, "Drink Empire Tea," 143.

38 Rappaport, "Drink Empire Tea," 150.
39 Katherine Mansfield, "A Cup of Tea," in Kimber and O'Sullivan, *Collected Fiction*, 461.
40 Anne Friedberg, "Les Flâneurs du Mal(l): Cinema and the Postmodern Condition," *PMLA* 3, no. 106 (1991): 422, quoted in Elizabeth Outka, *Consuming Traditions: Modernity, Modernism and the Commodified Authentic* (Oxford: Oxford University Press, 2009), 147.
41 Mansfield, "A Cup of Tea," 461.
42 Mansfield, "A Cup of Tea," 462.
43 Mansfield, "A Cup of Tea," 465.
44 Markman Ellis, Richard Coulton, and Matthew Mauger, *Empire of Tea: The Asian Leaf that Conquered the World* (London: Reaktion Books Ltd, 2015), 9.
45 Joanna de Groot, "Metropolitan Desires and Colonial Connections: Reflections on Consumption and Empire," in *At Home with Empire: Metropolitan Culture and the Imperial World*, ed. Catherine Hall and Sonya O. Rose (Cambridge: Cambridge University Press, 2006), 173.
46 D. Forrest, *Tea for the British* (London: Chatto & Windus, 1973), 184, quoted in de Groot, "Metropolitan Desires," 184–85.
47 Stuart Hall, "Old and New Identities, Old and New Ethnicities," in *Theories of Race and Racism: A Reader*, ed. Les Back and John Salamos (London: Routledge, 2000), 147.
48 Mansfield, "A Cup of Tea," 465.
49 Mansfield, "A Cup of Tea," 465.
50 Mica Nava, "Modernity's Disavowal: Women, the City and the Department Store," in *Modern Times: Reflections on a Century of English Modernity*, ed. Mica Nava and Alan O'Shea (London: Routledge, 1996), 49.
51 Nava, *Visceral Cosmopolitanism*, 31.
52 John Drummond, "A Creative Crossroads. The Revival of Dance in Fergusson's Paris," in Scottish Arts Council (1985): 22, quoted in Peter Brooker, *Bohemia in London: The Social Scene of Early Modernism* (Houndmills, Basingstoke, Hampshire: Palgrave MacMillan, 2004), 82.
53 Brooker, *Bohemia in London*, 175.
54 Katherine Mansfield, "Marriage à la Mode," in Kimber and O'Sullivan, *Collected Fiction*, 332.
55 Mansfield, "Marriage à la Mode," 332.
56 Mansfield "Marriage à la Mode," 330.
57 Mansfield, "Marriage à la Mode," 331.
58 Mansfield, "Marriage à la Mode," 334.
59 Virginia Woolf, "Bloomsbury," in *Moments of Being*, ed. Jeanne Schulkind, 2nd ed. (San Diego: Harcourt Brace Jovanovich, 1985), 185, quoted in Rosner, *Modernism and Architecture*, 130.

60 Mansfield, "Marriage à la Mode," 331.
61 Mansfield, "Marriage à la Mode," 330.
62 Mansfield, "Marriage à la Mode," 337.
63 Mansfield, "Bliss," 144.
64 Sir Christopher Ondaatje, *Woolf in Ceylon: An Imperial Journey in the Shadow of Leonard Woolf, 1904–1911* (London: Harper Collins, 2005), 238–39, quoted in Gerzina, "Bloomsbury and Empire," 113. Expressing his reservations about their proclaimed radicalism, Ondaatje asserts that they "were not radical enough to take seriously a viewpoint utterly removed from their own … even through the literary filter of one of their own" (Gerzina, "Bloomsbury and Empire," 113).
65 Katherine Mansfield to John Middleton Murry, May 19, 1913, in *The Collected Letters of Katherine Mansfield, 1903–1917*, vol. 1, ed. Vincent O'Sullivan and Margaret Scott (Oxford: Clarendon Press, 1984), 124.

12

Performances of Knowledge in Mansfield's Bloomsbury Satires

Alex Moffett

It is a truism of modernist scholarship to say that Katherine Mansfield had a complex relationship to the Bloomsbury group. She moved in the same circles as many Bloomsbury members in the mid- to late 1910s and had a famously productive professional friendship with Virginia Woolf. But Mansfield often expressed a feeling of alienation from other Bloomsbury members, and even her friendship with Woolf was marked by wariness. Modernist scholars have often discussed the Bloomsbury snobbery and Mansfield's reaction to it, both of which helped to fuel this dynamic. However, the precise parameters of her own critique of Bloomsbury, regardless of their personal reception of her, are less frequently explored. What aspects of the Bloomsbury group did Mansfield object to, and how are those objections incarnated in her fiction?

We can see the beginnings of answers to these questions in an excerpt from a letter from Mansfield to Woolf in August 1917. This letter is well known among Mansfield scholars for two reasons: it has the famous "[w]e have got the same job, Virginia" profession of friendship with Woolf, and it provides evidence that Mansfield had read, and the two of them had discussed, Woolf's short story "Kew Gardens," an important text in the development of Woolf's career and of British modernist literature more generally.[1] However, this warmth is set in the context of Mansfield's hesitancy about Woolf and her set. It was only the week before that Mansfield had exclaimed "[t]o Hell with the Blooms Berries" in a letter to Ottoline Morrell.[2] And in the paragraph *between* Mansfield's profession of a shared calling and her affirmation of "Kew Gardens," Mansfield expresses this wariness directly to Woolf:

> Don't let THEM ever persuade you that I spend any of my precious time swapping hats or committing adultery—I'm far too arrogant & proud. However,

let them think what they like. Theres [sic] a most wonderful greengage light on the tree outside and little white clouds bobbing over the sky like rabbits. And I wish you could see some superb gladioli standing up in my studio very proud and defiant like Indian braves.[3]

The editors of Mansfield's collected letters, Vincent O'Sullivan and Margaret Scott, propose that the "THEM" of the letter could refer to Clive Bell, John Maynard Keynes, and/or Desmond McCarthy.[4] At any rate, Mansfield's message is quite clear: do not let your opinion of me be swayed by idle Bloomsbury gossip. However, she is also making another point. It doesn't matter precisely what the likes of Bell and Keynes think of her; it is the communication and propagation of those opinions that matter. And then, within the very same paragraph, Mansfield switches subjects and talks about the light on the tree outside and the flowers in her studio. While this might seem like the nonlinear flittings of the conscious mind, it also functions as a corrective to the matter that preceded it. Untrue Bloomsbury gossip, publically disseminated, yields to a truer, private sort of knowledge, possessed of greater value than rumors of Mansfield's love affairs.

I want to propose that this sort of dichotomy is also present in Katherine Mansfield's celebrated short fiction, and particularly when that fiction depicts artistic figures similar to members of the Bloomsbury group. Her representations of these sorts of figures are often satirical, and that satire frequently manifests itself in a specific way. These characters produce performances of knowledge: a knowing quotation here, a reference to a contemporary event, or a bit of gossip there. We see this dynamic in Bloomsbury satires such as "Marriage à la Mode" (1921) and "Bliss" (1918), in which bohemian figures are all too willing to perform their knowingness to others in social situations. In this chapter, I analyze the performance of knowingness in these two stories and in "A Dill Pickle" (1917). In doing so, I want to propose that these showy performances comprise a large part of Mansfield's satire of Bloomsbury mores. However, there's another half of this equation. In the stories I'll discuss, these performances of knowledge coexist with another mode of knowing, that which Angela Smith calls "writing the secret self."[5] This mode is a familiar one to both Mansfield scholars and fans; it is marked by interiority, by sudden awareness. The protagonist becomes aware of an emotion or a memory or an observation. However, this knowledge is frequently incommunicable to other characters in the story, even when circumstances insist that it become known. Privileged by Mansfield's literary technique of free indirect discourse, only readers can potentially have access to these truths; indeed Mansfield's development of a modernist technique—one that relies on silences, ellipses, the things left unsaid—is the only way in which these truths might be articulated. This way of knowing is equivalent to what Morris Beja and others have called the epiphanic tendency of modernist literature.[6] What I'd like to suggest is that in these three stories such epiphanies are juxtaposed against shallow public performances of knowledge. In each of these stories, Mansfield contrasts such moments of ostentatious performativity with other diametrically oppositional modes of knowing characterized by quiet interior revelation. In essence, these stories juxtapose knowing and knowingness, bringing them into conflict with one another, and never fully resolving the tension between truth and the way that truth is publically conveyed.

I want to turn to another letter of Mansfield that illustrates this dynamic in a way that is helpful for reading the three stories I will be discussing. This document is Mansfield's most noteworthy documents on the state of modern literature. In a November 1919 letter to her husband, John Middleton Murry, Katherine Mansfield follows her negative opinion of Virginia Woolf's novel *Night and Day* by considering the aims of the novel in an environment that has been shattered by the Great War. She posits the problem of the novel's role in a postwar world as being fundamentally epistemological in nature:

> Now we know ourselves for what we are. In a way its a tragic knowledge. Its as though, even while we live again we face death. [...] We see death in life as we see death in a flower that is fresh unfolded. Our hymn is to the flower's beauty—we would make that beauty immortal because we *know*.[7]

What's important here is that Mansfield feels that the novel should be associated with a certain kind of knowledge, one that is characterized by an indirect and oblique relationship between the knowing of a thing and the telling of it. The knowledge of ourselves and our mortality becomes transmuted to a hymn about the flower's beauty—a kind of telling. There is a considerable gap, therefore, between what's known and what's told. And of course these are the sort of textual lacunae that make literary modernism what it is; it's why we admire Mansfield and Woolf and Joyce and others. So knowledge isn't quite incommunicable, but strictly denotative modes of communication just won't do. And Mansfield emphasizes precisely this point to Murry in the next paragraph of the letter. After quoting Andrew Marvel's famous phrase, "deserts of vast eternity," to describe the kind of knowledge she means, she then proceeds to clarify what precisely this means for literature: "I couldn't tell anybody *bang out* about those deserts: they are my secret. I might write about a boy eating strawberries or a woman combing her hair on a windy morning, and that is the only way I can ever mention them. But they *must* be there."[8] Once again, the knowing is there, but simply communicating that knowledge by straightforward discourse—talking "bang out" about it—cannot adequately convey it. There is a palpable tension between knowing and telling.

This emphasis on knowing is consonant with the narrative arc of her short fictions, many of which culminate in some sort of epiphanic moment in which a protagonist achieves a greater degree of knowledge. Such moments are often unutterable within the diegetic world of the narrative itself. In a particularly famous instance of this incommunicability, Laura Sheridan can only haltingly speculate "Isn't life—" in "The Garden Party" (1921). However, Mansfield often contrasts these episodes with other moments in which characters deliberately display an excess of superficial and insignificant knowledge. A different sort of knowingness arises in these occasions, one marked by showiness, performance, and most of all by meaninglessness; these instances of dialogue primarily function to demonstrate a character's casual mastery of the cultural and social spheres in which he or she moves. In two of the stories I'll discuss—"Bliss" and "Marriage a la Mode"—these sorts of characters are read by most critics as being sharp satires of the Bloomsbury group. I would also argue that the other story in this chapter, "A Dill Pickle," has more than a whiff of Bloomsbury about it. Mansfield felt drawn to Bloomsbury even as she felt apart from it, and as Sydney Janet Kaplan has said, Mansfield's portrayals of the group in these stories "reflect her persistent awareness of exclusion."[9] It's also worth noting that "Bliss" and "Marriage à la Mode" were written at a literal distance from Bloomsbury, in France and Switzerland respectively, and this separation adds to the sharpness of the satire.

"Marriage à la Mode" very conspicuously mocks Bloomsbury values in its depiction of Isabel's new friends, a set of poets and artists who parasitically have attached themselves to the household of her and her husband, William. These friends are largely characterized by their excessive and gratuitous demonstrations of knowingness, a desire to demonstrate to others their own store of witty references. They quote literature and scripture in order to be witty; for example, Moira Morrison's address of Isabel as "Titania" or Dennis Green's quotation of Ecclesiastes: "'We shall have to anoint ourselves with butter,' said Dennis. 'May thy head, William, lack not ointment.'"[10] Likewise they are completely au courant in their appreciation of Nijinksy and the comic operetta *The Maid of the Mountains*. These characters perform this cavalcade of references in a completely affected manner, exaggerating the intensity of the emotions that they are feeling. The chasmal juxtaposition between the intensity of their performances and the insignificant referentiality of their remarks is the driving engine of the satire of the story; we sense these characters to be ridiculous because of the discrepancy between the content of what they are expressing and the register in which they express it.

However, this binary relationship is, in its totality, the first term of a larger binary within "Marriage à la Mode": that between the triviality of Isabel's set and the sincerity of William's distress about the state of their marriage. Alarmed by the distance between himself and Isabel, and frustrated by his inability to spend time with his family without the presence of Isabel's artsy friends, William writes his wife a sincere letter, apparently indicating both his love for her and his dissatisfaction with the direction their relationship has taken. This letter is antithetical to the blatherings of Isabel's friends in both the genuineness of its sentiments and in the private mode in which it expresses them. These two opposing forms of communication come into collision with one another in the climactic moment of the story when Isabel proceeds to read the letter aloud to her hangers-on:

> It was absurd, of course, it must be absurd, ridiculous. "Ha, ha, ha! Oh dear!" What was she to do? Isabel flung back in her chair and laughed till she couldn't stop laughing.
> "Do, do tell us," said the others. "You must tell us."
> "I'm longing to," gurgled Isabel. She sat up, gathered the letter, and waved it at them. "Gather round," she said. "Listen, it's too marvellous. A love-letter!"
> "A love-letter! But how divine!" *"Darling, precious Isabel."* But she had hardly begun before their laughter interrupted her.
> "Go on, Isabel, it's perfect."
> "It's the most marvellous find."
> "Oh, do go on, Isabel!"
> *"God forbid, my darling, that I should be a drag on your happiness."*
> "Oh! oh! oh!"
> "Sh! sh! sh!"
> "You must let me have it just as it is, entire, for my new book," said Dennis firmly. "I shall give it a whole chapter."[11]

Their mockery precipitates a crisis with Isabel, who, at least momentarily, perceives the shallowness of her behavior; she lies on her bed and mutters, "how vile, odious, abominable, vulgar" to herself.[12] What Mansfield has done in this episode is to take a moment of private revelation shared in a letter and demonstrate that its public airing corrupts it. As readers, we don't even fully know what is in William's letter or to what degree it's a love letter, an ultimatum, or both. By reading it and therefore transforming the letter to public knowledge, it's clear that Isabel has vulgarized it. The assembled artistic crowd can only see it through ironic eyes as an example of a clichéd textual form, a view that culminates in Dennis's statement that he is going to include it without emendation in his book. Dennis has gone from being a financial parasite to a literary parasite, and in doing so is attempting to represent a piece of private knowledge by performing it, by going "bang on" about it, as Mansfield put it in her earlier letter to Murry. The sanctity of William's private expression is in imminent danger of being violated and commercialized in an act of literary piracy that's very far from Mansfield's own literary technique.[13]

"Marriage à la Mode" at least retains the possibility that its private knowledge can be potentially communicable to other characters through language—the letter that William writes to Isabel—even if it is not revealed to the reader. In Mansfield's earlier story, "A Dill Pickle," this situation is reversed. The private knowledge that Vera has about her former relationship with the unnamed man is never shared with him, but it is known to the reader through her thoughts. However, "A Dill Pickle" resembles "Marriage à la Mode" in that this private knowledge is directly juxtaposed against the man's very public performance of knowledge, both of their previous romantic relationship and of his life after their relationship concluded. There are two episodes in "A Dill Pickle" in which this dynamic operates. The first occurs early in the story when the man, having encountered Vera unexpectedly, shares with his former lover a memory of the time they spent together in Kew Gardens. The reader has already gained a sense of the man's character from this recollection of Vera's:

> But she was thinking how well she remembered that trick of his—the trick of interrupting her—and of how it used to exasperate her six years ago. She used to feel then as though he, quite suddenly, in the middle of what she was saying, put his hand over her lips, turned from her, attended to something different, and then took his hand away, and with just the same slightly too broad smile, gave her his attention again.... Now we are ready. That is settled.[14]

This moment clearly indicates the power dynamics of their previous relationship; Vera perceived the man as actively trying to assert control over her communication. And immediately after Vera recalls this tendency, this dynamic resurrects itself, except with more complexity. The man recalls a moment of happiness from their previous relationship:

> Do you remember that first afternoon we spent together at Kew Gardens? You were so surprised because I did not know the names of any flowers. I am still

just as ignorant for all your telling me. But whenever it is very fine and warm, and I see some bright colours—it's awfully strange—I hear your voice saying: "Geranium, marigold, and verbena." And I feel those three words are all I recall of some forgotten, heavenly language.[15]

Inwardly, Vera responds by recalling a different memory of that afternoon:

Yet, what had remained in her mind of that particular afternoon was an absurd scene over the tea table. A great many people taking tea in a Chinese pagoda, and he behaving like a maniac about the wasps—waving them away, flapping at them with his straw hat, serious and infuriated out of all proportion to the occasion. How delighted the sniggering tea drinkers had been. And how she had suffered.[16]

While his recollection of the event is simply a romanticized moment from the afternoon, hers is more meaningful, perhaps containing a synecdochal account of why the couple split. Her silent embarrassment at his poor public behavior has remained with her over the years. However, when placed in opposition to his account of the day in Kew Gardens, hers seems to diminish: "But now, as he spoke, that memory faded. His was the truer. Yes, it had been a wonderful afternoon, full of geranium and marigold and verbena, and—warm sunshine."[17] Somewhat ironically, the force of his publically performed recollection seems to overpower her privately held memory of his previous public performance. However, the image created by his memory then engenders a new one in her which "unfolds [...] in the warmth." Vera then recalls a different scene, perhaps also at Kew Gardens:

She saw herself sitting on a lawn. He lay beside her, and suddenly, after a long silence, he rolled over and put his head in her lap.
"I wish," he said, in a low, troubled voice, "I wish that I had taken poison and were about to die—here now!"
At that moment a little girl in a white dress, holding a long, dripping water lily, dodged from behind a bush, stared at them, and dodged back again. But he did not see.
She leaned over him.
"Ah, why do you say that? I could not say that."
But he gave a kind of soft moan, and taking her hand he held it to his cheek.
"Because I know I am going to love you too much—far too much. And I shall suffer so terribly, Vera, because you never, never will love me."[18]

Within Vera's remembered scene is another depiction of the man's exaggerated performativity: an excess of expressive emotion that casts into relief his behavior in the narrative present. What also emerges from the dialogue that is currently taking place between them is a complex interaction between his public declamation of knowledge of the past and her private contestation of that knowledge. Mansfield depicts the man's public declamation of his memory as being something of a paper tiger. It has a seeming strength, one that comes into conflict with Vera's thought but unexpressed recollections. Neither of these private memories are uttered, but they exist in a competitive tension with the man's spoken memory, which seems to eradicate her first memory, and yet in doing so provide a fertile environment in which the second can grow. Vera's privately held truth retains its legitimacy both in spite and because of the mastery that the man tries to publically perform in opposition to it.

The second moment in the story where his publicly expressed knowledge collides with her privately held thoughts occurs when the man tells Vera about the trip to Russia he has taken in the days since their relationship ended. It's this moment that generates the image that gives the story its title:

> "You'd like almost everything about Russian life," he said warmly. "It's so informal, so impulsive, so free without question. And then the peasants are so splendid. They are such human beings—yes, that is it. Even the man who drives your carriage has—has some real part in what is happening. I remember the evening a party of us, two friends of mine and the wife of one of them, went for a picnic by the Black Sea. We took supper and champagne and ate and drank on the grass. And while we were eating the coachman came up. 'Have a dill pickle,' he said. He wanted to share with us. That seemed to me so right, so—you know what I mean?"[19]

The man's patronizing tone as he recounts his journeys suggests that Mansfield fully understood the phenomenon of "mansplaining" many decades before it had a name, but it also generates a similar effect as his memory of Kew Gardens: it is oppressive and yet simultaneously generative. As he talks about Russia, Vera experiences an eidetic vision of the landscape he describes: "And she seemed at that moment to be sitting on the grass beside the mysteriously Black Sea, black as velvet, and rippling against the banks in silent, velvet waves."[20] However, one thing is missing: she doesn't know what a dill pickle actually is. Her vision ends up substituting a symbolically laden image for that of an actual pickle:

> "Have a dill pickle," said he, and although she was not certain what a dill pickle was, she saw the greenish glass jar with a red chili like a parrot's beak glimmering through. She sucked in her cheeks; the dill pickle was terribly sour.
>
> "Yes, I know perfectly what you mean," she said.[21]

The wonderfully Mansfieldian image of the pickle—suggestive of phallic menace—is somehow truer than the denotative image of the pickle it replaces. It also betokens a gendered aspect to the two ways of expressing knowledge presented in the story; in contrast with "Marriage à la Mode," the excessive performance of knowledge practiced by the man is a specifically masculine practice. And also in contrast with "Marriage à la Mode," these two ways of expressing knowledge have a closely intertwined relationship. It is too simplistic merely to say that Vera and her former lover are talking past one another. In both of the instances I've detailed above, the relationship between the two modes is marked by antagonism, and yet also generative codependence. Vera's private knowledge—marked by semiotic dislocation— resists the overtly demonstrative and heavily denotative performances of the man, and ends up being, as Vera says, a more perfect knowledge, despite her knowledge being indirect. However, in both of these episodes, Vera's private knowledge gains strength from the excessively knowing statements of her former lover. Private knowledge grows in the space where knowledge is publically performed. This possibility complicates the binary between knowing and knowingness, suggesting perhaps that the former requires the latter as a way of strengthening itself, so that we might approach a more perfectly formed truth,

Another story that juxtaposes private and public modes of knowledge within the context of a romantic relationship is "Bliss," which Mansfield wrote a few months after "A Dill Pickle" was published.[22] I'll start with what are probably two obvious points about the story. First, the emotion indicated by the title, that, as Mansfield puts it, feeling of "absolute bliss!—as though you'd suddenly swallowed a bright piece of that late afternoon sun and it burned in your bosom, sending out a little shower of sparks into every particle, into every finger and toe?…" is an awareness privately held by Bertha Young.[23] Bertha's feeling of bliss is never fully expressed by her to any other character in the story. It can only be rendered by the narrator to the reader, and only through figurative language, as in the passage quoted above. Second, the desire that this feeling encodes—an erotic yearning that ultimately finds its most powerful object in Pearl Fulton, a woman who attends her dinner party—is absolutely an unutterable sentiment in British society at the time the story was written. However, erotic desire of the kind Bertha is experiencing demands some sort of outlet. In contrast with the private memories held by Vera in "A Dill Pickle," Bertha's feeling of bliss requires that it be conveyed in some form to another human being.

Consequently, it is unsurprising that Mansfield simultaneously emphasizes both the sheer incommunicability of Bertha's private feeling and the insistent demands that the feeling be somehow communicated. There are many incidences of what we might call thwarted speech in the story, moments where Bertha tries to say something or thinks about saying something but for whatever reason does not. Almost all of these moments have to do with this feeling of absolute bliss she is experiencing. For instance, immediately after that first description, Mansfield's narrator, voicing the consciousness of Bertha, registers frustration that the feeling can't be properly voiced: "Oh, is there no way you can express it without being 'drunk and disorderly'? How idiotic civilisation is!"[24] This proto-Freudian idea of civilization being the primary impediment to Bertha's desires returns a few pages later when Bertha attempts to convey the desire to her husband, Harry, when he telephones her at the house:

> "Oh, is that you, Ber? Look here. I'll be late. I'll take a taxi and come along as quickly as I can, but get dinner put back ten minutes—will you? All right?"
> "Yes, perfectly. Oh, Harry!"
> "Yes?"
> What had she to say? She'd nothing to say. She only wanted to get in touch with him for a moment. She couldn't absurdly cry: "Hasn't it been a divine day!"
> "What is it?" rapped out the little voice.
> "Nothing. *Entendu*," said Bertha, and hung up the receiver, thinking how much more than idiotic civilisation was.[25]

Once again, Bertha attempts and fails to communicate something of the feeling she is experiencing. The prosaically informative message of her husband is the utterable speech act, one that seems to steamroll her attempt to convey her bliss. Other moments of thwarted speech include when she wants to say something, for instance, to her nanny about her child, or to her dinner guest Eddie Warren, but checks herself, or finds herself unable to speak.

The contrast between Bertha's private, insistent yet unutterable bliss and Harry's briskly denotative phone message is one that will recur in the story. The same dynamic that occurs in "Marriage à la Mode" and "A Dill Pickle" also takes place in "Bliss": private ways of knowing are juxtaposed against public performances of knowingness. Harry Young is a prime example of this. The manner in which he is primarily characterized in the story is by his knowing snarkiness about others, first manifested in a recollected conversation he and his wife had about Pearl Fulton:

> "No, the way she has of sitting with her head a little on one side, and smiling, has something behind it, Harry, and I must find out what that something is."
> "Most likely it's a good stomach," answered Harry.

He made a point of catching Bertha's heels with replies of that kind ... "liver frozen, my dear girl," or "pure flatulence," or "kidney disease,"... and so on. For some strange reason Bertha liked this, and almost admired it in him very much.[26]

These comical diagnoses clearly emphasize the bodiliness of the individuals he is talking about, but they also present himself as possessing an almost medical authority. Harry reduces elements of personality to mere biological malfunction, while presenting himself as a witty font of knowingness.

There are also the friends that Harry and Bertha have over for dinner: the Mr. and Mrs. Norman Knights and Eddie Warren, who, like Isabel's coterie in "Marriage a la Mode," are often read as being satirical of Bloomsbury figures. We are first told by the narrator that the Norman Knights are "a very sound couple" and that Eddie is a poet much in demand in their social set. Bertha tells herself that she is very pleased with the friendships she has: "And friends—modern, thrilling friends, writers and painters and poets or people keen on social questions—just the kind of friends they wanted."[27] However, when they actually appear at Bertha's party, these friends are, like Isabel's coterie in "Marriage à la Mode," marked by their performative knowingness, a savvy that most typically applies to artistic and literary topics. For instance, just as Dennis will do in the later story, Norman Knight quotes scripture: "and so was Mug, smoking a cigarette and saying as he flicked the ash: 'Why doth the bridegroom tarry?'"[28] And Eddie Warren is personified as a showy aesthete, exaggeratedly declaiming on such subjects as his taxi driver and his socks.[29] As Kate Fulbrook rightly observes in her reading of "Bliss," "[t]he group is wrapped in conventions, though it takes itself to be frightfully liberated and knowing."[30]

Mansfield directly foregrounds this juxtaposition between Bertha's incommunicable and yet profound inner knowledge and the performed knowingness of her husband and her guests in two key scenes in the story, both of which have to do with the connection between Bertha and Pearl Fulton. The first time Bertha experiences this connection, the narrator conveys it as a moment of inexpressible communion between the two of them: "But Bertha knew, suddenly, as if the longest, most intimate look had passed between them—as if they had said to each other: 'You too?'—that Pearl Fulton, stirring the beautiful red soup in the grey plate, was feeling just what she was feeling."[31] Narrating her conscious thoughts in free, indirect discourse, Mansfield then signals Bertha's attention being turned to the rest of the group: "And the others?" What the reader then gets is an outbreak of performed knowingness from the other four figures in the room:

Face and Mug, Eddie and Harry, their spoons rising and falling—dabbing their lips with their napkins, crumbling bread, fiddling with the forks and glasses and talking.

"I met her at the Alpha show—the weirdest little person. She'd not only cut off her hair, but she seemed to have taken a dreadfully good snip off her legs and arms and her neck and her poor little nose as well."

"Isn't she very *liée* with Michael Oat?"

"The man who wrote *Love in False Teeth*?"

"He wants to write a play for me. One act. One man. Decides to commit suicide. Gives all the reasons why he should and why he shouldn't. And just as he has made up his mind either to do it or not to do it—curtain. Not half a bad idea."

"What's he going to call it—'Stomach Trouble'?"

"I *think* I've come across the *same* idea in a lit-tle French review, *quite* unknown in England."[32]

This sample of conversation, unmediated by narration, focuses on the gossip of the artistic coterie in which the interlocutors move and is characterized by all their typical traits: knowingness, vacuity, and petty snideness. All this time the question of Bertha's feeling of bliss and whether or not it was experienced by the others has been, as it were, on the table. Following this snippet, that question is simply answered: "No, they didn't share it...."[33] We see the shallowness of the world of the Norman Knights and Eddie Warren in direct and stark contrast to the depth, the vibrancy of Bertha's feeling. Mansfield has directly juxtaposed these two epistemic modes.

She repeats this device in the famous moment in "Bliss" when Bertha and Pearl Fulton gaze upon the pear tree in Bertha's garden and experience what Bertha imagines is a moment of communion between the two of them:

How long did they stand there? Both, as it were, caught in that circle of unearthly light, understanding each other perfectly, creatures of another world, and wondering what they were to do in this one with all this blissful treasure that burned in their bosoms and dropped, in silver flowers, from their hair and hands?

For ever—for a moment? And did Miss Fulton murmur: "Yes. Just *that*." Or did Bertha dream it?[34]

The essence of this moment is one of understanding and communication. A secret knowledge about a privately held emotion has been shared (or so Bertha imagines). It cannot be conveyed denotatively, in so many words, but under this special set of circumstances, surrounded by such symbols of fertility, it can potentially be imparted. However, the moment of communion is dispelled with an abruptness bordering on violence by the empty blather of the other dinner guests:

> Then the light was snapped on and Face made the coffee and Harry said: "My dear Mrs. Knight, don't ask me about my baby. I never see her. I shan't feel the slightest interest in her until she has a lover," and Mug took his eye out of the conservatory for a moment and then put it under glass again and Eddie Warren drank his coffee and set down the cup with a face of anguish as though he had drunk and seen the spider.
>
> "What I want to do is to give the young men a show. I believe London is simply teeming with first-chop, unwritten plays. What I want to say to 'em is: 'Here's the theatre. Fire ahead.'"
>
> "You know, my dear, I am going to decorate a room for the Jacob Nathans. Oh, I am so tempted to do a fried-fish scheme, with the backs of the chairs shaped like frying-pans and lovely chip potatoes embroidered all over the curtains."
>
> "The trouble with our young writing men is that they are still too romantic. You can't put out to sea without being seasick and wanting a basin. Well, why won't they have the courage of those basins?"
>
> "A *dreadful* poem about a *girl* who was *violated* by a beggar *without* a nose in a lit-tle wood."[35]

Just as in the previous moment in which Bertha recognized that Pearl Fulton felt as she felt, we have her private knowledge juxtaposed against the publically performed knowingness of her husband and her dinner guests. However, the two moments differ in that the previous interrupting conversation had the benefit of cohesion. Here, we just get disconnected fragments of dialogue. This may be because Bertha, whose consciousness the narrator is inhabiting, is in such emotional turmoil that she is not able to perceive the coherence in the conversation. Regardless, if this is the case, the effect is to emphasize the meaninglessness of the world of her husband and dinner guests; bereft of marks of continuity, the statements of Harry, Eddie, and the Norman Knights are revealed as being so much nonsense.

And then this juxtaposition between Bertha's and Pearl Fulton's private sharing of knowledge and the others' all-too-public conveyance of it yields to a second juxtaposition: that between Bertha's desire for Miss Fulton and Harry's very public, very gauche pursuit of her.

At times in the story Bertha's erotic desires seem to have no particular object, and toward the end of "Bliss" she briefly registers, for the first time in her life, a sexual desire for her husband. However, most scholars read the story as centrally conveying her desire for Pearl Fulton. This desire is rendered primarily through the figurative language of metaphor and symbol, so much so that mid-twentieth-century scholars, writing at a time when such desire was not an acceptable topic of scholarly conversation, felt able to ignore the matter entirely. Harry's sexual desire for Pearl Fulton is expressed in an altogether dissimilar manner. He offers to help Miss Fulton put on her coat and follows her into the hall. Bertha is momentarily distracted by the nattering of Eddie Warren, but nonetheless witnesses her husband profess his desire in his own particular manner:

> While he looked it up she turned her head towards the hall. And she saw ... Harry with Miss Fulton's coat in his arms and Miss Fulton with her back turned to him and her head bent. He tossed the coat away, put his hands on her shoulders and turned her violently to him. His lips said: "I adore you," and Miss Fulton laid her moonbeam fingers on his cheeks and smiled her sleepy smile. Harry's nostrils quivered; his lips curled back in a hideous grin while he whispered: "Tomorrow," and with her eyelids Miss Fulton said: "Yes."
>
> "Here it is," said Eddie. "'Why Must it Always be Tomato Soup?' It's so *deeply* true, don't you feel? Tomato soup is so *dreadfully* eternal."
>
> "If you prefer," said Harry's voice, very loud, from the hall, "I can phone you a cab to come to the door."[36]

Harry's mode of expressing his desire is antithetical to that of Bertha's. It is specifically verbal and traffics in all the clichés of a romance novel: the feigned indifference, the self-consciously masculine assertiveness, the overt expression of desire, the arranging of a secret rendezvous. Yet despite the seeming furtiveness of Harry's approach, there is something terribly public about the affair. He expresses his desire to his lover in the middle of a busy house, just as guests are milling about preparing to leave. His cover dialogue to Miss Fulton is delivered at an almost comically high volume. All the subtleties of Bertha's desire, all the profundity and the mystery, are absent from Harry's vulgar behavior. It is a courtship very much in keeping with his world and the company he keeps. And yet, there is a certain power to this mode of expressing his affection. The felt reciprocity of the moment Bertha and Miss Fulton were having earlier is revealed to be an illusion—perhaps, as Clare Hanson and Andrew Gurr suggest, an example of Bertha's naiveté.[37] That privately held knowledge of "Bliss" was not conveyed after all, and the conclusion of the story—with Bertha's plaintive cry of "[o]h, what is going to happen now?"—gives us nothing with which to replace the previous certitude.[38] In this way, Mansfield's depiction of the conflict between knowing and knowingness in "Bliss" is perhaps more pessimistic than it was when treated in "A Dill Pickle." The only suggestion that there might be a possibility for Bertha's mode of knowing to take root once again, the fertile territory that existed in the previous story, is in the return of the primary symbol in its concluding sentence: "But the pear tree was as lovely as ever and as full of flower and as still."[39] I propose that a lot hinges on the opening conjunction of that final sentence. The logical relationship—one of opposition—it supplies to the uncertainty that Bertha had previously expressed implies that perhaps her mode of knowledge, characterized by privacy and incommunicability, is the more valid after all.

There's the risk for readers, I think, of taking a little too much pleasure in Mansfield's depictions of the likes of Eddie Warren in "Bliss," or Moira and the others in "Marriage à la Mode," the same kind of risk we take as we might when laughing at a bearded hipster in a chic local coffee shop. We point out the person who is attending a little too closely to modish social conventions, not realizing the ways in which our own behavior might also be implicated. It is true that Moira, Eddie Warren, and the rest of them represent Mansfield's indictment of a certain artistically inclined social set, one most prominently identified with the Bloomsbury group. But Mansfield is also making a larger observation about the social networks that encourage such behavior and the strategies that we employ to negotiate them, for another trait that these performers of knowledge have in common is that they are all, in a worldly sense, *successful*. Eddie Warren does indeed have a book published and Norman Knight is an apparently in-demand theater producer. Vera's ex-lover in "A Dill Pickle," we are told, has apparently made money and travelled to all the places to which he used to dream of taking them. Even Moira, Dennis, Bill, and Bobby, in "Marriage à la Mode," have found a moderately wealthy, upper-middle-class patron who is willing to subsidize their lifestyle in exchange for the bohemian stimulation they provide. In the social circles in which Mansfield and her protagonists move—circles where both financial and cultural capital are inextricably intermingled—a showy performance of knowingness is a strategy that can reap rewards. So while Mansfield may be poking fun at Bloomsbury, she is simultaneously articulating a larger critique of a world increasingly celebratory of such public performances. The presence of the same dichotomy between knowing and knowingness in a story that is set, geographically and conceptually, about as far from Bloomsbury as it is possible to get bears out this speculation. In one of her final stories, "A Doll's House," Mansfield juxtaposes Isabel Burnell's showy possessiveness about the titular toy with Kezia's silent joy in the beautiful little lamp that is in one of the dollhouse bedrooms. Popular

Isabel shows all her friends the dollhouse, while Kezia secretly shows it to the social outcast Kelvey girls: Lil and our Else. In so many episodes in Mansfield's Burnell stories, the behavior of the children becomes a blueprint for later models of adult behavior, and this aspect of "A Doll's House" says something about epistemic propagation in the adult world. It is Isabel's performance of knowledge that, says Mansfield, is the key to worldly success. However, these stories then assert the value of holding on to knowledge in the face of knowingness, despite the pressure of a modern society that sends the opposite message. They celebrate the perceptions and experiences of those of us who, like our Else, have seen the little lamp.

Notes

1 Katherine Mansfield to Virginia Woolf, c. August 23, 1917, in *The Collected Letters of Katherine Mansfield*, 5 vols., ed. Vincent O'Sullivan and Margaret Scott (Oxford: Clarendon Press, 1984–2008), 1:327. Published under the title "Kew Gardens," this story is referred to as "Flower Bed" in Mansfield's letter. All subsequent letters from Mansfield are from this source.
2 Katherine Mansfield to Ottoline Morrell, August 15, 1917, 1:326.
3 Mansfield to Woolf, c. August 23, 1917, 1:327.
4 Mansfield to Woolf, c. August 23, 1917, 1:327.
5 Angela Smith, introduction to *Katherine Mansfield: Selected Stories*, ed. Angela Smith (Oxford: Oxford University Press, 2002), xxi.
6 Morris Beja, *Epiphany in the Modern Novel: Revelation as Art* (London: Peter Owen Limited, 1971), 13–14.
7 Katherine Mansfield to John Middleton Murry, November 16, 1919, 3:97.
8 Mansfield to Murry, November 16, 1919, 3:97.
9 Sydney Janet Kaplan, *Katherine Mansfield and the Origins of Modernist Fiction* (Ithaca: Cornell University Press, 1991), 12.
10 Katherine Mansfield, "Marriage à la Mode," in *The Collected Works of Katherine Mansfield, The Collected Fiction*, 2 vols., ed. Gerri Kimber and Vincent O'Sullivan (Edinburgh: Edinburgh University Press, 2012), 2:333.
11 Mansfield, "Marriage à la Mode," 2:337.
12 Mansfield, "Marriage à la Mode," 2:337.
13 It should be mentioned that "Marriage à la Mode" itself is sometimes considered to be an excessively commercial work since it was written for the popular illustrated paper the *Sphere*, a more remunerative publication than those that typically published Mansfield's work. See Jenny McDonnell, "'The Famous New Zealand

Mag. Story Writer': Katherine Mansfield, Periodical Publishing and the Short Story," in *Katherine Mansfield and Literary Modernism*, ed. Janet Wilson, Gerri Kimber, and Susan Reid (London: Bloomsbury, 2011), 46.
14 Katherine Mansfield, "A Dill Pickle," in Kimber and O'Sullivan, *Collected Fiction*, 2:98.
15 Mansfield, "A Dill Pickle," 2:99.
16 Mansfield, "A Dill Pickle," 2:99.
17 Mansfield, "A Dill Pickle," 2:99.
18 Mansfield, "A Dill Pickle," 2:99.
19 Mansfield, "A Dill Pickle," 2:100–1.
20 Mansfield, "A Dill Pickle," 2:101.
21 Mansfield, "A Dill Pickle," 2:101.
22 Roger Norburn, *A Katherine Mansfield Chronology* (Basingstoke: Palgrave MacMillan, 2008), 44; 48.
23 Katherine Mansfield, "Bliss," in Kimber and O'Sullivan, *Collected Fiction*, 2:142.
24 Mansfield, "Bliss," 2:142.
25 Mansfield, "Bliss," 2:144.
26 Mansfield, "Bliss," 2:144–45.
27 Mansfield, "Bliss," 2:145.
28 Mansfield, "Bliss," 2:147.
29 In a 1918 letter to Murry, Mansfield described Eddie Warren as being "a fish out of the Garsington pond," a reference to Ottoline Morrell's residence Garsington Hall, and the sorts of artists and poets whom Morrell invited there. Mansfield to Murry, February 28, 1918, 2:98.
30 Kate Fulbrook, *Katherine Mansfield* (Bloomington: Indiana University Press, 1986), 97.
31 Mansfield, "Bliss," 2:148.
32 Mansfield, "Bliss," 2:148.
33 Mansfield, "Bliss," 2:148.
34 Mansfield, "Bliss," 2:149.
35 Mansfield, "Bliss," 2:149–50.
36 Mansfield, "Bliss," 2:151–2.
37 Clare Hanson and Andrew Gurr, *Katherine Mansfield* (London: Macmillan, 1981), 62.
38 Mansfield, "Bliss," 2:152.
39 Mansfield, "Bliss," 2:152.

13

An Invitation to the Table: Katherine Mansfield's "A Cup of Tea" and Literary London

Richard Cappuccio

In January 1922, Katherine Mansfield was in Switzerland far from the Bloomsbury group and Garsington circle, but let us consider them in relation to "A Cup of Tea." Mansfield was settled for the time in Montana-sur-Sierre, and it was a time that has been referred to as "the most fruitful period of her life."[1] While "A Cup of Tea" was not published in book form until John Middleton Murry brought out the posthumous *The Doves' Nest and Other Stories* (1923), the story is from the same period as "At the Bay" and "The Garden Party," work that was published that spring in *The Garden Party and Other Stories* (1922). It should strike the contemporary reader as strange that Antony Alpers omitted "A Cup of Tea" from his "Definitive Edition" of her stories. He based his decision on Mansfield's speedy composition of the story and its popular market: it "was quickly sold by K.M.'s percipient agent [J. B. Pinker] to a pulp magazine called the *Story-Teller*."[2] Now that Gerri Kimber, Vincent O'Sullivan, Angela Smith, and Claire Davison have restored all of Mansfield's work and Kathleen Jones has rehabilitated the term "Story-Teller," it is important to view "A Cup of Tea" as the sophisticated story it is and, more importantly, to read it for the insight it gives into Mansfield's alienation from London literary circles.

Mansfield gives a clear picture of her writing process at this point in her life. Yes, she records that she wrote the story quickly: "Wrote & finished *A Cup of Tea*. It took about 4–5 hours."[3] By comparison, she wrote her next story, "Taking the Veil," with even greater speed: "It took me about three hours to write, finally."[4] She stresses the word "finally" because much of her revision took place before she actually sat down to write; she explains, "I had been thinking over the decor and so on for weeks—nay—months, I believe."[5] She adds, "I can't say how thankful I am […] to know Wellington as I do and to have it to range about in. Writing about the convent seemed so natural. I suppose I have not been in the grounds more than twice. But it is one of the places that remain as vivid as ever."[6] Let us be clear: it had been fourteen years since Mansfield had been in Wellington, and this entry clarifies that her rapid writing time is preceded by a period, months in her estimation, of recalling stored details. Acknowledging Mansfield's deep memory when writing, one can better reconsider the sophistication of "A Cup of Tea."[7]

As she states in her notebook, Mansfield's immediate motivation for writing the story might have been Elizabeth von Arnim's visit on January 11, 1922, when she thoughtlessly reduced "At the Bay" by calling it a "pretty little story."[8] The anger that sparked the composition and resulted in the story, however, is quickly dispelled four days later when Mansfield received a letter from Elizabeth that Mansfield says is "so generous, so sweet […] that I am ashamed of what I said or thought the other day."[9] Mansfield's diary memorializes frustration with her cousin, but her subsequent cautionary tale of deceptiveness, "A Cup of Tea," is no more a simple story of that specific squabble than "Prelude" is merely a story of a change of address.

In addition to reading "A Cup of Tea" as a reaction to her cousin's visit, one can read it as a commentary on Mansfield's relationship with the London literary elite, particularly Ottoline Morrell and Virginia Woolf. These circles were also ones, as Mansfield reflects on the composition of "A Cup of Tea," in which "we were sincere but at the back there was nothing but falsity."[10] For Mansfield, being true to her craft but feeling like an outsider to the literary circles of Garsington and Bloomsbury weighed heavily on her. In this context, "A Cup of Tea" examines the relationship of a powerful and privileged host to a powerless and expendable outsider. There are multiple references throughout the story, for example, to Miss Smith as "the other," a phrase repeated with such frequency that it designates her not only as an outsider but as a diminished figure. Mansfield writes of Miss Smith, with emphasis added, that

> Rosemary [Fell] drew *the other* into the hall. […] *The other* scarcely helped her at all; She gave *the other* her lace handkerchief. […] Now at last *the other* forgot to be shy […] *The other* did stop [crying] just in time for Rosemary to get up before the tea came. [… Rosemary] smoked and looked away tactfully so that *the other* should not be shy.[11]

There is an irony with Miss Smith's depiction as the social outcast, especially if we consider Mansfield in a similar role. The circle of those at *Rhythm*, as opposed to the elite in Bloomsbury, would have embraced the outsider as one source for new art.[12] The bohemian is a force of creativity rather than what Rosemary sees as inferior, a "foreigner … [and] childlike."[13] Instead of giving the help that is really needed, Rosemary promotes the idea that Miss Smith is fortunate to be in her company: "Don't you see," Rosemary Fell stresses, "what a good thing it was that you met me?"[14] In these characters, Mansfield creates the dynamics of her experience both at Garsington and Bloomsbury. Rosemary Fell serves as a collector—of flowers, antiques, and guests—much in the same way that Ottoline Morrell collected artists. But Mansfield also demonstrates how those collected are alienated and objectified in the process. Her reflections on sincerity and falsity, the compelling themes for "A Cup of Tea," were very much a part of her first visit to Garsington: her nervousness about the visit had been preceded by the "letters she [… had] written to Ottoline [… that were false in their] fawning and reverent" tone.[15] Yet, her visit revealed a different and unsettling reality.

Mansfield has the reader of "A Cup of Tea" experience the shock of entering this world with the jarring first impression of the major character: Mansfield's opening line, "Rosemary Fell was not exactly beautiful," is a simple sentence that summons an image of Ottoline Morrell, whose appearance was both unconventional and immediately noticeable.[16] Portraits of Ottoline by Augustus John and Simon Bussy accentuate her arresting image. Aldous Huxley, who used Garsington for the basis of his satiric novel *Crome Yellow*, describes Priscilla Wimbush, his fictional counterpart to Ottoline, as a woman with a "masculine […] large square, middle-aged face, with a massive projecting nose and little greenish eyes, the whole surmounted by a lofty and elaborate coiffure of a curiously improbable shade of orange."[17] Huxley ends his description with a comparison that blends gender: she is likened to the British comic music hall singer "Wilkie Bard as the cantatrice."[18]

When Woolf describes Morrell, she may have written with greater skill but also describes a person who does not invite immediate comfort. Woolf does not evoke the masculine, but rather chooses language that accentuates a complex figure, a mythological female that is powerful, frightening, and simultaneously possessing a certain beauty, at least when it comes to her sympathies for the arts. Woolf describes Ottoline with "the head of a Medusa"; however, Woolf completes that image with language that stresses Morrell's virtue and high-mindedness: she "is very simple and innocent in spite of it, and worships the arts."[19] In a letter to Vanessa Bell, Woolf further acknowledges Morrell's otherworldly appearance while conveying her passion for the arts: "I was so much overcome by her beauty that I really felt as if I'd suddenly got into the sea, and heard the mermaids fluting on their rocks."[20]

Unlike Huxley's simple caricature, Mansfield's intricate characterization of Rosemary Fell is more in tune with Woolf's observations. Mansfield conveys Morrell's complexity that sets the stage for the reader to critically consider Rosemary: while one could not call Rosemary "beautiful," she is pretty "if you took her to pieces."[21] Mansfield includes a depth that echoes Woolf's multilayered impressions: Rosemary Fell is "brilliant, [...] modern, [...] well dressed, [... and] well read in the newest of the new books"; Mansfield adds that "her parties were the most delicious mixture of the really important people and ... artists—quaint creatures, discoveries of hers."[22]

Consider further that it was through Ottoline Morrell that Mansfield became acquainted with Woolf's writing. Before Mansfield and Woolf met, Morrell had lent Mansfield a copy of *The Voyage Out* (1915). Mansfield read it on her return to England from France, where she had gone first for her brief affair with Francis Carco and later to start *The Aloe*, which the Hogarth Press would publish as *Prelude*.[23] Lytton Strachey, a regular guest at Garsington, wrote to Woolf about Mansfield's "great enthusiasm" for that novel and suggested that the writers meet: Strachey writes to Woolf that Mansfield wants "to make your acquaintance more than anyone else's. [...] I really believe you'd find her entertaining."[24]

The literary gatherings at the Fells' home, then, might be inspired by events at Garsington or the Morrells' home in Bloomsbury or the salons hosted by the Woolfs. For Mansfield, these groups would have been one and the same. Ottoline and Philip Morrell saw themselves not just as patrons of the "Blooms Berries" but as part of the group: "You cannot ignore [... Ottoline Morrell] in the 'Blooms Berries' because the Bloomsbury group revolved around her, and it revolved around Garsington in a way it didn't revolve around any other house or any other person."[25]

Mansfield leads her reader to enter a new environment with uncertainty and assume the position of an outsider; her collaboration with and involvement in London's literary salons was an uncomfortable one. Beatrice Campbell records Mansfield's sense of her outsider status during their first visit to one of Morrell's London gatherings:

> Katherine and I found ourselves wandering round the large drawing-room examining pictures and furniture, and she said softly to me, "Do you feel that we are two prostitutes and that this is the first time we have ever been in a decent house?" I knew she was acting a part and wanted me to join in the game. It had been raining on our way there and we were rather damp and bedraggled, which helped the illusion.[26]

While Campbell observes a dramatic flair in Mansfield's suggestion, Mansfield appears to have played up the role of the wanton in the face of the airs of those who made her feel alienated. Mansfield's sexuality resulted in vile talk that cemented her outsider status. Karen Usborne writes of Alexander Frere's recollection of Elizabeth von Arnim and Murry discussing what they referred to as the "problem of Katherine":

> Frere recalled hearing them discuss how in a fit of self-destruction, or madness even, Katherine had dressed herself up as a *poilu* or French soldier during the war as did the whores and camp followers. She went down into the trenches and, as a result of what happened there, contracted syphilis.[27]

There is, of course, no factual basis for this story, but what is most striking is that others could share this gossip as something within the realm of possibility.

Similarly, in "A Cup of Tea," Mansfield links a woman's sexuality with the status of one who is treated as a social inferior. Philip Fell jokes in a manner that echoes Alexander Frere's gossip when Philip tells Rosemary, "Let me know if Miss Smith is going to dine with us in time for me to look up *The Milliner's Gazette*."[28] His reference to Miss Smith as a "milliner," a "profession with a dubious reputation," adds the subversive subtext of sexual commerce and an important class distinction.[29] Angela Smith discusses J. D. Ferguson, an artist for whom Woolf did not share Mansfield's admiration, and his interest in the models he found in the Paris cafés: "They were chiefly girls employed by dressmakers and milliners and wore things they were working at, mostly too extreme [...] but with that touch of daring that made them *very helpful*."[30] Smith observes that Ferguson "felt at home with the dressmakers and milliners in the café [...] because they were not preoccupied by respectability." Further, "milliner" is a word loaded with a connotation of the cold and hungry *grisette*, a character type that remains in the popular consciousness with Puccini's sympathetic and consumptive heroine Mimì. In "A Cup of Tea," Mansfield revives the character of the impoverished, lower-class woman who may resort to prostitution.[31] Miss Smith is initially described in the "dark [...] shadowy" gray tones that suggest the word *grisette*.[32] Mansfield intensifies the image of the prostitute throughout the story, concluding with Philip questioning his wife's motivations in bringing Miss Smith into the house: "I think you're making a ghastly mistake. Sorry, darling, if I'm crude and all that."[33] Rosemary and the reader may simply read Philip's words that Miss Smith is "so astonishingly pretty" as a statement of his desire.[34] However, reading Rosemary's and Philip's interest in the same person harkens back to the complexity Mansfield had explored more overtly in "Bliss" (1918).

The hint of sexual encounter may help explain Miss Smith's initial fear that she may have opened herself up to the threat of arrest.[35] Rosemary's thoughts of taking the young beggar home are charged with a sexual undertone: "Supposing [Rosemary] ... did do one of those things she was always reading about or seeing on the stage, what would happen? It would be thrilling."[36] Rosemary's invitation to her home is coy and seductive: she tells the young stranger, "I want you to. To please me. Come along."[37] Miss Smith's reaction also signals that this conversation should stay secret: "The girl put her finger to her lips and her eyes devoured Rosemary."[38] This interchange not only echoes Beatrice Campbell's account of the visit to the Morrells' Bloomsbury home but reinforces Mansfield's impressions of the established class's view of "the other." Woolf's initial impressions of Mansfield were particularly harsh: she describes Mansfield as common, "hard & cheap," and one who "had taken to street walking."[39] Mansfield's sympathies were with the woman whose reputation was unfairly determined. Because of her own experiences feeling like an outsider in London social circles, she knew what it was to be labeled as socially inferior.

Readers of Mansfield know well this motif of the woman whose reputation has been unfairly spoiled. One may think of "The Little Governess," written in 1915, but just collected in *Bliss and Other Stories* (1920).[40] That story begins with a warning: the woman at the bureau counsels the young governess: it is "better to mistrust people at first rather than trust them, and it's safer to suspect people of evil intentions rather than good ones.... It sounds rather hard but we've got to be women of the world, haven't we?"[41] The old German, like Rosemary Fell, builds trust with an offer of food and drink and the reassurance that "It goes easier [...] if you take my arm."[42] Both the governess and the reader prefer to see these actions as those of a kindly grandfather figure. When Mansfield repeats this pattern in "A Cup of Tea," readers also are taken in by the author's manipulation; the ruse results in a willingness to accept that Rosemary Fell is indeed a "fairy godmother" rather than a character who dominates the hungry and penniless Miss Smith.[43]

With Rosemary Fell, Mansfield constructs a female protagonist who builds a false sense of trust in her willingness to exploit another woman. During the ride back to her home, Rosemary articulates very little to Miss Smith. Despite an interior monologue, she utters little other than the single word "There!"[44] Everything else is a window into her private thoughts: Rosemary "had a feeling of triumph as she slipped her hand through the velvet strap. She could have said, 'Now I've got you,' as she gazed at the little captive she had netted."[45] Rosemary rationalizes her motivation, convincing herself that this is an act of compassion. Even then, she has trouble completing her thought:

> But of course she meant it kindly. Oh, more than kindly. She was going to prove to this girl that—wonderful things did happen in life, that—fairy godmothers were real, that—rich people had hearts, and that women *were* sisters. She turned impulsively, saying: "Don't be frightened. After all, why shouldn't you come back with me? We're both women. If I'm the more fortunate, you ought to expect ..." But happily at that moment, for she didn't know how the sentence was going to end, the car stopped.[46]

The passage echoes a scene in Woolf's *The Voyage Out*, another narrative about mentorship. There, Helen Ambrose makes a case for trust to her niece, Rachel Vinrace; she argues, "After all [...] it's silly to pretend that because there's twenty years' difference between us we therefore can't talk to each other like human beings."[47] Mansfield uses Woolf's approach but takes it farther and exposes Rosemary's untrustworthiness through a series of interrupted thoughts, a halting interior monologue as she constructs an argument to convince herself, and, if necessary, her new charge that she is principled.

"A Cup of Tea" already hinted at Rosemary's self-deception with her penchant for floral decorations in the face of the realities of a landscape that she describes as "bitter [... and] sad," with dim lamps on the houses that are filled with regret.[48] Her outer concern with flowers and antiques for her fashionable home shifts to the uncomfortable interior life in which she feels trapped. When Rosemary Fell is at the antiques dealer, she is not simply taken by a decorative box; she is aware of her hands against "the tiny square of blue velvet," a soft, palatable image of the boundaries of the comfortable home that she wants to ornament with "quaint creatures."[49] Even if Mansfield's reader were to believe, at first, that Rosemary is benevolent, her insincerity is exposed through self-congratulatory flattery: her actions are not simply "kindly" but "more than kindly."[50] As her mind races, she eventually runs out of ideas: Rosemary will "prove to this girl that—"; she is unable to finish the thought. The pause gives her time to invent two reasons: "wonderful things did happen in life," and the most unconvincing argument, "fairy godmothers ... [are] real."[51] Even for Rosemary Fell that idea is ridiculous to consider for long. She revises her rhetoric, first to "rich people had hearts" and finally to "women *were* sisters."[52] When Rosemary finally speaks, she opts for the egalitarian statement "Don't be frightened ... We're both women."[53] Once inside her home, however, Rosemary's thoughts reveal a lack of empathy for the woman she claims to be nurturing, and it is nothing less than alarming: "To be quite sincere, she looked rather stupid."[54]

That shift from consoling and empathetic to privately dismissive reveals Rosemary as either oblivious to or totally accepting of hypocrisy originating in class difference. However, Rosemary's tone draws more from Woolf than from Morrell. Mansfield had learned to read a manipulative mixture of jealousy, anger, and self-centeredness in Woolf's condescending overtures. Mansfield would have recognized the same tone in Woolf's voice in her letter from February of 1921. That letter is one that Mansfield apparently never answered, but it is one that she kept.[55] "A Cup of Tea" can be read as Mansfield's response to Woolf. Woolf writes with a chatty, gossipy, and aggressive tone that gives insight about her conversational style, and her tone exposes an untrustworthiness similar to that of Rosemary Fell. Joanne Trautmann Banks writes that Woolf, in her letters, not only exemplifies the "hostess," but her content combines both praise and "tangential insults."[56] Woolf opens her letter to Mansfield with polite pleasantries, invoking a welcoming image of sitting at the table: "I was so delighted to get your letter. It came while I was having my tea alone."[57] Woolf, however, soon cuts to the quick: "I'm wondering what you think about your book—what people have said about it."[58] Woolf appears to elicit Mansfield's reaction to the reviews of *Bliss*, but in straightforward language, Woolf fires out her own feelings: "The reviews are enthusiastic, but then the reviews are stupid."[59] The harsh tone of the word "stupid" has a long sustain, and one can't help but compare its powerful dismissive effect both here and when Mansfield repeats its use in Rosemary's thoughts about Miss Smith. Mansfield is aware that the strongest use of such juvenile diction is to put it into the thoughts of an overbearing character.

Woolf continues her letter with a series of appeals that foreshadow the duplicitous observations of Rosemary Fell. Woolf next offers a peer's assessment that is simultaneously solicitous and threatening with a less-than-subtle jab at Mansfield's review of *Night and Day* (1919): "Shall I write you a criticism yet one of these days."[60] Woolf's attempt to speak to Mansfield as a peer about the difficulties the writer faces results in flattery that Mansfield would have been more wary of than seduced by, especially with the question she asks Mansfield after describing the difficulty she is facing with *Jacob's Room* (1922):

> I sometimes think that though we're so different we have some of the same difficulties. ... What I admire in you so much is your transparent quality. My stuff gets muddy; & then in a novel we must have continuity, but in this one I'm always chopping and changing from one level to another. I think what I'm at is

to change the consciousness, & to break up the awful stodge. Does this convey anything to you?[61]

Woolf's question would have hung heavily in the air for Mansfield, the writer who had conversed freely with Woolf about writing and, as Alpers first argued, even offered Woolf the idea for a new form which Woolf used in "Kew Gardens."[62] Woolf's question is in sharp contrast with her recollections after Mansfield's death. Woolf writes of mutual sympathies and understanding in their craft talks: "Most days I think we reached that kind of certainty, in talk […] about our writings, which I thought had something durable about it."[63]

Perhaps most shocking in this letter, though, is the manner in which Woolf juxtaposes her flattery with leaden words of dismissal: "And you seem to me to go so straightly & directly—ah clear as glass and spiritual. But I must read them over again properly."[64] Woolf's praise, tempered with a qualification that she must reconsider *Bliss and Other Stories* with a "proper" critical reading, is much like Rosemary Fell in the antiques shop when she admires an object but walks away from it in her attempt to diminish its value.

By contrast, Woolf's only other surviving letter to Mansfield was written three months earlier right after the publication of *Bliss* and has an effusive congratulatory tone:

> My dearest Katherine,
> I wish you were here to enjoy your triumph—still more that we might talk about your book—For what's the use of telling you how glad and indeed proud I am? However, I must to please myself send a line to say just that.[65]

Just as Mansfield kept her real criticism of *Night and Day* to her private writings, in her diary Woolf not only admits she has not read *Bliss* but also reveals her thoughts, which range from jealousy to an outright dismissal of Mansfield's talent:

> I've plucked out my jealousy of Katherine by writing her an insincere-sincere letter. Her books praised for a column in the Lit Sup—the prelude of paeans to come. I foresee editions; then the Hawthornden prize next summer. So I've had my little nettle growing in me, & plucked it as I say. I've revived my affection for her somehow, & don't mind, in fact enjoy [it]. But I've not read her book.[66]

Woolf's reflection on her "insincere-sincere" letter is a candid acceptance of a duplicity of emotion that encompasses both "jealousy [and …] affection." One must also remember that "Bliss" is a story about which Woolf had reservations as far back as 1918; she was so incensed by the story that she unleashed an angry appraisal of Mansfield as a writer: "I threw down Bliss with the exclamation,

'She's done for!' Indeed I dont see how much faith in her as a woman or writer can survive that sort of story. [... H]er mind is a very thin soil, laid an inch or two deep upon very barren rock."[67] Woolf continues to criticize the story as "poor, cheap, not the vision [...] of an interesting mind"; evaluating Mansfield's skill as an artist, Woolf adds that Mansfield "writes badly too. And the effect was as I say, to give me an impression of her callousness & hardness as a human being."[68] Two days later, in a letter to Vanessa Bell, Woolf is more guarded but still critical of the story: "I'm a little disturbed by a story of hers in the English Review. Its—well I wont say."[69]

Woolf's dislike of "Bliss" and her expressed loss of faith in Mansfield "as a woman" and her decision to keep details of that criticism from her sister could have been driven by the story's Sapphic content and frank exploration of sexual desire. Years later, in a letter to Vita Sackville-West, Woolf continues to reflect about her relationship with Mansfield: "I thought her cheap, and she thought me priggish. [...] But the fact remains—I mean that she had a quality I adored, and needed; I think her sharpness and reality—her having knocked about with prostitutes and so on, whereas I had always been respectable—was the thing I wanted then."[70] Her harsh criticism appears to be guided by Mansfield's openness toward her sexuality despite an observation of Woolf biographer Quentin Bell: in a conversation with Antony Alpers, Bell thought Woolf felt "a little love affair" with Mansfield, a fascination driven by "Katherine's elusive personality and all her wide 'experience.'"[71]

Although Woolf is regarded as a feminist icon today, her attitude toward women's confident sexuality, at the time she knew Mansfield, was disapproving of the bohemian women with whom she associated. In her diary she freely disparages them: Woolf described Ottoline Morrell as "brilliantly painted, as garish as a strumpet"[72]; after meeting Ida Baker, Woolf described her as "another of these females on the border land of propriety, & naturally inhabiting the underworld [...] without any attachment to one place rather than another."[73] Woolf famously wrote that her first impression of Mansfield was that "she stinks like a—well civet cat that has taken to street walking"; Woolf adds, "In truth, I'm a little shocked by her commonness."[74] One cannot imagine that such class-driven attitudes stayed private, especially because Woolf's jealousy runs throughout her diaries: "I was happy to hear K[atherine] abused the other night. Now why? ... how bad the Athenaeum stories are; yet in my heart I must think her good, since I'm glad to hear her abused."[75] It might very well be that Woolf was able to hide such negative feelings from Mansfield; then again, Mansfield, like Woolf herself, was an astute observer of character. Contrasting spoken words with a character's unspoken observations, after all, is an important characteristic of Mansfield's fiction and private writing as well as a key to understanding the duplicity of Rosemary Fell; it also explains why Mansfield would have decided to address Woolf's unanswered letter in her fiction.

Antony Alpers perceptively observes "the end of the friendship, on [... Mansfield's] side at least," in her last letter to Woolf. Mansfield closes not only with a note of finality but with a puzzling question: "Farewell, dear friend (may I call you that?)."[76] Alpers suggests that Mansfield's questioning of the term friend "sounds as though Katherine had heard something she didn't like."[77]

Woolf's perception of Mansfield's illness was something to which Mansfield would have been particularly sensitive. While living in Hampstead, a period when Woolf visited Mansfield regularly, her health, of course, had declined.[78] In her notebook, Mansfield writes about her consumption straightforwardly: "There is still a great deal of moisture (& pain) in my BAD lung."[79] Mansfield's descriptions of the progression of her illness in July 1920 become even more intense:

> I cough and cough and at each breath a dragging boiling bubbling sound is heard. I feel that my whole chest is boiling.... I can't expand my chest—it's as though the chest had collapsed. Life is—getting new breath.... I had a sensation of UTTER cold.... What a fate to be so self imprisoned!! What a ghastly fate.... It's like [...] trying not to drown.[80]

Woolf, however, comes across as indifferent to Mansfield's physical condition. As early as 1918, Woolf describes Mansfield as "feeble, crawling about the room like an old woman" and obliviously adds, "How far she is ill, one cant say."[81] While Mansfield may feel the outsider in social circles, Woolf's apparent lack of empathy for Mansfield's illness marks her as an outsider to Mansfield's world. Woolf unsympathetically complains about the disruption of her own social activity: "I asked Murry whether she would like a visit; to which he replied cordially & without the shadow of hesitation. I proposed to go yesterday. About eleven she, or rather the female who keeps house, rang up & put me off, saying that K. M. was too unwell for my visit; but making no suggestion of another time, nor have I any word from her or K. this morning."[82] Woolf further notes another "rather stiff tea" with Mansfield, Murry, his brother Richard, and "the Rhodesian woman" because "Katherine [was] haggard & powdered."[83]

Just as Woolf does not seem to fully comprehend the extent of Mansfield's illness, Mansfield's characterization of Rosemary Fell explores her perception of a woman that is not simply protected by the stability of a home but isolated from a real understanding of the fragile state of "the other"; Rosemary has never known and will never understand the full effects of the destructiveness of the cold. Moments before Miss Smith approaches her, Rosemary thinks about getting to the protection of her motorcar; discomfort consists of only "moments, horrible moments in life, when one emerges from shelter and looks out, and it's awful."[84] However, Miss Smith's cold, impoverished state is real and by the end of the story has no effect on Rosemary. Dismissing Miss Smith into the cold and rain is particularly resonant if one reads her impoverished existence as a parallel to Mansfield's outsider status created by her illness. Susan Sontag, in her analysis of the consumptive, writes that "TB is often imagined as a disease of poverty and deprivation—of thin garments, thin bodies, unheated rooms, poor hygiene, inadequate food."[85] The narrative voice in "A Cup of Tea" similarly records Rosemary's impressions of the beggar's weakness, cold, and hunger. Rosemary, however, never fully comprehends the seriousness of what she sees: the "battered creature [...] had] reddened hands, and shivered as though she had just come out of the water" and is so weak by the time she gets to the Fells' home that she can barely "whisper." Rosemary Fell focuses instead on Miss Smith's socially unacceptable "crushed hat."[86] There were times when Mansfield similarly felt a basic human need for health and physical comfort: "How I envy Virginia; no wonder she can write. There is always in her writing a calm freedom of expression as though she were at peace—her roof over her—her own possessions round her—and her man somewhere within call. Boge what have I done that I should have all the handicaps—plus a disease."[87]

Even though both Woolf and Mansfield record admiration for one another, what lingers most in Woolf's final letter to Mansfield is an undercurrent of dismissiveness that Mansfield dramatizes with Rosemary Fell. In another attempt to indicate a mutual bond, Woolf shares an anecdote from a recent literary event. She tells Mansfield that a member of the forum rose to his feet to say he has "no use for [...] Katherine Mansfield, or Virginia Woolf."[88] She tells Mansfield that E. M. Forster added his voice: "Morgan Forster said that Prelude & The Voyage Out were the best novels of their time."[89] Woolf comes across as more petty than lighthearted in her reaction: "I said Damn Katherine! Why can't I be the only woman who knows how to write?"[90] The answer, of course, seems simple: she was not. Mansfield writes a similar sentiment into the final lines of "A Cup of Tea" when Rosemary, after dismissing Miss Smith, who has turned more into a threat than anticipated, asks her husband, "Am I pretty?"[91] The question remains unanswered by Philip; the answer, however, is there for the reader who has taken Rosemary "to pieces" just as Mansfield had examined Woolf's letter. Revealing her own jealousy, when she wrote to Murry about her dreams for home, Mansfield says that Woolf's stability allows a "calm freedom of expression as though she were at peace."[92] Mansfield's words, as always, are carefully chosen. She knows that this too is an illusion: "as though she were at peace" is a far cry from saying Woolf *is* at peace.

There are lasting lessons that Mansfield learned at the tables of Ottoline Morrell and Virginia Woolf. They were both dedicated to the arts, but they also exhibited behavior that motivated Mansfield to withdraw from them. Mansfield was ever aware of the ways of the world and the dangers women face. When Miss Smith disappears from the Fells' home, it is she who has the reader's sympathy: she may return to her difficult life, but she is her own person, free not just from exploitation as a temporary amusement but, more importantly, free from any delusion about what constitutes a bond between women: it is not a hostess and her guest sharing a cup of tea. Like Miss Smith, who is sent back into the cold and rain, Mansfield faces the elements and navigates life. Mansfield's records in her journal a dream in which she faces a tempestuous sea: "It was a marvellous sight."[93] She draws strength, like her counterpart Miss Smith, not from a false sense of security but from her willingness to face the storm.

Notes

1 Katherine Mansfield, *The Montana Stories* (London: Persephone, 2001), v.
2 Antony Alpers, ed., *The Stories of Katherine Mansfield* (Auckland: Oxford University Press, 1984), 576.
3 Margaret Scott, ed., *The Katherine Mansfield Notebooks*, 2 vols. (Minneapolis: University of Minnesota Press, 2002), 2:315.
4 Scott, *Mansfield Notebooks*, 2:319.
5 Scott, *Mansfield Notebooks*, 2:319.
6 Scott, *Mansfield Notebooks*, 2:320.
7 Katherine Mansfield, "A Cup of Tea," in *The Collected Works of Katherine Mansfield, The Collected Fiction*, ed. Gerri Kimber and Vincent O'Sullivan, 2 vols. (Edinburgh: Edinburgh University Press, 2012), 2:461–67.
8 Scott, *Mansfield Notebooks*, 2:315.
9 Scott, *Mansfield Notebooks*, 2:317.
10 Scott, *Mansfield Notebooks*, 2:315–16.
11 Mansfield, "A Cup of Tea," 2:464–65.

12 Michael Sadler, writing in *Rhythm*, quotes from a letter Gauguin wrote to Strindberg: "Your civilization is your disease, […] my barbarism is my restoration to health." See "L'Esprit Veille," *Rhythm* 1, no. 3 (Winter 1911): 32.
13 Angela Smith, *Katherine Mansfield: A Literary Life* (New York: Palgrave, 2000), 3.
14 Mansfield, "A Cup of Tea," 2:465.
15 Kathleen Jones, *Katherine Mansfield: The Story Teller* (Edinburgh: Edinburgh University Press, 2010), 277.
16 Mansfield, "A Cup of Tea," 2:461.
17 Aldous Huxley, *Crome Yellow* (1921; repr., New York: Barnes and Noble, 2004), 8.
18 Huxley quotes from one of Bard's signature songs, "I Want to Sing in Opera."
19 Virginia Woolf to Madge Vaughan, May 1909, in *The Letters of Virginia Woolf*, ed. Nigel Nicolson and Joanne Trautmann, 6 vols. (New York: Harcourt Brace Jovanovich, 1975–1980), 1:395. Unless otherwise noted, all subsequent letters from Woolf are from this source.
20 Virginia Woolf to Vanessa Bell, May 22, 1917, 2:156.
21 Mansfield, "A Cup of Tea," 2:461.
22 Mansfield, "A Cup of Tea," 2:461.
23 Jones, *Story Teller*, 280.
24 Jones, *Story Teller*, 280–81.
25 "Rachel Johnson on Ottoline Morrell," *Great Lives*, BBC4, April 17, 2015, Radio Broadcast. http://www.bbc.co.uk/programmes/b05qgch9 (accessed December 17, 2016).
26 Beatrice [Campbell], Lady Glenavy, *Today We Will Only Gossip* (London: Constable, 1964), 80.
27 Karen Usborne, *Elizabeth* (London: The Bodley Head, 1986), 230.
28 Mansfield, "A Cup of Tea," 2:466.
29 Kathleen Jones, *A Passionate Sisterhood* (New York: St. Martin's Press, 2000), 5. In her discussion of Sarah and Edith Fricker, Jones notes that "It was Byron who made the sarcastic remark about Coleridge and Southey marrying 'two milliners from Bath,' gossip repeated by Thomas De Quincey, who added, 'Everybody knows what is meant to be conveyed in that expression'" (5).
30 Angela Smith, *Katherine Mansfield*, 12.
31 Mansfield also explored the situation of Miss Moss in the short play "The Common Round," originally published in *The New Age* (1917), revised as "The Pictures" (1919), and included as "Pictures" in *Bliss and Other Stories* (1920).
32 Mansfield, "A Cup of Tea," 2:462.
33 Mansfield, "A Cup of Tea," 2:466.
34 Mansfield, "A Cup of Tea," 2:466.
35 Paula Bartley, *Prostitution: Prevention and Reform in England, 1860–1914* (London: Routledge, 2000). Bartley notes,

Prostitution was not illegal but it was a stigmatised activity, socially unacceptable and surrounded by so many legal restrictions as to be illegal in all but name. [...] Actions which would not constitute an infringement of the law by "respectable" women were illegal if committed by known prostitutes: loitering for example was not in itself a criminal offence and became so only if practised by women thought to be prostitutes. (4)

36 Mansfield, "A Cup of Tea," 2:463.
37 Mansfield, "A Cup of Tea," 2:463.
38 Mansfield, "A Cup of Tea," 2:463.
39 Anne Olivier Bell, ed., *The Diary of Virginia Woolf*, 5 vols. (New York: Harcourt Brace & Company, 1977–1984), 1:58.
40 Katherine Mansfield, "The Little Governess," in *The Collected Fiction*, ed. Kimber and O'Sullivan, 1:422–33.
41 Mansfield, "Governess," 1:422.
42 Mansfield, "Governess," 1:430.
43 Mansfield, "A Cup of Tea," 2:463.
44 Mansfield, "A Cup of Tea," 2:463.
45 Mansfield, "A Cup of Tea," 2:463.
46 Mansfield, "A Cup of Tea," 2:463–64.
47 Virginia Woolf, *The Voyage Out* (1915, repr., London: Hogarth, 1971), 95.
48 Mansfield, "A Cup of Tea," 2:462.
49 Mansfield, "A Cup of Tea," 2:461.
50 Mansfield, "A Cup of Tea," 2:463.
51 Mansfield, "A Cup of Tea," 2:463.
52 Mansfield, "A Cup of Tea," 2:463–64.
53 Mansfield, "A Cup of Tea," 2:464.
54 Mansfield, "A Cup of Tea," 2:464.
55 While some might speculate that there could have been a meeting between Mansfield and Woolf when Mansfield returned to London, it would be difficult to explain why Woolf would not have recorded the event in her diaries.
56 Joanne Trautmann Banks, introduction to *Congenial Spirits: The Selected Letters of Virginia Woolf*, ed. Joanne Trautmann Banks (San Diego: Harcourt Brace Jovanovich, 1989), vii–viii.
57 Virginia Woolf to Katherine Mansfield, February 13, 1921, in Trautmann, *Congenial Spirits*, 127. A facsimile of the letter is available in the *Woolf in the World, A Pen and a Press of Her Own*, Online Exhibit, Mortimer Rare Book Room, Smith College.
58 Woolf to Mansfield, February 13, 1921, in Banks, *Congenial Spirits*, 127.
59 Woolf to Mansfield, February 13, 1921, in Banks, *Congenial Spirits*, 127.
60 Woolf to Mansfield, February 13, 1921, in Banks, *Congenial Spirits*, 127.

61 Woolf to Mansfield, February 13, 1921, in Banks, *Congenial Spirits*, 127–28.
62 Antony Alpers, *The Life of Katherine Mansfield* (New York: Viking Press, 1980), 250–52. See also Angela Smith, *Katherine Mansfield: A Public of Two* (Oxford: Clarendon, 1999), 136–40.
63 Bell, *Diary of Virginia Woolf*, 2:226.
64 Woolf to Mansfield, February 13, 1921, in Banks, *Congenial Spirits*, 128.
65 Woolf to Mansfield, December 19, 1920, 2:449.
66 Bell, *Diary of Virginia Woolf*, 2:80.
67 Bell, *Diary of Virginia Woolf*, 1:179.
68 Bell, *Diary of Virginia Woolf*, 1:179.
69 Woolf to Vanessa Bell, August 9, 1918, 2:266.
70 Virginia Woolf to Vita Sackville-West, August 8, 1931, in Banks, *Congenial Spirits*, 293.
71 Alpers, *Life*, 288.
72 Bell, *Diary of Virginia Woolf*, 1:201.
73 Bell, *Diary of Virginia Woolf*, 1:58.
74 Bell, *Diary of Virginia Woolf*, 1:58.
75 Bell, *Diary of Virginia Woolf*, 2:78–79.
76 Alpers, *Life*, 260.
77 Alpers, *Life*, 260.
78 "Cherie Rogers—An Oddly Complete Understanding," BBC4, November 30, 2015, Radio Broadcast. http://www.bbc.co.uk/programmes/b06qsngj (accessed December 17, 2016). Rogers states that Woolf made seven visits to Mansfield's Hampstead home.
79 Scott, *Mansfield Notebooks*, 2:173.
80 Scott, *Mansfield Notebooks*, 2:219.
81 Bell, *Diary of Virginia Woolf*, 1:216.
82 Bell, *Diary of Virginia Woolf*, 1:243.
83 Bell, *Diary of Virginia Woolf*, 1:268.
84 Mansfield, "A Cup of Tea," 2:462.
85 Susan Sontag, *Illness as Metaphor* (New York: Farrar, Straus and Giroux, 1977), 15.
86 Mansfield, "A Cup of Tea," 2:463–64.
87 Katherine Mansfield to John Middleton Murry, November 30, 1919, in *The Collected Letters of Katherine Mansfield*, 5 vols. ed. Vincent O'Sullivan and Margaret Scott (Oxford: Clarendon Press, 1984–2008), 3:127–28.
88 Woolf to Mansfield, February 13, 1921, in Banks, *Congenial Spirits*, 128.
89 Woolf to Mansfield, February 13, 1921, in Banks, *Congenial Spirits*, 128.
90 Woolf to Mansfield, February 13, 1921, in Banks, *Congenial Spirits*, 128.
91 Mansfield, "A Cup of Tea," 2:437.
92 Mansfield to Murry, November 30, 1919, 3:127.
93 Scott, *Mansfield Notebooks*, 2:317.

Selected Bibliography

Alpers, Antony. *The Life of Katherine Mansfield*. London: Jonathan Cape, 1980.
Beal, Wesley. *Networks of Modernism: Reorganizing American Narrative*. Iowa City: University of Iowa Press, 2015.
Bell, Anne Oliver and Andrew McNeillie, eds. *The Diary of Virginia Woolf*. 5 vols. London: Hogarth Press, 1977–1984.
Binckes, Faith. *Modernism, Magazines, and the British Avant-Garde: Reading Rhythm 1910–1914*. Oxford: Oxford University Press, 2010.
Boddy, Gillian. *Katherine Mansfield: The Woman and the Writer*. Victoria: Penguin Books, 1988.
Bradshaw, David, ed. *Aldous Huxley between the Wars: Essays and Letters*. Chicago: Ivan R. Dee, 1994.
Brooke, Jocelyn. *Aldous Huxley*. London: Longmans, Green & Co., 1968.
Brooker, Jewell Spears and Ronald Schuchard, eds. *The Complete Prose of T. S. Eliot: The Critical Edition: Apprentice Years, 1905–1918*. Baltimore: The Johns Hopkins University Press, 2014.
Brooker, Peter. *Bohemia in London: The Social Scene of Early Modernism*. New York: Palgrave Macmillan, 2007.
Edel, Leon. *Bloomsbury: A House of Lions*. Philadelphia and New York: J. B. Lippincott Company, 1979.
Eliot, Valerie and Hugh Haughton, eds. *The Letters of T. S. Eliot*. vol. 1, rev. ed. London: Faber, 2009.
Fulbrook, Kate. *Katherine Mansfield*. Bloomington: Indiana University Press, 1986.
Gathorne-Hardy, Robert, ed. *Ottoline at Garsington: Memoirs of Lady Ottoline Morrell 1915–1918*. London: Faber and Faber, 1974.
Gordon, Lyndall. *T. S. Eliot: An Imperfect Life*, 2nd ed. London: Vintage, 1998.
Hammond, Meghan Marie. *Empathy and the Psychology of Literary Modernism*. Edinburgh: Edinburgh University Press, 2014.
Hankin, C. A., ed. *Letters between Katherine Mansfield and John Middleton Murry*. London: Virago, 1988.
Hankin, C. A., ed. *The Letters of John Middleton Murry to Katherine Mansfield*. London: Constable, 1983.
Hanson, Clare and Andrew Gurr. *Katherine Mansfield*. London: Macmillan, 1981.
Holroyd, Michael. *Lytton Strachey*. London: Chatto & Windus, 1994.
Jerrold, Douglas. *Georgian Adventure*. London: Collins Pall Mall, 1937.
Jones, Kathleen. *Katherine Mansfield: The Story Teller*. Edinburgh: Edinburgh University Press, 2010.

Kaplan, Sydney Janet. *Circulating Genius: John Middleton Murry, Katherine Mansfield and D. H. Lawrence*. Edinburgh: Edinburgh University Press, 2010.

Kaplan, Sydney Janet. *Katherine Mansfield and the Origins of Modernist Fiction*. Ithaca: Cornell University Press, 1991.

Kaščáková, Janka and Gerri Kimber, eds. *Katherine Mansfield and Continental Europe: Connections and Influences*. London: Palgrave, 2015.

Kimber, Gerri and Janet Wilson, eds. *Celebrating Katherine Mansfield*. New York: Palgrave Macmillan, 2011.

Kimber, Gerri, Vincent O'Sullivan, Angela Smith, and Claire Davison, eds. *The Collected Works of Katherine Mansfield*. 4 vols. Edinburgh: Edinburgh University Press, 2012–2016.

Latour, Bruno. *Reassembling the Social: An Introduction to Actor-Network-Theory*. Clarendon Lectures in Management Studies. Oxford: Oxford University Press, 2005.

Lea, F. A. *John Middleton Murry*. New York: Oxford University Press, 1960.

Lee, Hermione. *Virginia Woolf*. New York: Vintage-Random House, 1999.

McDonnell, Jenny. *Katherine Mansfield and the Modernist Marketplace*. New York: Palgrave Macmillan, 2010.

McNeillie, Andrew and Stuart Clarke, eds. *The Essays of Virginia Woolf*. 6 vols. London: Hogarth Press, 1987–2000.

Meyers, Jeffrey. *Katherine Mansfield: A Darker View*. 1978. Reprinted with a new introduction. New York: Cooper Square Press, 2002.

Murry, Nicholas. *Aldous Huxley: An English Intellectual*. London: Abacus, 2003.

Nathan, Rhoda B., ed. *Essays on Katherine Mansfield*. New York: R. K. Hall, 1993.

New, W. H. *Reading Mansfield and Metaphors of Form*. Montreal and Kingston: McGill-Queen's University Press, 1999.

Nicolson, Nigel and Joanne Trautmann, eds. *The Letters of Virginia Woolf*. 6 vols. London: Hogarth Press, 1975–1980.

Noë, Alva and Evan Thompson, eds. *Vision and Mind*. Cambridge, MA: MIT Press, 2002.

O'Sullivan, Vincent and Margaret Scott, eds. *The Collected Letters of Katherine Mansfield*. 5 vols. Oxford: Clarendon Press, 1984–2008.

Reed, Christopher. *Bloomsbury Rooms: Modernism, Subculture and Domesticity*. New Haven: Yale University Press, 2004.

Reed, Christopher, ed. *A Roger Fry Reader*. Chicago: University of Chicago Press, 1996.

Ricks, Christopher and Jim McCue, eds. *The Poems of T. S. Eliot: Collected and Uncollected Poems*, vol. 1. Baltimore: The Johns Hopkins University Press, 2015.

Robinson, Roger, ed. *Katherine Mansfield: In from the Margin*. Louisiana: Louisiana State University Press, 1994.

Rosenbaum, S. P. *Georgian Bloomsbury: The Early Literary History of the Bloomsbury Group 1910–1914*. vol. 3. Basingstoke: Palgrave Macmillan, 2003.

Rosner, Victoria, ed. *Cambridge Companion to the Bloomsbury Group*. Cambridge: Cambridge University Press, 2014.

Rubin, Adrianne. *Roger Fry's "Difficult and Uncertain Science": The Interpretation of Aesthetic Perception.* Cultural Interactions: Studies in the Relationship between the Arts 28. Oxford: Peter Lang AG, 2013.

Scheider, Elizabeth W. *T. S. Eliot: The Pattern in the Carpet.* Los Angeles: UCLA Press, 1975.

Scott, Margaret, ed. *The Katherine Mansfield Notebooks.* 2 vols. Minneapolis: University of Minnesota Press, 2002.

Sellers, Susan, ed. *The Cambridge Companion to Virginia Woolf.* Cambridge: Cambridge University Press, 2010.

Sexton, James, ed. *Aldous Huxley: Selected Letters.* Chicago: Ivan R. Dee, 2007.

Seymour, Miranda. *Ottoline Morrell: Life on a Grand Scale.* London: Hodder and Stoughton, 1998.

Sion, Robert T. *Aldous Huxley and the Search for Meaning: A Study of the Eleven Novels.* Jefferson, NC: McFarland, 2010.

Smith, Angela. *Katherine Mansfield: A Literary Life.* London: Palgrave Macmillan, 2000.

Smith, Angela. *Katherine Mansfield and Virginia Woolf: A Public of Two.* Oxford: Clarendon Press, 1999.

Smith, Grover, ed. *Letters of Aldous Huxley.* London: Chatto & Windus, 1969.

Spalding, Frances. *Roger Fry: Art and Life.* London: Granada, 1980.

Thody, Philip. *Aldous Huxley: A Biographical Introduction.* London: Studio Vista, 1973.

Todd, Pamela. *Bloomsbury at Home.* New York: Harry N. Abrahms, 1999.

Tomalin, Claire. *Katherine Mansfield: A Secret Life.* London: Penguin, 1988.

Valentine, Mark, ed. *Strangers and Pilgrims: Tales by Walter de la Mare.* Leyburn, North Yorkshire: Tartarus Press, 2007.

Waugh, Alec. *My Brother Evelyn, and Other Portraits.* New York: Farrar, Straus, and Giroux, 1968.

Whistler, Theresa. *Imagination of the Heart: The Life of Walter de la Mare.* London: Duckworth, 1993.

Wilson, Janet, Gerri Kimber, and Susan Reid, eds. *Katherine Mansfield and Literary Modernism.* London: Bloomsbury, 2011.

Contributors

Erika Baldt is an English instructor at Rowan College at Burlington County, a community college in New Jersey, where she teaches composition and literature. She earned a PhD in English and comparative literature from Goldsmiths, University of London, with a thesis on the work of Virginia Woolf, Katherine Mansfield, and their contemporaries of the Harlem Renaissance, Jessie Fauset and Nella Larsen. She has published essays on the work of Fauset, Mansfield, Woolf, and Vita Sackville-West. Her research interests include Anglo-American modernism and cosmopolitanism as well as service learning and its integration into the community college environment.

Richard Cappuccio has presented papers at the Katherine Mansfield Society's conferences in Wellington, Paris, Chicago, and Bandol as well as at the Virginia Woolf International Conference. His articles about Mansfield have appeared in the *New Zealand Journal of Literature*, *Katherine Mansfield Studies*, and *The Journal of Religious History*. The Katherine Mansfield Birthplace appointed him as ambassador in 2014. He enjoys gardening at his home in Charlottesville, Virginia; he also finds time to set type by hand at the Virginia Arts of the Book Center.

Christine Darrohn is Associate Professor of English at the University of Maine at Farmington. Her research centers on Victorian and modern British literature with an emphasis on representations of the possibilities and difficulties of forming human connections across social barriers. She has published articles on Katherine Mansfield and Virginia Woolf that focus on class, gender, and the Great War.

Mary Ann Gillies is a professor in the English Department at Simon Fraser University in Vancouver, Canada, where she teaches and publishes on late nineteenth- and early twentieth-century British literature and Anglo-American modernism. Among her publications are *Henri Bergson and British Modernism* (McGill-Queen's, 1995); *The Professional Literary Agent in Britain: 1880–1920* (Toronto, 2007); with Aurelea Mahood, *Modernist Literature: An Introduction*

(Edinburgh, 2007); and with Helen Sword and Steven Yao, *Pacific Rim Modernisms* (Toronto, 2009). She is currently at work on a book about Katherine Mansfield, Emily Carr, and Virginia Woolf and is beginning a project on trauma theory and detective fiction.

Sydney Janet Kaplan is Professor of English and Adjunct Professor of Gender, Women, and Sexuality Studies at the University of Washington in Seattle. She is the author of *Circulating Genius: John Middle Murry, Katherine Mansfield and D.H. Lawrence*; *Katherine Mansfield and the Origins of Modernist Fiction*; and *Feminine Consciousness in the Modern British Novel*, as well as numerous reviews and articles on modernist literature. She serves on the International Advisory Board of *Katherine Mansfield Studies*, and on the Advisory Board for *The Edinburgh Edition of the Collected Works of Katherine Mansfield*.

Gerri Kimber is Visiting Professor of English at the University of Northampton, UK. Her research focus has two main strands: early twentieth-century literary modernism, in particular Katherine Mansfield and the Bloomsbury group, and postcolonial studies, particularly the literature of New Zealand Aotearoa. She is Chair of the Katherine Mansfield Society and coeditor of Katherine Mansfield Studies, the society's annual book series. She is the author of *Katherine Mansfield: The Early Years* (2016), *Katherine Mansfield and the Art of the Short Story* (2015), and *Katherine Mansfield: The View from France* (2008). She is also the series editor of the four-volume *Edinburgh Edition of the Collected Works of Katherine Mansfield* (2012–2016).

Ann Herndon Marshall earned her BA from Hollins College and her doctorate in English from the University of Virginia in 1987. She taught for twenty-five years at The Hill School, Pottstown, Pennsylvania. Her article "Winckelmann and the Anti-Essentialist Thrust in *Dorian Gray*" appeared in *Oscar Wilde: The Man, His Writing, and His World* (2003). She has presented three papers on Vita Sackville-West at the International Virginia Woolf Conference. She is currently writing an article on Elizabeth von Arnim, "Act Natural: Dubious Proposals in *The Mill on the Floss*, *Vera*, and *Rebecca*." Ann lives in Charlottesville, Virginia.

Todd Martin is Professor of English at Huntington University where he currently holds the Edwina Patton Chair of Arts and Sciences. His area of expertise is modern British and American literature, and he has published on such varied authors as John Barth, E. E. Cummings, Clyde Edgerton, Edwidge

Danticat, Julia Alvarez, and Katherine Mansfield. He is Membership Secretary of the Katherine Mansfield Society and coeditor of Katherine Mansfield Studies, the society's annual book series.

Jenny McDonnell lectures in critical theory, modernism, and postmodernism in the Department of Humanities & Arts Management, Dún Laoghaire Institute of Art, Design and Technology (IADT), Dublin, Ireland. Her primary research is in the field of modernism, in particular, modernist publishing histories; she has additional research interests in gothic studies. She is the author of *Katherine Mansfield and the Modernist Marketplace: At the Mercy of the Public* (Palgrave, 2010), as well as several essays on Mansfield, Robert Louis Stevenson, and Samuel Butler. She worked on the *Katherine Mansfield Society Newsletter* from 2008 to 2014 (first as coeditor and subsequently as editor), and was coeditor of *The Irish Journal of Gothic and Horror Studies* between September 2012 and November 2015.

Alex Moffett is Assistant Professor of English at Providence College, where he teaches twentieth-century British and Irish fiction. His articles have been recently published in *The Journal of Modern Literature*, *Katherine Mansfield Studies*, and *The Journal of Literature and Science*.

Chris Mourant is a teaching fellow in twentieth-century literature at the University of Birmingham. He has published articles on Katherine Mansfield in the *Times Literary Supplement* and the peer-reviewed journal *Katherine Mansfield Studies*, winning the Katherine Mansfield Society Essay Prize in 2014. Mourant's research primarily focuses on early twentieth-century print cultures and modernist women's writing; he is currently preparing his first monograph for publication, titled *Katherine Mansfield and Periodical Culture*.

Ruchi Mundeja is Associate Professor in the Department of English at Lakshmibai College, University of Delhi. She is currently enrolled as a PhD candidate at Jawaharlal Nehru University, New Delhi. As part of a research opportunity, she recently spent one semester as a doctoral scholar at King's College, London. She is now working toward completing her dissertation on "The Politics of the Sneer: Jean Rhys and the Milieu of Modernist Iconoclasm." Her research is primarily in the areas of modernist and postcolonial literature.

Janet Wilson is Professor of English and Postcolonial Studies at the University of Northampton, UK. She has published widely on the literature and cinema of the white settler societies of Australia and New Zealand. Her current research interests are in Katherine Mansfield, postcolonial studies more generally, diaspora writing, and criticism. Her recent publications include "Katherine Mansfield and Anima Mundi: France and the Tradition of Nature Personified" in *Katherine Mansfield's French Lives* (2016) and "Discoursing on Slums: Representing the Cosmopolitan Subaltern" in *Reworking Postcolonialism: Globalization, Labour and Rights* (2015). She is Vice-Chair of the Katherine Mansfield Society.

Index

Abercrombie, Lascelles 98
Achilles 30
Adelphi, The 92
"Album Leaf, An" (Mansfield, K.) 74, 85
Aldington, Richard 85
Aloe, The (Mansfield, K.) 76, 222
Along the Road (Huxley, A.) 67
Amores (Lawrence, D. H.) 55
"Anatomy of Fiction, The" (Woolf, V.) 40, 43
Antic Hay (Huxley, A.) 65
Arabian Nights 82
Arnold, Matthew 39
Art (Bell, C.) 165
Asheham 19, 22
Asquith, Margot 54
Athenaeum 9–10, 39–44, 46, 60, 62–4, 66–7, 83, 85, 94–5, 136, 149, 155, 161, 163–5, 167, 170–1, 173–4, 228
"At the Bay" (Mansfield, K.) 65, 93, 117, 119, 152–3, 219–20
Austen, Jane 44, 162
"Awake" (de la Mare, W.) 93

Bad Wörishofen 110
Baillot, Juliet 60
Baker, Ida 119, 228
Ballet Russes 82
Bandol, France 54, 60, 62
"Baron, The" (Mansfield, K.) 110
Bates, H. E. 85
Beauchamp, Annie 151
Beauchamp, Harold 151
Bedford Square 3–4, 6
Bed of Roses, A (George, W.) 127, 129
Bell, Clive 1, 6, 95, 161, 165, 202
    Art 165
Bell, Quentin 228
Bell, Vanessa 1, 60, 182, 185, 187, 192, 221, 228
Bennett, Arnold 162
Beresford, J. D. 40, 48, 171–2
Bergson, Henri 79

Bertha Mason *(Jane Eyre)* 195
Bishop and Other Stories, The (Garnett, C.) 174
"Black Cap, The" (Mansfield, K.) 76
Blind Alley (George, W.) 135, 137
"Bliss" (Mansfield, K.) 7, 10, 23–4, 29, 45, 60–1, 65, 67, 75, 85, 92, 111, 113–14, 126–8, 131–3, 174, 182–3, 186, 188–9, 194–5, 202, 204, 209–15, 223, 226–8
Bliss and Other Stories (Mansfield, K.) 85, 94, 224, 227
Bloomsbury Group 1–12, 22, 40, 42, 73, 76, 81–2, 85, 91, 94–5, 97–8, 103, 146, 148–9, 154, 156–7, 161, 165, 181–6, 188, 192–5, 201–2, 204, 211, 215, 219–22, 224
Blue Review, The 44, 96–7
Boxing Day 56
Bretherton, R. H 171
Brett, Dorothy 56, 60, 65–6, 73, 78, 107, 115, 119, 169
Bronte, Charlotte 195
    Bertha Mason *(Jane Eyre)* 195
Brooke, Rupert 97–8, 131
Burlington Magazine, The 149
Bussy, Simon 221
"By Moonlight" (Mansfield, K.) 102
"Byron & Mr Briggs" (Woolf, V.) 177n

Café Royal 55
Caliban (George, W.) 132, 135–7
Cambridge 97, 149
Campbell, Beatrice 127, 130, 222–4
Canada 29
"Canary, The" (Mansfield, K.) 100
Cannan, Gilbert 40, 96
Carco, Francis 65, 222
Carr, Emily 146
Carrington, Dora 56, 65
Cézanne, Paul 150
Chancery Lane 44

"Changeling, The" (de la Mare, W.) 97
Chatto and Windus 47
Chekhov, Anton 46–7, 68, 73, 93, 162–3, 173–4
  Cherry Orchard, The 174
  "Steppe, The" 174
Chelsea Palace 58
Cherry Orchard, The (Chekhov, A.) 174
Church Street 58
Classicism 76, 175
Collected Poems (Thomas, E.) 64
Common Reader, The (Woolf, V.) 162
"Condition of English Poetry, The" (Murry, J. M.) 104n, 177n
Confession of Ursula Trent, The (George, W.) 136
Conrad, Joseph 164, 168
  Rescue, The 164
Constable & Co. 94
Continental Times 131
"Conversation Galante" (Eliot, T. S.) 74
Couperus, Louis 156, 172–3
Craft of Fiction, The (Lubbock, P.) 165
Cramb, John 54
Cresswell, D'Arcy 62
Criterion 83–4
Critic in Judgement, The (Murry, J. M.) 40
Crome Yellow (Huxley, A.) 55, 59, 61, 64–7, 221
"Cup of Tea, A" (Mansfield, K.) 10–11, 24, 186, 189, 194–5, 219–21, 223–6, 230

Daily Mirror 131
Daily News 136
de la Mare, Walter 1, 6, 9, 91–102
  "Awake" 93
  "Changeling, The" 97
  Down-Adown-Derry: A Book of Fairy Poems 93
  "Epitaph, An" 93
  "Green Room, The" 98–100
  "Horse in a Field (To Katherine Mansfield)" 100–1
  Memoirs of a Midget 93
  "Mocking Fairy, The" 97
  "Revenant, A" 98–9
  "Song of the Mad Prince, The" 97
  "Three Mulla-Mulgars, The" 93
  "To K. M." 100
Derrida, Jacques 9, 18, 23–4, 31, 34n

"Dill Pickle, A" (Mansfield, K.) 10, 79, 84, 202, 204, 206, 209–10, 215
"Doll's House, The" (Mansfield, K.) 24–6, 33, 152
Doves' Nest and Other Stories, The (Mansfield, K.) 92, 101–3, 219
Down-Adown-Derry: A Book of Fairy Poems (de la Mare, W.) 93
"Dragonflies" (Mansfield, K.) 170
Drey, Raymond 134
Drinkwater, John 96
Duckworth, George 22
Dunning, Bill 107
Dunning, Millar 1, 6, 9, 107–20
  Earth Spirit, The 108–9
  "English Village, An" 108
  "London" 108–9
  "Red Lion Square" 108, 111, 113, 121n
  "Sanatana Dharma" 109, 116, 119
  "Subconscious Influence of Nature, The" 118–19
  "Three Vignettes" 117
  "Women and War" 120n

"Early Spring" (Mansfield, K.) 111, 113
Earth Spirit, The (Dunning, M.) 108–9
Ecclesiastes 204
"Eeldrop and Appleplex" (Eliot, T. S.) 77, 81, 83
Elephant, The 101
Eliot, T. S. 1, 9, 40–1, 73–85, 95, 115, 150, 161, 165
  "Conversation Galante" 74
  "Eeldrop and Appleplex" 77, 81, 83
  "Hamlet and his Problems" 165
  "Love Song of J. Alfred Prufrock, The" 74, 76
  Poems 40
  "Preludes" 75
  "Rhapsody on a Windy Night" 74–5
Eliot, Vivien 82–3, 85
"English Village, An" (Dunning, M.) 108
"Epitaph, An" (de la Mare, W.) 93
"Escape, The" (Mansfield, K.) 85
"Essay in Aesthetics, An" (Fry, R.) 150
Esther Waters (Moore, G.) 155

Fauvism 146, 148, 154–5
Fergusson, J. D. 154–5

"Feuille d'Album" (Mansfield, K.) 74–6, 78, 80, 82, 84–5
Fielding, Henry 162
Fitzgerald, F. Scott 66
Fontainbleau 53, 114, 119
Ford, Ford Maddox 184
Forster, E. M. 11, 40, 63, 94, 161, 230
Fortnightly Review, The 149
France 54, 56, 59–60, 77, 79, 134, 204, 222
Frere, Alexander 223
"Freudian Fictions" (Woolf, V.) 171
Fry, Roger 1, 5, 10, 75, 145–6, 148–52, 156–7, 161
   "Essay in Aesthetics, An" 150
   "Giotto" 150
   Last Lectures 150
   "Philosophy of Impression, The" 145
   "Post Impression" 151
   "Retrospect" 150
   Vision and Design 146, 150

Galsworthy, John 162
"Garden Party, The" (Mansfield, K.) 92, 100–2, 204, 219
Garden Party and Other Stories, The (Mansfield, K.) 219
Garnett, Constance 174
   Bishop and Other Stories, The 174
Garnett, David *(Bunny)* 66
Garsington 3–7, 11, 13n, 53–6, 58–60, 64–7, 73, 75–6, 94, 107, 125, 161, 184, 219–22
George, Lloyd 63
George, W. L. 1, 6, 10, 40, 60, 125–38
   Bed of Roses, A 127, 129
   Blind Alley 135, 137
   Caliban 132, 135–7
   Confession of Ursula Trent, The 136
   Intelligence of Woman, The 128–9
   Making of an Englishman, The 132
   "Negress, The" 130
   Woman and To-Morrow 128
Georgian 2, 94–8, 103, 125
Georgian Poetry 95, 97
"Germans at Meat" (Mansfield, K.) 110
Gertler, Mark 55, 65
Gibson, Wilfrid Wilson 96, 98
Gift of the Dusk, A (Prowse, R. O.) 167
"Giotto" (Fry, R.) 150
Gissing, George 47

Gordon, John 42
Grafton Galleries 149
Grant, Duncan 1, 187
"Green Room, The" (de la Mare, W.) 98–100
Gurdjieff, George 10, 83, 114, 137

"Hamlet and his Problems" (Eliot, T. S.) 165
Happy Family, The (Swinnerton, F.) 43
Hardy, Thomas 93, 167–9
   Moments of Vision 167–8
Hastings, Beatrice 96, 175
Heinemann 98
Hergesheimer, Joseph 166–7
   Java Head 166
Heritage (Sackville-West, V.) 169
Hermes 119
Hogarth Press 41, 43, 76, 81, 95, 222
"Horse in a Field (To Katherine Mansfield)" (de la Mare, W.) 100–1
Hours, The (Woolf, V.) 176
"How It Strikes a Contemporary" (Woolf, V.) 164
Hudson, Stephen *(see Sydney Schiff)*
Hulme, T. E. 175
Hunt, Violet 184
Hutchinson, Jack 74–5
Hutchinson, Mary 74–5, 84
Huxley, Aldous 1, 9, 53–69, 73, 161, 221–2
   Along the Road 67
   Antic Hay 65
   Crome Yellow 55, 59, 61, 64–7, 221
   Limbo 63
   Point Counter Point 53, 65, 67
   Those Barren Leaves 62, 65, 67
   "Traveler's Eye View, The" 67
Huxley, Julian 56
Hyde, Robin 100

Ibsen, Henrik 56
Iliad, The 30
Imagistes, Des 97
Impressionists 145
"In Confidence" (Mansfield, K.) 58
"In the Botanical Gardens" (Mansfield, K.) 153
"Indiscreet Journey, An" (Mansfield, K.) 79
Institute for the Harmonious Development of Man 83

Intelligence of Woman, The (George, W.) 128–9
Interim (Richardson, D.) 170
"Is there a New Generation" (Murry, J. M.) 171
Italy 64

Jacob's Room (Woolf, V.) 18, 30, 226
James, William 171
Jane Eyre (Bronte, C.) 195
Java Head (Hergesheimer, J.) 166
"Je ne parle pas français" (Mansfield, K.) 65
Jerrold, Douglas 126, 131–2
John, Augustus 221
Jonson, Ben 78
Journal (Mansfield, K.) 66
Joyce, James 162, 203
Juliet (Mansfield, K.) 65

Kant, Immanuel 59
Karori 152–3
Kaziany, Florence 56
Keats, John 75–6
"Kew Gardens" (Woolf, V.) 41, 169, 201, 227
Keynes, John Maynard 1, 6, 202
Koteliansky, S. S. 93, 163, 174

Lady Chatterley's Lover (Lawrence, D. H.) 48
"Lady's Maid, The" (Mansfield, K.) 93
Laforgue, Jules 73, 79–80
Last Lectures (Fry, R.) 150
Laurels, The (Mansfield, K.) 56
Lawrence, D. H. 6–7, 40, 48, 54–5, 64, 67–8, 92, 97
  Amores 55
  Lady Chatterley's Lover 48
  "Snapdragon" 97
  Sons and Lovers 40
  Women in Love 55, 64
Lawrence, Frieda 62
Levinas, Emmanuel 9, 18, 24–5, 27–32, 33n
Limbo (Huxley, A.) 63
"Little Governess, The" (Mansfield, K.) 77, 224
Little Review, The 81
"London" (Dunning, M.) 108–9

London 6, 21, 40, 53, 55, 58, 60, 69, 74, 79, 82, 115, 121n, 125–7, 135, 138, 149, 152, 154, 193, 213, 219–20, 222, 224
London Mercury 93–4
"Love Song of J. Alfred Prufrock, The" (Eliot, T. S.) 74, 76
Lubbock, Percy 165
  Craft of Fiction, The 165
Lynd, Robert 136
Lynd, Sylvia 100

Maid of the Mountains, The 204
Making of an Englishman, The (George, W.) 132
"Man Without a Temperament, The" (Mansfield, K.) 50
Mansfield, Katherine 1, 6–11, 17–25, 28–30, 33, 39–50, 51n, 53–69, 73–85, 91–103, 107–8, 110–20, 125–37, 146, 148, 151–7, 161, 163–76, 181–8, 190–5, 201–6, 208–12, 214–16, 219–31
  "Album Leaf, An" 74, 85
  Aloe, The 76, 222
  "At the Bay" 65, 93, 117, 119, 152–3, 219–20
  "Baron, The" 110
  "Black Cap, The" 76
  "Bliss" 7, 10, 23–4, 29, 45, 60–1, 65, 67, 75, 85, 92, 111, 113–14, 126–8, 131–3, 174, 182–3, 186, 188–9, 194–5, 202, 204, 209–15, 223, 226–8
  Bliss and Other Stories 85, 94, 224, 227
  "By Moonlight" 102
  "Canary, The" 100
  "Cup of Tea, A" 10–11, 24, 186, 189, 194–5, 219–21, 223–6, 230
  "Dill Pickle, A" 10, 79, 84, 202, 204, 206, 209–10, 215
  "Doll's House, The" 24–6, 33, 152
  Doves' Nest and Other Stories, The 92, 101–3, 219
  "Dragonflies" 170
  "Early Spring" 111, 113
  "Escape, The" 85
  "Feuille d'Album" 74–6, 78, 80, 82, 84–5
  "Garden Party, The" 92, 100–2, 204, 219
  Garden Party and Other Stories, The 219
  "Germans at Meat" 110

"In Confidence" 58
"In the Botanical Gardens" 153
"Indiscreet Journey, An" 79
"Je ne parle pas français" 65
Journal 66
Juliet 65
"Lady's Maid, The" 93
Laurels, The 56
"Little Governess, The" 77, 224
"Man Without a Temperament, The" 50
"Marriage à la Mode" 10, 23, 186, 192–4, 202, 204–6, 209–11, 215, 216n
"Marriage of Passion, A" 127–9
"Night-Scented Stock" 75
"Pictures" 75
"Prelude" 24, 65, 76, 81, 95, 102, 118, 152, 220, 222, 230
"Sister of the Baroness, The" 110–1
"Something Childish but Very Natural" 77
"Sunday Lunch" 125, 130, 138
"Taking the Veil" 219
"Tales of a Courtyard" 111, 114
"Two Tuppenny Ones, Please" 76
"Wind Blows, The" 153
Mansfield: A Novel (Stead, C. K.) 74
Maori 21–2
"Mark on the Wall, The" (Woolf, V.) 43
"Marriage à la Mode" (Mansfield, K.) 10, 23, 186, 192–4, 202, 204–6, 209–11, 215, 216n
"Marriage of Passion, A" (Mansfield, K.) 127–9
Marsh, Edward 94–7
Marvel, Andrew 203
Matisse, Henri 154–5
McCarthy, Desmond 1, 202
McCarthy, Mollie 6
Mediterranean 62
Memoirs of a Midget (de la Mare, W.) 93
Menton 101
Millin, Sarah Gertrude 7
"Mocking Fairy, The" (de la Mare, W.) 97
"Modern Fiction" (Woolf, V.) 162
"Modern Novels" (Woolf, V.) 43, 161–3, 166, 168–9, 171–4
Modernism 2–4, 8–9, 18, 22, 42, 44, 48, 69, 74–6, 78, 84–5, 94, 96–7, 127–8, 131, 145–6, 149–50, 153, 156–7, 161–2, 164, 167, 169, 171–2, 174–6, 181, 184–6, 188–93, 195, 201–3, 211, 216, 222
Moments of Being (Woolf, V.) 35n, 178n, 198n
Moments of Vision (Hardy, T.) 167–8
Monkhouse, Allan 156
Monro, Harold 94, 97
Montana-sur-Sierre, Switzerland 64, 219
Moore, George 155, 166
  Esther Waters 155
Morrell, Ottoline 2–4, 6–8, 11, 13n, 53–8, 60, 62–7, 73–5, 93–5, 107, 125–7, 137, 168, 201, 220–2, 224, 226, 228, 231
Morrell, Phillip 41, 222
Mother Goose 93
"Mr Bennett and Mrs Brown" (Woolf, V.) 145
"Mr Conrad: A Conversation" (Woolf, V.) 164
Mrs Dalloway (Woolf, V.) 176
Murry, John Middleton 6, 9, 39–44, 46, 49, 53–4, 56, 58, 60, 62–4, 66–9, 73, 76, 78, 83, 85, 91–6, 99–101, 107, 114–16, 119, 126–7, 129–34, 136–7, 161, 165, 167–9, 171, 173–4, 184, 203, 206, 219, 223, 229, 231
  "Condition of English Poetry, The" 104n, 177n
  Critic in Judgement, The 40
  "Is there a New Generation" 171
  "Poetry of Mr. Hardy, The"
  Problem of Style, The 165
  Things We Are, The 69

Nation, The 136, 149
"Negress, The" (George, W.) 130
Network theory 3–5, 13n
New Age, The 107, 109
New Statesman 64
New Woman 128–9, 138
New Zealand 7, 10, 21–2, 54, 73, 85, 107, 146, 148, 152–3
Nietzsche, Frederich 154
Night and Day (Woolf, V.) 41, 44, 46, 161, 203, 226–7
"Night-Scented Stock" (Mansfield, K.) 75
Nijinsky, Vaslav 82
Nys, Maria 56

O'Connor, Frank 98
"Old Bloomsbury" (Woolf, L.) 2, 22
"Old Bloomsbury" (Woolf, V.) 2, 22
"On Being Ill" (Woolf, V.) 164
Orage, A. R. 92–3, 115
Orpheus 108
Ospedaletti 44, 49
Ouspensky, Peter 107
Oxbridge 154
Oxford 53, 55, 60

Paris, France 77, 79, 110, 126, 131, 154, 190, 192, 223
Patanjali 116
Pater, Walter 154
"Philosophy of Impression, The" (Fry, R.) 145
"Pictures" (Mansfield, K.) 75
Pinker, J. B. 94, 219
Poe, Edgar Allan 99, 118
Poems (Eliot, T.) 40
"Poetry of Mr. Hardy, The" (Murry, J. M.)
Point Counter Point (Huxley, A.) 53, 65, 67
Portland Villa 43, 62
"Post Impression" (Fry, R.) 151
Post-Impressionism 10
Pound, Ezra 73, 81–4, 97, 175
"Prelude" (Mansfield, K.) 24, 65, 76, 81, 95, 102, 118, 152, 220, 222, 230
"Preludes" (Eliot, T.) 75
Priam 30
Prieuré, La 84
Problem of Style, The (Murry, J. M.) 165
Prowse, R. O. 167
    Gift of the Dusk, A 167

Quaker 148
Queen's College 54

Raja Yoga 116, 118–19
Rasputin 62
Raverat, Jacques 174
"Red Lion Square" (Dunning, M.) 108, 111, 113, 121n
Rescue, The (Conrad, J.) 164
"Retrospect" (Fry, R.) 150
"Revenant, A" (de la Mare, W.) 98–9
"Rhapsody on a Windy Night" (Eliot, T.) 74–5

Rhythm 42–4, 81, 94, 96–7, 111, 130, 154, 220
Richardson, Dorothy 39, 164, 170–1
    Interim 170
    Tunnel, The 164, 170
Riviera 64
Robinson, Gidley 62
Romanticism 76, 78
Room of One's Own, A (Woolf, V.) 21, 195
Rothermere, Lady Mary Lilian 83–4
Rowntree, Arthur 161
Royal Academy 43
Royde-Smith, Naomi 94
Russell, Bertrand 54–5, 65, 73, 82, 161

Sackville-West, Vita 228
    Heritage 169
Sadleir, Michael 94
St. John's Wood 125–7
St. Paul Daily News 66
"Sanatana Dharma" (Dunning, M.) 109, 116, 119
San Remo, Italy 41, 44
Sargeson, Frank 85
Saturday Westminster Gazette 43, 51n, 100, 106n
Scheherazade 82, 192
Schiff, Sydney 40, 83, 85
Schiff, Violet 63, 73, 75, 83, 85
Secret History of Modernism, The (Stead, C. K.) 74
Selfridges 192
September (Swinnerton, F.) 9, 43–50, 172
Sinclair, May 44, 171
"Sister of the Baroness, The" (Mansfield, K.) 110–1
"Sketch of the Past, A" (Woolf, V.) 168
Smollett, Tobias 62
"Snapdragon" (Lawrence, D. H.) 97
Sobienowski, Floryan 56
"Something Childish but Very Natural" (Mansfield, K.) 77
"Song of the Mad Prince, The" (de la Mare, W.) 97
Sons and Lovers (Lawrence, D. H.) 40
Stead, C. K. 74–5, 81, 84–5
    Mansfield: A Novel 74
    Secret History of Modernism, The 74
"Steppe, The" (Chekhov, A.) 174

Stevenson, Robert Lewis 47
Story Teller 123n, 232n
Strachey, James 97
Strachey, Lytton 1, 4, 6–7, 11, 43, 53, 55, 66, 73, 82, 161, 184–5, 222
"Subconscious Influence of Nature, The" (Dunning, M.) 118–19
Suhrawardy, Husyen 55
Sullivan, J. W. N. 60, 63–4, 115
Sumurûn 82
"Sunday Lunch" (Mansfield, K.) 125, 130, 138
Swinnerton, Frank 9, 40, 43–9, 51n, 172
  Happy Family, The 43
  September 9, 43–50, 172
Switzerland 64, 67, 204, 219
Symons, Arthur 73, 154

"Taking the Veil" (Mansfield, K.) 219
"Tales of a Courtyard" (Mansfield, K.) 111, 114
"Talk about Memoirs, A" (Woolf, V.) 164
Thackeray, William Makepeace 162
Things We Are, The (Murry, J. M.) 69
Thomas, Edward 64, 98
  Collected Poems 64
Those Barren Leaves (Huxley, A.) 62, 65, 67
"Three Mulla-Mulgars, The" (de la Mare, W.) 93
"Three Vignettes" (Dunning, M.) 117
Times Literary Supplement 41, 43–4, 93, 161, 171
Tinakori Road 151
"To K. M." (de la Mare, W.) 100
Tomlinson, H. M. 40, 63, 93
To the Lighthouse (Woolf, V.) 29–30, 182
"Traveler's Eye View, The" (Huxley, A.) 67
Tunnel, The (Richardson, D.) 164, 170
"Two Tuppenny Ones, Please" (Mansfield, K.) 76

United States 73

Village in the Jungle, The (Woolf, L.) 195
Vision and Design (Fry, R.) 146, 150
Vivekananda, Swami 116, 118
von Arnim, Elizabeth 40, 62, 136, 220, 223
Voyage Out, The (Woolf, V.) 222, 225, 230

Waterlow, Sydney 75, 78
Waugh, Alec 126–7, 130
Weekly Westminster Gazette 100, 106n
Wellington 8, 151–4, 219–20
Wells, H. G. 126, 136, 162
West, Rebecca 64
Westminster Gazette 94, 98
Wilde, Oscar 79, 154
"Wind Blows, The" (Mansfield, K.) 153
Woman and To-Morrow (George, W.) 128
"Women and War" (Dunning, M.) 120n
Women in Love (Lawrence, D. H.) 55, 64
Woolf, Leonard 1–2, 6, 37n, 53, 76, 81, 95, 222
  "Old Bloomsbury" 2, 22
  Village in the Jungle, The 195
Woolf, Virginia 1, 4, 6, 8–12, 17–23, 29–30, 32–3, 37n, 39–44, 46–50, 59–62, 66, 73, 76, 81, 94–7, 107, 134, 145–6, 149, 157, 161–76, 182–4, 188, 193, 195, 201, 203, 220–31
  "Anatomy of Fiction, The" 40, 43
  "Byron & Mr Briggs" 177n
  Common Reader, The 162
  "Freudian Fictions" 171
  Hours, The 176
  "How It Strikes a Contemporary" 164
  Jacob's Room 18, 30, 226
  "Kew Gardens" 41, 169, 201, 227
  "Mark on the Wall, The" 43
  "Modern Fiction" 162
  "Modern Novels" 43, 161–3, 166, 168–9, 171–4
  Moments of Being 35n, 178n, 198n
  "Mr Bennett and Mrs Brown" 145
  "Mr Conrad: A Conversation" 164
  Mrs Dalloway 176
  Night and Day 41, 44, 46, 161, 203, 226–7
  "Old Bloomsbury" 2, 22
  "On Being Ill" 164
  Room of One's Own, A 21, 195
  "Sketch of the Past, A" 168
  "Talk about Memoirs, A" 164
  To the Lighthouse 29–30, 182
  Voyage Out, The 222, 225, 230
World War I 30, 42, 49, 98, 109, 167, 203

Yeats, W. B. 54

CPSIA information can be obtained
at www.ICGtesting.com
Printed in the USA
LVHW021744070820
662646LV00004B/59